# Medical Law in the Netherlands

# Medical Law in the Netherlands

**Second Edition**

**Herman Nys**

This book was originally published as a monograph in the International Encyclopaedia of Laws/Medical Law.

Founding Editor: Roger Blanpain
General Editor: Frank Hendrickx
Volume Editor: Herman Nys

Wolters Kluwer

*Published by:*
Kluwer Law International B.V.
PO Box 316
2400 AH Alphen aan den Rijn
The Netherlands
E-mail: international-sales@wolterskluwer.com
Website: lrus.wolterskluwer.com

*Sold and distributed by:*
Wolters Kluwer Legal & Regulatory U.S.
7201 McKinney Circle
Frederick, MD 21704
United States of America
Email: customer.service@wolterskluwer.com



ISBN 978-94-035-3333-9

e-Book: ISBN 978-94-035-3334-6
web-PDF: ISBN 978-94-035-3335-3

# The Author

Emeritus Professor Dr Herman Nys (born on 20 January 1951) studied Law at KU Leuven University (1969–1974) and Radboud University Nijmegen (1974–1975). From 1975–1980, he worked as an assistant, specialising in healthcare law, at the Centre for Hospital Sciences in Leuven, where he received his doctoral for his thesis on Legal Aspects of Healthcare Planning in 1980. During 1981–1989, he was affiliated with the Law School in Leuven, first as Lecturer of Medical Law and from 1985 to 1996, he worked as an associate professor. He was the Director of the Centre of Biomedical Ethics and Law in Leuven from 1989 to 2015. In 1992, he was appointed as a professor, and he retired on 1 October 2016.

Between 2000–2006, he was also the Professor of International Health Law at the University of Maastricht, the Netherlands. Prof. Nys is the author of numerous books and articles on medical law and healthcare policy. He is a member of the editorial boards of several learned journals and editor-in-chief of the *European Journal of Health Law*.

He was also the co-founder and director of the European Association of Health Law (2008–2017) and vice-president of the World Association of Medical Law (2010–2012).

He is the first deputy chairman of the European Group of Ethics in Science and New Technologies (2017–2022).

## The Author

# Table of Contents

# List of Abbreviations

| | |
|---|---|
| COPD | Chronic Obstructive Pulmonary Disease |
| DMA | Dutch Medical Association |
| ECHR | European Convention on Human Rights |
| EU | European Union |
| GDPR | General Data Protection Regulation |
| GP | General Practitioner |
| IHCP Act | Individual Healthcare Professions Act |
| NJ | Nederlandse Jurisprudentie |
| OJ | Official Journal of the European Union |
| QCDHC Act | Quality, Complaints and Disputes in Healthcare Act |

# General Introduction

## Chapter 1. The General Background of the Country

### §1. Geography and Climate

*1.* The Netherlands consists of mainly flat land, with some hilly areas in the south and east. The northern and western areas are partially below sea level. The maritime climate is moderate, with an average temperature of 16°C–17°C in summer and 2°C–3°C in winter.

The Netherlands comprises an area of 41,532 $km^2$ (33,889 $km^2$ of land and 7,643 $km^2$ of water), which lies between the North Sea in the north and west, Germany in the east and Belgium to the south. The Netherlands' highest point lies in the extreme south, where the borders of Germany, Belgium and the Netherlands meet.

### §2. Population

*2.* The Netherlands is one of the world's most densely populated countries with an average of more than 500 inhabitants/$km^2$. The total population is over 17 million (17,476,159) as of December 2020. A total of 60% of the population lives in the urban core known as the *Randstad*, comprising the main cities of Amsterdam (the capital), The Hague (seat of government), Rotterdam and Utrecht.

*3.* The language spoken in the Netherlands is Dutch, a Germanic language. Apart from Dutch, the inhabitants of the province of Friesland speak Frisian, a Germanic language related to Dutch. Many people throughout the country are fluent in English as well.

### §3. Political and Judicial System

*4.* The Netherlands is a parliamentary democracy under a constitutional monarch, who is the head of state. Legislature, Judiciary and Executive functions are strictly separate. The Parliament shares the legislative power with the monarch and the ministers; the monarch and the ministers are the executive power; the judiciary is independent and entrusted to judges who are appointed for life. The first Constitution of the Netherlands dates back to 1814. It has been through fourteen revisions since then, the most important being the 1848 revision (the Year of Revolution). The most recent revision being the 1983 revision.

*5.* Till the nineteenth century, the Netherlands was a republic, governed by the United Provinces. The Republic came to an end during the French Occupation (1810–1813). In the years that followed, the foundation was laid for a constitutional monarchy with the House of Orange. For a brief period, the monarch reigned supreme (1815–1848). The revision of the Constitution of 1848 changed the concept of monarchial legislative power into the concept of ministerial responsibility: 'The monarch is inviolable, the ministers are responsible.' Any act of the monarch requires the permission of the Cabinet Council (ministerial responsibility), which implies that the monarch cannot be held politically responsible. The revised Constitution of 1848 is the first to use the word 'government' instead of 'King'; the government being the monarch acting in conjunction with the ministers (Article 42.1 Constitution). The Constitution does not define the monarch's task within the government, but it is tacitly agreed that the monarch has the following rights: the right to be consulted, the right to encourage and the right to admonish.

*6.* The ministers together form the Cabinet Council, which is one of the country's main executive bodies, deliberating and deciding upon the general policy and stimulating its unanimity. The definition of 'general policy' is left to the interpretation of the Cabinet Council.

*7.* A Cabinet Minister is usually the Head of a Ministry. Ministries are separate administrative bodies responsible for certain elements of the general policy. Apart from Cabinet Ministers, there are also Secretaries of State who are responsible for specific aspects of a Ministry's policy. Secretaries of State are not in the Cabinet Council and are therefore not entitled to vote in Council. Secretaries of State, as well as Cabinet Ministers, are accountable to Parliament regarding their specific responsibilities. Secretaries of State manage aspects of a Ministry's task and, are held politically responsible; the ultimate political responsibility for the entire Ministry, however, rests with the Cabinet Minister.

*8.* The Prime Minister, who is the chairman of the Cabinet Council, is responsible for the cohesion and coordination of the government policy. His position is one of '*primus inter pares*', which renders him powerless to make any changes in the Cabinet. The Cabinet Council's duties and competencies are regulated by the Standing Orders of the Cabinet Council.

*9.* In compliance with the Constitution, the monarch appoints and administers the oath to new Cabinet Ministers and Secretaries of State. This led to common practice for the monarch to supervise the formation of Cabinet while observing his political neutrality. In order to safeguard the latter, the monarch appoints a 'formateur' (a person in charge of forming a government that will be assured of the support of a Parliamentary majority), who does the actual formation of Cabinet.

*10.* The monarchy is hereditary with the right of primogeniture in both the male and female lineages (since 1983, Revised Constitution). King Willem-Alexander is the official head of state. The government always consists of a coalition of different political parties since a multitude of parties are elected to Parliament, and none of them has ever had an absolute majority. The political climate in the Netherlands in the past fifteen years has been influenced considerably by the rise of far right-wing parties, such as the Party for Freedom (Partij voor de Vrijheid). Issues brought up by such parties, in particular concerning immigration and anti-Islam or antiterrorism measures, now dominate political discourse in general.

*11.* The Dutch Parliament is known as the States-General, which represents the entire Dutch population (Article 50 Constitution). The States-General (Parliament) consists of two Houses, the First and Second Chamber. The First Chamber or Senate has 75 members who are elected by the members of the Provincial Councils, who in turn are directly elected. The Second Chamber has 150 members who are directly elected by the enfranchised: all Dutch citizens of 18 years and above and non-residents who have been legally accepted.

*12.* Both Chambers serve four-year terms (Article 52.1 Constitution), as do the elected members of the Provincial Councils (Article 129.4 Constitution). The members of the Second Chamber represent a large number of political parties. Members of one particular party within the First and Second Chambers form a 'fractie' (group). Members of the States-General are elected according to a system of proportional representation (Article 53 Constitution). There is no compulsory attendance at the polls. Simultaneous membership of both Chambers is impossible (Article 57.1 Constitution).

*13.* Both Chambers select a chairman among their members (Article 61.1 Constitution). The Chairman of the Second Chamber is mostly a member of the largest 'fractie', the Chairman of the First Chamber is usually a member of the second largest. Meetings held in either Chamber are public.

*14.* Members of the States-General, Cabinet Ministers, Secretaries of State and other participants in the deliberations cannot be prosecuted for any statements, written or oral, made in Chamber meetings or in Chamber committees (Article 71 Constitution). Decisions in both the First and Second Chambers are reached on the principle of majority vote (Article 67.2 Constitution). The First Chamber has the following rights: the right of interpellation, the right of enquiry and the right of budget. The Second Chamber has, besides these, the right of amendment and the right of initiative.

*15.* The right of interpellation is the right members have to ask for any information, oral or written, from Cabinet Ministers or Secretary of State they deem of importance to their task of supervising the government, providing the required information is not in contravention of the interests of state (Article 68 Constitution). The right of enquiry is the right the Chambers have to start an investigation without the government's knowledge or consent through an investigative committee. The Chambers may avail themselves of this right both separately and jointly.

*16.* The Council of State is the oldest state institution and serves the government in an advisory capacity. Not only is the government obliged to ask the Council's advice, but the Council itself may offer advice on its own initiative. The government usually has to ask advice on the following issues (Article 73 Constitution): all bills; all proposed measures of general administration; all agreements with supranational institutions; the intended reversal of decisions of institutions of public corporations; the denial of approval of certain decisions of Provincial Councils; all matters decreed by law. Since the coming into force of the Revised Constitution, the Council of State is competent to give advice directly to the States-General. The monarch presides over the Council of State whereas the vice-president actually chairs its meetings. The Council has a maximum of twenty-eight members who are appointed for life by Royal Decree.

*17.* The Netherlands Court of Audit is a central government body created to ensure that the democratic system works properly. The Court of Audit's tasks, powers and legal status are laid down in the Constitution (Articles 76–78) and the Government Accounts Act.

*18.* The Court of Audit investigates whether central government revenue and expenditure are received and spent correctly and whether central government policy is implemented as intended. The Court is obliged to carry out these tasks by law. It expresses an opinion on government policy that has already been adopted; it does not express political opinions.

*19.* The Court of Audit's principal 'customers' are the House of Representatives and the government. Its job is to provide the Parliament with useful and relevant information so that Parliament can decide whether a minister's policies are effective or not. Wherever possible, the Court matches his audits to parliament's wishes and needs.

*20.* The Court of Audit is an independent institution. That means that the Court decides what to audit. The Court often receives requests to carry out audits from Members of Parliament, ministers and state secretaries who need an independent expert opinion on a particular matter. But they cannot order the Court to do so. In practice, the Court of Audit usually honours requests made by members of parliament or government if the Court can add value.

*21.* The National Ombudsman of the Netherlands is independent and impartial. The existence of the National Ombudsman is guaranteed by the Dutch Constitution (Article 78a). The National Ombudsman investigates complaints brought to him by members of the public. He can also launch investigations on his own initiative. His remit includes almost the entire machinery of government: not just the ministries and their different sections, but also other administrative authorities (like the Social Insurance Bank), the police, the provinces and municipalities.

*22.* The National Ombudsman cannot deal with complaints about government policy or the content of laws. Complaints have to concern the actions of administrative authorities. For example, if the time taken to deal with a letter or request is too long, if the complainant has received no response to a question or if a law has been wrongly applied.

*23.* The National Ombudsman's decisions, recommendations and reports are not legally enforceable. However, the National Ombudsman has extensive investigative powers. By law, both administrative authorities and witnesses have to cooperate with his investigations. He investigates the facts, takes well-argued decisions and issues clear, readable reports. The National Ombudsman owes much of his authority to the meticulous way in which he works.

*24.* The government, as well as parliament, are aided in the execution of their duties by hundreds of Permanent Advisory Boards, some well-known ones being the Socio-Economic Council and the Scientific Council for Government Policy. The institution, the organisation, the composition and the competence of these Advisory Boards are regulated by law.

*25.* Article 81 of the Constitution states that the laws are established by the government and the States-General jointly. More often than not, the government takes the initiative to propose a Bill, although the Second Chamber is entitled to do so, as well. This right is called 'the right of initiative' (Article 82). The number of 'initiative Bills' proposed by members of the Second Chamber is, however, limited.

*26.* The Judiciary in the Netherlands is independent. Judges are appointed by the government for life by Royal Decree. The administration of justice is subdivided into the areas of criminal law, civil law and administrative law. Cases are initially dealt with and heard by Cantonal Courts and District Courts. The highest court in the Netherlands is the Supreme Court; its most important task is to ensure the uniform application of the law. The Supreme Court is qualified to reverse rulings of lower court judges (Cassation). Facts, as found by lower court judges, are admitted as such. In the Netherlands, the judiciary can only determine whether or not a governmental measure is at variance with the law or has no legal basis. The law itself is inviolable. The judiciary is not allowed to examine a law for compatibility with the Constitution (Article 120 Constitution).

*27.* The Netherlands can be described as a decentralised unity, which means certain legislative and administrative powers was transferred from State to province and municipality. The Netherlands has twelve provinces and hundreds of municipalities. In 1962, a Province Act was instituted, regulating the provinces' affairs. The Provincial States are the provincial authorities. Their task is the institution of provincial by-laws and deciding on matters of administrative importance.

*28.* The governing body of a province is completed with the Provincial Executive and the Royal Commissioner, who is appointed by Royal Decree. The Provincial Executive Board, together with the Royal Commissioner as its chairman are the executive body. Their special task is the supervision of the municipalities. On a provincial level, the various governing bodies are assisted by a registrar.

*29.* The Local Government Act regulates municipal affairs. Municipalities are presided over by Local Councils (Article 125.1 Constitution), which have legislative as well as executive powers. The Mayor and the Aldermen are the executives, who, amongst other matters, are responsible for the preparation of issues to be discussed in the Local Council meetings, as well as the implementation of the Council's decisions. Since 2015, major tasks in the area of social protection and support, self-care, social participation and sheltered living have been decentralised to the municipalities.

## §4. Population and Vital Statistics

*30.* In 1950, the total population of the Netherlands was around 10 million people. By 2017, the total population increased to over 17 million people. On 1 January 2017, there were approximately 3.8 million people younger than 20 years of age living in the Netherlands. The largest age group was formed by those between 40 and 65 years old. Together, they number approximately 6 million people. The retired population of the Netherlands consists of approximately 3 million people. In 2019, the life expectancy for men in the Netherlands increased by four months to 80.5 years, for women by three months to 83.6 years. Higher mortality due to COVID-19 may affect life expectancy developments.

*31.* Of the nearly 17.1 million people living in the Netherlands in 2017, roughly 13.2 million people had a Dutch background and 3.8 million people had a foreign background, defined as first- or second-generation migrants. Of the non-Western population, the majority of the inhabitants had a Turkish background. The second largest group is formed by the population with a Moroccan background. These groups consist roughly around 4 million and 3.91 million people respectively. According to a recent forecast, both the population with a Western background and the population with a non-Western background are likely to increase in the future. It is estimated that, by 2060, approximately 3 million people in the Netherlands will have a non-Western background.

*32.* In 2019, 169,680 babies were born alive in the Netherlands.

## §5. Social and Cultural Values Regarding Health

*33.* Cardiovascular disease is often seen as something that affects mainly men, but in fact, heart failure is now the number one cause of death among women, partially because the signs manifest differently in women and are not always recognised in time. Furthermore, figures show that women take more time off sick during their working life and incur higher medical expenses than men.

*34.* Women's organisations, the healthcare sector and researchers have therefore called for more 'gender awareness' in healthcare, taking account of differences between the sexes. This should improve the quality of life for both men and women, and save money. Working with pioneers in this field, the Ministry of Education, Culture and Science is taking measures to enhance the knowledge and awareness of stakeholders (physicians, insurance companies, employers, patients) concerning the need for gender-aware healthcare, and to actually develop such practices. An alliance has been forged for this purpose with pioneers from the field.

*35.* The 'Gender and Health Alliance' has drawn up a strategic plan for awareness-raising, teaching and research, with the aim of launching a widely supported programme in two years' time. This is being done in consultation with the Ministry of Health, Welfare and Sport and the Ministry of Social Affairs and Employment. The initiative will also tie in with other innovative developments, such as the Interministerial National Disease Prevention and Health Promotion Programme, which focuses on a healthy start (parenting and education), housing and life in healthy neighbourhoods, healthy working, health protection and disease prevention in the healthcare sector.

*36.* Sick and elderly people want to live in their own homes as long as possible. This is a clear social trend, which is reflected in the State Secretary for Health, Welfare and Sports reform of long-term care. This requires formal and informal care and support to be organised differently, with people in the patients' own network and community – informal carers and volunteers – playing a bigger role. Of the 3.5 million informal carers in the Netherlands, 2.6 million give intensive and/or long-term care. The majority of informal carers are women. Their share has remained constant over the past few years, at 60%. Qualitative studies have shown that men are often less directly involved in care, playing more of a support role than women. There are also at least 4.5 million volunteers who provide care and support in the Netherlands. Female volunteers are almost three times more active than men in the healthcare sector. There are more than 5.5 million active volunteers in the Netherlands, about 44% are of the adult population.

# Chapter 2. General Description of the Healthcare System

## §1. General Overview of the Dutch Healthcare System

*37.* Healthcare is mainly privately organised. Most hospitals, nursing homes and other intramural facilities are either foundations or societies and operate on a not-for-profit basis, as regulated in the Healthcare Facilities Act.

*38.* Till the late years of the nineteenth century, there was no clear-cut system of public healthcare. The roots of the present-day Dutch system of health insurance lay in the Middle Ages when the guilds played an important role in society as professional associations, they were the greater part concentrated in the urban areas and fulfilled a prominent socio-economic role from 1200 to 1900. One of the guilds' social objectives was to offer assistance to ill and needy members. At the end of the nineteenth century, Workers Funds came into being, established by the employees themselves, as well as Employers Funds, run by employers for the benefit of the employees. The latter offered medical aid by physicians engaged by the Funds: the premiums were paid partially by the employers, partially by the employees. Influenced by the notion of 'caritas', so-called Charity Funds were established as well, run largely by socially conscientious people and offering help in kind at a modest premium.

*39.* As the Funds grew, medical practitioners grew fearful of having to deal with more and more powerful groups at negotiations concerning, for instance, contracts. That is why, from the early years of the twentieth century onwards, the Medical Society started to advocate the establishment of so-called Society Funds, which were to incorporate the Doctors' Funds as well.

*40.* In 1913, the General Assembly of the Dutch Medical Association (DMA) resolved to no longer cooperate with those Funds not recognised by the Society. This was a binding resolution, which led to non-recognised Funds running the risk of being unable to contract physicians. Another consequence of the Resolution was, moreover, that physicians were no longer allowed to sign individual contracts with the Funds, as the Society itself would handle these matters in future. However, opposition from the Funds under communal management also grew stronger as they saw their very existence threatened. On 4 November of that same year, the National Federation for the Promotion of the Sickness Funds was founded. The conflict between physicians and Funds grew even grimmer: the Funds did not want the premiums raised, the physicians demanded higher fees and a free choice of physician. All this led to appeals to the government to provide legislation to regulate medical insurance. The need to do so increased for the government as well, but all efforts were to no avail because of the enormous conflicts of interest and lack of funds.

*41.* Where the Dutch legislator had failed after years of conflict, the German occupation of the country in 1941 succeeded: compulsory medical insurance for employees (and their families) by means of the Sickness Funds Decree. The insured person was not obliged to register with the service; he was, however, obliged to pay a premium.

*42.* Voluntary medical insurance remained side by side with the compulsory insurance, for those who were not insured compulsorily and whose income did not exceed the limit set by the Sickness Funds. After World War II, besides the Sickness Funds Act (1962, implemented 1966), the Exceptional Medical Expenses Act was effectuated (1967), national insurance for the entire population.

*43.* At first, the government had a limited task in the field of public health (a preconditioning and controlling task), but the rise of the welfare state caused public health and public healthcare to be regarded more and more as a matter of public interest, thus enlarging governmental duty and responsibility. Public healthcare increasingly became part of the public domain.

*44.* Structurally, the main feature of the organisation and policymaking of the Dutch healthcare system is the relationship of government, private initiative and insurance system. Government interference is mainly administrative, whereas healthcare as such largely rests with private initiative. Again the government is taking a back seat in the field of public healthcare. The care facilities thus created may be qualified as a system of regulated competition.

*45.* Due to expansion of scope in healthcare as well as in knowledge and specialisation, the healthcare system has, to a large extent, become differentiated: preventive as well as curative care, and primary and secondary healthcare. Primary healthcare consists of general practitioners (GPs), dentists, pharmacists, homecare, district nursing, social service, midwifery and maternity care, and paramedical professions (such as physiotherapists). The GP provides both treatment and referral to specialist care (secondary healthcare).

*46.* Most GPs work solo, although they and other primary healthcare workers increasingly tend to join forces (partly stimulated by the revision of the payment of the public health system), or they cooperate in a multidisciplinary home team or health centre. Secondary healthcare is, as a rule, only accessible after a GP's referral. Specialists almost exclusively practise in intramural institutions, where they give outpatient or clinical treatment.

*47.* Intramural care is offered within, or under the supervision of an institution, that is, within institutions for treatment (e.g., hospitals) and residential institutions (e.g., convalescent homes). The nursing homes combine the functions of both treatment and residential institutions. The nursing homes' population mainly consists of elderly people (90% above 70 years of age). Nursing home care offers an extension of hospital care. When a patient is no longer dependent on hospital care but needs the kind of nursing and care that cannot be provided at home, the nursing home fills the gap.

*48.* Hospitals are subdivided into teaching (university) hospitals, general hospitals and categorised hospitals. For the past thirty years, developments within the Dutch healthcare system have been characterised by expansion. Institutions are, on an average, twice the size they were in 1951, obliterating many small hospitals.

*49.* Mental healthcare is subdivided into extramural, semimural and intramural care. Extramural care is provided by regional institutions for ambulatory mental healthcare, health centres for alcohol and drugs, outpatients' clinics at psychiatric hospitals and self-employed psychiatrists and/or neurologists. Semimural facilities, also called in-between facilities, are difficult to classify. There are such facilities as crisis centres and shelters, protected housing and medical day nurseries. Intramural facilities are the general psychiatric hospitals, psychiatric wards in general hospitals, institutions for forensic patients, psychogeriatric (wards in) nursing homes. For a long time, a lack of cohesion has been characteristic of the mental healthcare system, which was expressed in an overlap in facilities and defective communication among the various providers of care.

*50.* Besides curative healthcare, there is preventive care, part of which is collective prevention, regulated in the Public Health Act 2008. Individual prevention is made effective within the system of individual curative healthcare. Collective prevention is a separate system which comprises all activities aimed at stimulating health and preventing illness for the entire population or groups of the population. Some major fields are basic public healthcare and occupational healthcare.

*51.* Basic public healthcare is, among others, preventive juvenile healthcare and tracing contagious diseases (like SARS or Avian Influenza). These tasks are currently carried out by the home nursing organisations, the regional health services, municipal medical and public health services and specific basic health services.

## §2. Regulation of the Healthcare System

*52.* The following governmental obligation was formulated in Article 22.1 of the Dutch Constitution: 'The Government takes measures to promote public health.' This implies a concrete task for the government. This constitutional obligation reflects the core elements of the social right to health: availability, accessibility and quality of individual healthcare.

*53.* Due to its 'programmatic goals', the social right to healthcare has a weaker legal status than individual (liberty) rights. The absence of a constitutional review by the courts makes it even more difficult to interpret this right. Statutory law is the most important legal source incorporating the right to healthcare. Translated into healthcare entitlements, access to healthcare has been made enforceable under social health insurance law. Healthcare litigation has reinforced the legal status of the right to healthcare and concerns both curative and long-term care.

§3. Financing of Healthcare

*54.* As a result of the incipient economic recession, the need to control the cost of the public healthcare sector became increasingly evident in the 1970s. During the 1980s, expenditure as a percentage of the Gross National Product was up to half a point higher than the European Union (EU) average. It rose from 7.5% in 1980 to 8.6% in 1993. After 1993, it decreased to 8.1% in 1998. Since 2001, there has been an upward trend; it had risen from 9.1% to 12.0% in 2009. In the Netherlands, 84.7% of current health spending was funded by public sources in 2009, well above the average of 71.9% in Organisation for Economic Co-Operation and Development countries.[1] These expenditures of the healthcare sector in the Netherlands are mainly financed by the health insurance system.

*55.* Under the Health Insurance Act, health insurance is funded by means of a fixed (nominal) premium charged to insured persons, as well as an income-related contribution, an employer's contribution and a number of government contributions. Health insurers are expected to generate 50% of the total cost of premiums via the nominal premium. All insured persons of 18 years and above are obligated to pay premiums, those under 18 years are not. Health insurers are free to set the amount of the nominal premium and to use it as a basis for competition on the market. Insurers must charge all insured persons the same premium, regardless of risk (i.e., risk equalisation). The amount of the premium may only vary in respect of the cover options selected by the insured person (e.g., benefits-in-kind policy, reimbursement policy, a combination of both and voluntary co-payments).

*56.* In addition to the nominal premium, an income-related contribution is levied on insured persons, designed to cover the remaining 50% of the total cost of premiums. Levied by the Dutch Tax and Customs Administration, this contribution is calculated over wages and comparable wage components. Equalisation is achieved within the system largely through the income-related contribution. Employers are obligated to compensate employees for the income-related contribution due. A similar obligation applies to Benefits Agencies for those depending on social assistance. A government grant is used to fund the premium for insured persons under the age of 18.

*57.* Originally, insured persons received a refund for part of the premium paid if no or little use was made of healthcare services. This no-claim refund should encourage a less healthcare-consuming attitude and, thus, an incentive to cost containment in healthcare. Although it may achieve the goal of cost reduction, there can be serious consequences for certain categories of patients (e.g., chronically ill) who will not benefit from that measure since they will certainly exceed the yearly limit. Given its discriminatory effect, in 2008, the no-claim rebate was replaced by a compulsory deductible. In addition, health insurers may offer insurance policy options with a limited number of voluntary deductibles. Insured persons receive a discount on their premium in return for accepting a level of financial risk. In any event, health

1. *Health Data* (OECD, 2011).

insurers are obligated to offer an option without their own risk. Also, health insurers can enter into group insurance schemes with employers for their employees and their dependents. The discount may exceed 10% of the premium base for each employee or dependent.

*58.* Finally, the (*ex ante*) equalisation payment is designed to prevent some health insurers from having to deal with a disproportionate number of poor people and consequently be confronted with a competitive disadvantage as a result of the obligation for health insurers to provide insurance cover pursuant to the Health Insurance Act.

*59.* Preventive care targets the whole population and is financed from general taxation and regulated under the Preventive Care Act. This comprises vaccinations, cancer screening programmes and preventive care for children under the age of 13.

## §4. Health Insurance

*60.* Dutch health insurance is based on the principles of equal access and solidarity. According to the principle of equal access, the government is obliged to establish a universally accessible healthcare system of appropriate quality, taking into account the need for healthcare and the available resources. The principle of equality forbids discrimination in the provision of healthcare and entails that access to healthcare is allocated solely according to medical criteria (i.e., medical need). Non-medical factors (e.g., insurance coverage, residency, etc.) play no role in deciding whether to admit or to treat a person (allocation of resources).

*61.* Solidarity between the rich and poor and among people with high and low risks formally guarantees equal access.[2] Solidarity is not a woolly notion about the common good. It has a specific meaning that a healthcare system is organised and managed on the basis of universal access, without risk selection, based on income-related premiums and with no significant differences in the benefits package. Both equal access and solidarity are enshrined in Dutch social health insurance law.

*62.* The Health Insurance Act 2006 introduced a compulsory health insurance scheme for the entire population, carried out by (for-profit) insurance companies.[3] Health insurance agreements have a private law character (indemnity insurance) and are therefore based on principles such as freedom of contract. However, the Act imposes certain restrictions on freedom of contracting, to protect the principle of equal access to healthcare. The prohibition of risk selection is one clear example of this. In addition, all health insurers must participate in a risk equalisation system. Such a levelling mechanism prevents direct or indirect risk selection of so-called

2. Traditionally, classified as risk and income solidarity, i.e., the strong (low health risk and high incomes) support the high risk and low incomes.
3. It came into force on 1 Jan. 2006, *State Journal* (2005), 358.

high risk insured (i.e., the chronically ill). Also, the nature of the insured entitlements is defined by law, whereas contracting parties agree about where and who will deliver the insured health services. For reasons of public health interest, freedom of contract does not exist in case of emergency care and highly specialised care. By law, health insurers are forced to contract both types of services. These, and other restrictions of the Health Insurance Act's free contracting principle, reflect this Act's hybrid character.

*63.* The Health Insurance Act provides coverage for essential curative care assessed according to the criteria of necessity, proven efficacy, cost-effectiveness, and own responsibility.[4] Under the insurance scheme, the insured may opt for a benefits-in-kind model, a reimbursement model or a combination of both models. Although these models guarantee a standard insurance policy, under the reimbursement model, the insured have free choice of provider. Under the benefits-in-kind variant, the insured are limited to the types of care provided by contracted health providers. In exceptional cases, the insured may opt for a non-contracted provider (cross-border), for instance, in case of long waiting periods, and will receive a cash benefit (reimbursement model). As explained, the health insurer has a statutory obligation to guarantee access to medical care under the benefit-in-kind insurance scheme and may be held accountable for non-compliance with this obligation. It is, therefore, a principle of sound management that the benefit-in-kind insurer purchases sufficient care in and/or outside its area of activity. Except for force majeure, the insurance company cannot be released from its obligation to provide access to healthcare. The insurer cannot defend itself on the basis that it had insufficiently contracted for care or allocated insufficient funds to a hospital facility.

*64.* Instead of a pre-established list of types of treatment for which payment will be guaranteed, the Health Insurance Act includes a 'functional description' of the care covered by the insurance package (i.e., primary care, medical specialist care, dental care, nursery care, maternity and pharmaceutical care, hospital admission, medical devices and medical transport). Whereas the Act sets legal requirements regarding what entitlement includes, it is up to the providers and the health insurer to agree on who provides the care and where. Furthermore, the legislature has enacted a general rule stating that the care provided will also be determined by 'the state of medical science and practice'. This criterion follows the principles of evidence-based medicine.

*65.* It is largely up to the discretion of the health insurer to decide which types of treatment satisfy that condition. However, in applying that criterion, the insurer must interpret the criterion on the basis of what is sufficiently tried and tested by international medical science. This could mean that where a certain treatment has sufficiently been tried and tested by international science, authorisation by the health insurer cannot be refused on the grounds that it is not presently provided in the

4. Based on the method for priority setting by the Dunning Committee, *Choices in Healthcare* (1991). This framework of criteria basically functions as sieves in order to separate care that should or should not be funded.

Netherlands. Proving that an alternative treatment satisfies the 'International Medical Science' test remains extremely difficult for the complainant. In most cases brought before the arbitral insurance body, complainants failed to show that that was the case, for reasons that scientific evidence was not available yet, or simply due to limited accessibility and understanding of scientific literature on new medical technologies.

*66.* Basic health insurance is obligatory for all Dutch residents. Those working in the Netherlands and paying income tax to the Tax Office but living abroad are also compulsorily insured. For two groups of persons, an exception is made. There are special regulations for persons who refuse to insure themselves on the grounds of religious beliefs or their philosophy of life and for undocumented migrants.

*67.* Children under the age of 18 are insured free of charge but have to be included in one of the parents' plans. Children are covered by a government contribution to the health insurance fund.

*68.* All Dutch residents are compulsorily insured for long-term care under the Long-Term Care Act.

# Chapter 3. Medical Law

## §1. Definition and Functions of Medical Law

*69.* Medical law (health law) became a specialised subject in the 1970s. The two events that played an important role in the development of health law were the establishment of the Association of Health Law (*Vereniging voor Gezondheidsrecht*) in 1968 and the introduction of the Journal of Health Law (*Tijdschrift voor Gezondheidsrecht*) in 1977. Significant for the development of health law as a scientific discipline were the inclusions in 1970 of this field of research as a teaching chair at the University of Amsterdam (1970) as well as the creation of a special chair at the University of Leiden in 1972.

*70.* Health law can be defined as an entity of legal rules and regulations, directly connected to and a determining factor for the health in which a person finds himself. This definition indicates that health law cannot be classified as belonging to one of the traditional fields of law, criminal, civil, administrative or constitutional law, but it can be considered to be a horizontal specialism, transversing all fields of law.

*71.* The term medical law is not used very often in the Netherlands. Medical law can be considered to be one aspect of health law, as described in the above definition. As a result of the establishment in 1968 of the Association of Health Law, the discussion regarding medical or health law has been laid to rest and health law has become a general conception.

*72.* Health law consists of medical law and patients' rights, but not solely. Nowadays, health lawyers also concern themselves with the way healthcare is financed. Therefore, health law consists of the rules and principles regarding the relationships between patients and healthcare providers (i.e., the law of healthcare provision), between healthcare providers (in the broadest sense) and healthcare financiers (i.e., the law of healthcare finance) and between healthcare financiers and their clients (i.e., the law of healthcare insurance).[5]

*73.* The rules of health law provision deal with a variety of things. They cover the quality of care, confidentiality, medical records, patients' rights, etc. The rules pertaining to the law on healthcare finance cover planning, licensing, competition, tariffs, etc. Healthcare insurance law consists of rules concerning access to healthcare, the protection of informational privacy and so on. The unity of health law at the level of rules is not currently a subject of debate. They are distinguished from other rules by the fact that they consider the behaviour of the parties involved. Furthermore, while no one would deny the existence of principles underlying these rules, whether there is unity at the level of principles remains debatable.

---

5. M. Buijsen, 'Human Dignity and the Concept of Health Law', in A. den Exter (ed.), *European Health Law* (Antwerp, Maklu, 2017) 17–18.

*74.* According to one school of thought, health law has principles of its own. Its representatives, i.e., those who accept unity on both levels, usually regard health law as a separate branch of jurisprudence. The other school of thought denies the unity at the level of principles. Its representatives tend to maintain that the principles of health law are simply those of penal law, civil law and administrative law. Health law is a mishmash of rules of civil, penal and administrative law, which are similar in only one respect, namely their concern with the behaviour of parties engaged in healthcare. It goes without saying that they do not consider health law as a branch of jurisprudence.

## §2. Sources of Medical Law

*75.* Except for the principles as sources of health law, identifying the sources of health law, one should not forget to mention the norms codified by positive (national) law. Until a short time ago, the discussion regarding the fundamentals of health law took into consideration two constitutionally embedded concepts: the right to self-determination and the right to healthcare. However, several other mainstays have recently been introduced in the literature regarding health law. Some people have indicated that the mainstays of health law, the right to self-determination and the right to healthcare, are somewhat debatable.

*76.* Besides the classical civil rights, there are also social rights laid down in the Constitution. With regard to healthcare, one can hereby mention the right to healthcare. An entirely different significance can be attributed to social rights than can be attributed to the above-mentioned classical and individual rights. On the grounds of this section of the law, the government is obligated to support public healthcare. The government should use its powers to establish the necessary healthcare provisions. Should one wish to concretise such social rights, then it is essential that legislation be enacted in which this right is given in the real form. Under certain circumstances, a combination of the principle of equality as laid down in Article 1 of the Constitution and the social rights as laid down in Article 22 can give greater scope to the latter right than it was initially intended on the grounds of the character of a social right. The Constitution does not contain any provision that refers to the inviolability of human dignity.[6]

*77.* International documents also contain important sources of health law, such as the European Convention on Human Rights (ECHR) of 4 November 1950, ratified by the Netherlands on 28 July 1954. National and international regulations with regard to health law are strongly influenced by the procedures pursued by the European Commission of Human Rights and the European Court of Human Rights.

6. J.-P. Loof, 'Human Dignity in the Netherlands', in P. Becchi and K. Mathis (eds), *Handbook of Human Dignity in Europe* (Cham, Springer Nature Switzerland, 2019) 644.

*78.* The Netherlands has not ratified the ECHR and Biomedicine. On 20 March 2015, the then Dutch Government informed the Second Chamber that the Netherlands would not ratify the Convention. This came as a surprise as the Netherlands have played a pioneering role in the preparation of the Convention.

*79.* EU law has increasingly become important as a source of law in the field of healthcare. Apart from the EU public health provision and public health-related provisions, a relatively new source of law concerns the free movement provisions, in particular, the free movement principles (i.e., of persons, goods and services).

# Part I. The Medical Profession

## Chapter 1. Access to the Medical Profession

### §1. Medical Education

#### I. Historical Note

*80.* The profession of physician has been protected in the Netherlands since 1818 (Act of 12 March 1818 regulating the different branches of medicine). Before that time, there were no specific requirements for a medical degree. This situation changed in 1849, after the establishment of the DMA, and in 1949 the Royal DMA was added, which was the starting point for the reorganisation of medical education. Members of the DMA, all university graduates, played a decisive part in the effectuation of the most important piece of legislation concerning the practice of the profession in public healthcare: the Medical Practice Act of 1 June 1865. The Act provided for uniform university education and improved legal protection of the profession (profession and title protection). The Act only recognised university-educated physicians. This legislation remained unchanged in outline for a long time. It has been revised by the Individual Healthcare Professions Act of 11 November 1993 (IHCP Act) which regulates the qualifications of healthcare professionals wanting to practice in the individual healthcare sector. The Act imposes rules upon healthcare professionals and protects patients against incompetent and negligent acts (*See* below paragraphs 95 et seq.). The Act became effective for the professional domain of physicians on 1 December 1997.

#### II. Undergraduate Medical Education

*81.* Today, universities make use of a so-called numerus fixus for access to medical studies. This means that only a limited number of students are admitted. The greater part of available places are assigned by lottery, after categorisation of the applicants on the basis of their average marks: the ones with the highest average of final examination marks are more likely to draw a place.

*82.* The study of medicine nowadays has been phased: the first phase provides the education for a Master's Degree, including the first year (propaedeutic) and the senior years (second to the fourth year), both parts being concluded with an examination. The Academic Statute mentions the following subjects to be taken for the propaedeutic examination: introduction to the build and vital functions of the human being in a biological and psychosocial sense and their developments; introduction to the disorders of the build and the vital functions of the human being; introduction to public healthcare; the scientific fundamentals of the said subjects.

*83.* The Master's examination adds the subjects dealing with the recognition and influencing of abnormalities or disorders of the build and vital functions of the human being as well as public healthcare, including primary healthcare.

### III. Graduate Medical Education

*84.* The second phase of the study of medicine takes two years (the fifth and sixth) and is concluded with the Doctor of Medicine examination. During the second phase, students are introduced into the clinic. The degree of Doctor of Medicine qualifies a person to start practising medicine. In the Netherlands, medicine can be studied at eight different universities: Amsterdam (two universities), Groningen, Leiden, Maastricht, Nijmegen, Rotterdam and Utrecht.

*85.* Those who have passed their Doctor of Medicine examination but have not (yet) taken supplementary courses are fully qualified to practise medicine, all the same. They are, however, to stay within the limits of their own knowledge and competence. They may call themselves doctors and are legally qualified to prescribe medicines and provide medical certificates, such as the death certificate.

## §2. Licensing of Medical Specialists and GPs: Postgraduate Medical Education

*86.* There are a number of supplementary courses available after the Doctor of Medicine examination: specialist training, GP training, research and PhD programmes and practitioners of social medicine training. The professional associations concerned have formulated their own regulation for the recognition and registration of medical specialists, practitioners of social medicine and GPs. Although this is a private law arrangement, it had a wider social impact which is why it is seen as semi-statutory.

### I. Medical Specialists

*87.* The legal regulation of the licensing of medical specialists is based on a balance between self-regulation and public regulation. Article 14.1 of the IHCP Act leaves the licensing to professional organisations, but Article 14.2 states that the law determines the conditions that these organisations have and the rules they apply to satisfy. Such organisations have to enjoy full legal capacity and be representative of the professions concerned (Article 14.2a). No licensure as a specialist may be delivered to persons who are not registered (*see* paragraph 101) and may not be made dependent upon membership of an organisation (Article 14.2b). The rules applied by the organisations have to comply with the EU Directives (Article 14.2e).

*88.* Depending on the specialism, medical specialist training takes four to six years. Specialist training is given by recognised instructors in recognised institutes. Recognition and registration of medical specialists are taken care of by the following bodies: the Central College, the Specialist Registration Committee and the Committee of Appeal. The Central College has ordinary members (representatives of medical departments of universities and recognised specialists), as well as advisory members (representatives of the Ministry, the National Hospital Council and two assistant physicians). They determine which parts of medicine are recognised as specialisms and what demands are to be made of courses, instructors and institutes. Decisions on these matters are given legal force when approved by the Minister of Education and Science. The minister may veto any decision. The Specialist Registration Committee consists of representatives of the recognised specialisms; it settles the registration and carries out the decisions of the Central College, that is, the factual recognition of certain specialists as instructors, the recognition of institutes and the visitation. A specialist will be struck off the register if he/she has not practised his/her specialism for five years on a regular basis. Those in training to be specialists are called assistant physicians. They are fully qualified to practise medicine within the limits of his/her own abilities. Their legal position is covered by a training regulation and a model training contract which is linked with their employment contract with a hospital. The contract provides rules to strike a balance between their various duties, working hours, responsibilities, conflicts, etc.

## II. General Practitioners

*89.* In 1973, the DMA added to their domestic rules a regulation to recognise and register GPs, which since April 1989 has been extended to nursing home doctors. GP training is given by GP instructors in cooperation with the universities through the Academic GPs' Institutes. The GPs and Nursing Home Physicians Council determine the demands to be met by instructors and training courses. The GP Registration Committee supervises the implementation of the decisions and registers recognised GPs. The Committee of Appeal GP and Nursing Home Physicians hears appeals against the decisions of the GP Registration Committee.

*90.* To secure a contract with the Dutch healthcare insurers, registration in the GP register is compulsory; simultaneous registration in the GP and the medical specialists and/or practitioners of social medicine registers is not allowed. A GP may be struck off the register if he/she has not practised as a GP on a regular basis for five years.

*91.* GP training has a practical and a theoretical part and a waiting list of two and a half to four years. No lots are drawn for admission.

### III. Practitioners of Social Medicine

*92.* In 1930, the General Dutch Association for Social Medicine was founded. In 1956, the DMA added to its domestic rules and regulations concerning recognition and registration of practitioners of social medicine. At the same time, the Foundation for the Training in Social Medicine was founded in order to define the demands to be met by medical officers' training courses.

*93.* Social medicine has seven branches: labour and occupational medicine (1961), juvenile healthcare (1962), insurance medicine (1964), general healthcare (1965), special forms of social medicine (1974), general social medicine (1984) and sports medicine (1986). In 1986, the experimental branch of environmental medicine was started.

## §3. Manpower Planning: Freedom of Establishment

*94.* Access to undergraduate medical education has been limited (*see* paragraph 81). There exist no legal restrictions regarding the freedom of establishment.

## Chapter 2. Practice of Medicine

### §1. Historical Note

*95.* The Medical Practice Act of July 1865 had been the main body of legislation for the practice of medicine for a very long time. This Act has been replaced by the IHCP Act that, among others also, regulates the practice of medicine. The Act came into force in 1997.[7] On 1 April 2019, the law of 11 July 2018 in order to modify the IHCP Act to ameliorate the disciplinary law and the functioning of the Act entered into force.[8]

*96.* The IHCP Act has a long history. In December 1967, the State Commission on Medical Practice was established.[9] The Commission regarded medical professions as those which are concerned with individual (or personal) healthcare. Excluded were those professions which are concerned primarily with environmental hygiene and with health information. The existing regulations concerning medical practice were in need of revision because many professions other than physicians were involved in the treatment of patients and because of the high degree of specialisation within the medical and the related professions.

*97.* The 1865 Act made it an offence to practice medicine for those who were not legally qualified to practice medicine to combat so-called quack medicine. According to the Commission, however, this Act did not achieve this aim, for infringement of the prohibition was usually not prosecuted. For this reason, it proposed to limit the general prohibition to practice medicine by unqualified persons to areas which are a real danger to a patient's health (the so-called reserved procedures, *see* paragraph 107). The opinion of the State Commission is the basis of the IHCP Act. In 1986, the Healthcare Professionals bill was introduced in the Second Chamber of the States-General. The First Chamber endorsed the bill on 9 November 1993.[10]

*98.* A revision of the existing Medical Practice Act and other legislation was considered to be necessary because of the following:

- The Medical Practice Act 1865 was obsolete: a citizen's choice of treatment or diagnostic method for his/her disease should be respected. Strict application of the Medical Practice Act restricted this freedom of choice.

7. N. de Bijl and I. Nederveen-van de Kragt, 'Legal Safeguards Against Medical Practice by Not Suitably Qualified Persons: A Comparative Study in Seven EU-Countries', *European Journal of Health Law*, 4 (1997) 5–18.
8. *State Journal* (2018), 260.
9. Ministerie van Volksgezondheid en Milieuhygiëne, *Rapport van de Staatscommissie Medische Beroepsuitoefening* (Staatsuitgeverij 1973) with an English summary at pp. 142–144.
10. *State Journal* (1993), 655.

- The qualifications of nurses and other (para) medical staffs to carry out medical acts required legislation in order to replace the so-called prolonged arm construction (nurses carrying out medical activities based on a physician's implied or explicit authorisation).
- Over the years, a number of medical specialisations had come into existence; the option of legal recognition was desirable.
- Medical disciplinary jurisdiction was in need of adaptation to developments in society as regards the effectuation of a better position of the plaintiff, more up-to-date formulation of the disciplinary norms, more open nature of the sessions and adaptation of the composition of the disciplinary councils.

## §2. Procedures in the Field of Medicine and Healthcare

*99.* Medicine is defined as the domain of individual healthcare in the context of which procedures are practised that: (a) seek to cure a person of disease; (b) are intended to protect a person from developing a disease; (c) serve to assess the health status of a person; (d) are intended to provide obstetric assistance to a person; (e) are aimed at taking blood or removing tissue from a person for other purposes than those referred under a to d; (f) are aimed at removing tissue from a deceased person and performing an autopsy; (g) are directed at the application, modification, restructuring and removal of tissue from a person for other purposes than those mentioned under a to d (cosmetic procedures). (Article 1, fourth indent IHCP Act).

*100.* Individual healthcare is care that relates directly to a person and is intended to promote or monitor his/her health, including examinations and advice (Article 1, fifth indent IHCP Act). From this definition, it follows that individual healthcare is a broader concept than medicine.

## §3. Constitutive Registration and Professional Titles

*101.* Article 3.1 IHCP Act sets up registers in which those who meet the legal conditions are inscribed as either physician, dentist, pharmacist, healthcare psychologist, psychotherapist, physical therapist, midwife, nurse, physician assistant, orthopedagogic-generalist or clinical technologist. The family name, first names, gender, date of birth, nationality and address of the person concerned and the number and date of registration are stated in the register, profession and speciality of the registered (Article 3.2 IHCP Act). The name, initials, gender, IHCP number and the relevant profession and speciality of the registered person are public. A ministerial decree may provide that other registered data are public in order to make it possible to find a professional in the register (Article 3.3). A ministerial decree may determine the cases and the way in which a healthcare professional may make public under which IHCP number he is registered (Article 4a). Upon request, everyone is informed whether a person is registered (Article 12.2a).

*102.* Only those inscribed in a register may use the professional title corresponding with the profession. Others should not use this title (so-called title protection) (Article 4.1 and 4.2 IHCP Act).

*103.* In order to be registered as a physician, one had to obtain a certificate testifying that one fulfils all training requirements for a physician determined by a royal decree (Article 18 IHCP Act).

*104.* Registration is in principle for an undetermined period. However, Article 8.1. IHCP Act provides that a royal decree may determine that the registration is not valid anymore when a certain period of time has elapsed. This means that the healthcare professional concerned has to re-register to continue using his or her professional title. This so-called periodic registration aims to stimulate renewal of knowledge and competences. Since 1 January 2018, physicians have to re-register every five years. According to the Minister of Health, this obligation has reduced the number of registered physicians with 18,000 (or 20%).[11] The obligation to re-register already existed for physical therapists, midwives, nurses, pharmacists, dentists, healthcare psychologists and psychotherapists.

*105.* Registration gives the right to use a protected professional title and is therefore called 'constitutive registration'.

## §4. Competence of Physicians

*106.* The legal competence of physicians consists of the procedures in the field of medicine (*see* above paragraph 99). In case a GP is allowed to prepare or deliver medicinal products on the basis of the Medicine's Act, the preparation and the delivery of medicines also belongs to his or her legal competence (Article 19.1 and 19.2 IHCP Act).

## §5. Reserved Procedures

*107.* The most important and innovative aspect of the IHCP Act were the rules concerning the so-called reserved procedures (Articles 35–39). This Act has replaced the absolute prohibition of the practice of medicine by others than physicians by a system of so-called reserved procedures (medical acts which may only be performed by physicians or other designated persons such as dentists). This list of reserved procedures is supposed to describe the most hazardous acts which may only be performed by competent persons.

*108.* Article 36 IHCP Act contains an enumeration of the reserved procedures and refers to the healthcare profession(s) that are legally competent to practice them.

11. A. Hendriks, 'Kroniek van het gezondheidsrecht', *NJB* (2019) 1107.

*109.* The following are legally authorised to perform surgical actions – which are understood to mean actions in which the cohesion of body tissues is disrupted, and this does not recover immediately – (a) physicians, (b) dentists, (c) midwives, (d) physician assistants, (e) certain categories of nurses, and (f) clinical technologists. For dentists, midwives, physician assistants and clinical technologists, this competence is limited to the activities that belong to their legal domain of competence (Article 36.1 IHCP Act). The practice of obstetrical actions is the legal competence of physicians and under certain conditions of midwives (Article 36.2 IHCP Act). The practice of endoscopies is the legal competence of physicians and under certain conditions of physician assistants and certain categories of nurses (Article 36.3 IHCP Act). The practice of catheterisations is the legal competence of physicians and under certain conditions of midwives, physician assistants, certain categories of nurses and clinical technologists (Article 36.4 IHCP Act). The practice of injections is the legal competence of physicians, and under certain conditions of dentists, midwives, physician assistants, certain categories of nurses and clinical technologists (Article 36.5 IHCP Act). The practice of punctures is the legal competence of physicians and under certain conditions of midwives, physician assistants, certain categories of nurses and clinical technologists (Article 36.6 IHCP Act). The practice of anaesthetising patients is the legal competence of physicians and under certain conditions of dentists (Article 36.7 IHCP Act). The practice of activities in the field of individual healthcare by making use of radioactive or ionising radiation is the legal competence of physicians and under certain conditions of dentists and clinical technologists (Article 36.8 IHCP Act). The practice of electronic convulsion is the legal competence of physicians and under certain clinical technologists and certain categories of nurses (Article 36.9 IHCP Act). The practice of applying defibrillation is the legal competence of physicians and under certain conditions of clinical technologists and certain categories of nurses (Article 36.10 IHCP Act). The practice of electroconvulsive therapy is the legal competence of physicians (Article 36.11 IHCP Act). The practice of using a lithotripter for medical purposes is the legal competence of physicians (Article 36.12 IHCP Act). The practice of activities with human reproductive cells and human embryos not aimed at accomplishing a natural pregnancy is the legal competence of physicians (Article 36.13 IHCP Act). The prescription of medicinal products is the legal competence of physicians, dentists, and under certain conditions of midwives, nurses and physician assistants (Article 36.14 IHCP Act). It is prohibited to prescribe medicinal products via the internet to persons who the prescriber has never personally met or whom the prescriber does not know or from whom the prescriber has no medication history at his disposal (Article 67 Medicine's Act). Off label prescription of medicinal products is only allowed according to protocols or standards developed by the medical profession. If such standards or protocols are still in development, consultation between the treating physician and the pharmacist is required (Article 68.1 Medicine's Act).

*110.* According to Article 35a.1 IHCP Act, these persons are only legally authorised in so far as that they can reasonably assume that they have the competence for the proper performance of those acts (the so-called only competence gives legal authority rule).

*111.* Article 36a provides that notwithstanding Article 36, a royal decree may by way of experiment and for a period of maximal five years allow other healthcare professions than those referred to in Article 36 to practice certain reserved procedures. Article 36a has been inserted in the IHCP Act by the law of 7 November 2011.[12] Article 7.1 of the temporary royal decree of 7 April 2017[13] allows bachelors medical care providers to practice the following reserved procedures: subcutaneous, intramuscular and intravenous injections; catheterisation of the bladder of adults and the insertion of a gavage or an intravenous drip; a venepuncture; elective cardioversion and the practice of the following procedures in a setting of acute care: defibrillation; intubate or extubate the trachea with an oral or nasal tube and apply a drainage puncture in case of a tension pneumothorax. According to Article 7.2, this competence is limited to activities with limited complexity, routinely activities, activities with foreseeable risks and activities practised according to national applicable guidelines, standards and protocols. Article 8 of the royal decree of 17 May 2019 on the temporary autonomous competence of registered dental hygienists[14] allows them to perform the following reserved procedures: surgical procedures, injections and activities in which use is made of radioactive products or ionising radiation in so far as these procedures fall within their field of competence and are performed according to national applicable guidelines, standards and protocols.

*112.* Article 37 of the IHCP Act makes it possible to expand or to amend the list of reserved procedures by a royal decree provided a bill has been introduced in Parliament within six months after the royal decree in order to remain valid. According to Article 37a inserted by the law of 11 July 2018 the chapter on reserved procedures of the IHCP Act is not applicable to procedures referred to in Article 36 in so far as they are governed by other legal rules. In the explanatory memorandum to the bill, the use of material for tattoos and piercings is given as an example.

*113.* One may draw attention to the fact that Article 36 does not include in the list of reserved procedures for the diagnosis of a disease. Neither are activities in the field of human genetics because they require highly specialised equipment. Also, psychotherapy is not a reserved procedure.

*114.* Other activities in the field of medicine are reserved to physicians by other legislation. Terminating a pregnancy (abortion) is not liable to punishment if it is practised by a physician in a hospital or clinic authorised to do so according to the Termination of Pregnancy Act (*see* paragraph 405).

*115.* If reserved procedures are carried out by a person unqualified to do so according to Articles 35–39, in a professional way and without necessity, he/she is liable to legal action under Articles 35.1 and 97 IHCP Act (three months' imprisonment at the most and/or a second category fine). Whether a person has acted in a professional way depends upon the circumstances. Relevant circumstances are

12. *State Journal* (2011), 568.
13. *State Journal* (2017), 162.
14. *State Journal* (2019), 192.

acting on a regular basis, the way one presents him or herself to the public and asking a fee for the services provided. There is little jurisprudence in this regard. The placing of a drip needle in the context of a 'self-help' training by a soldier did not infringe the IHCP Act.[15]

15. Tribunal Gelderland, 3 Feb. 2020, ECLI:NL:RBGEL:2020:760.

# Chapter 3. Control over the Practice of Medicine

## §1. Disciplinary Liability

*116.* The disciplinary liability of physicians is regulated in Chapter VII IHCP Act.

### I. Historical Note

*117.* In the Netherlands, disciplinary law was introduced for physicians in 1928. The report of the State Commission on Medical Practice of 1973 (*see* paragraph 96) contained proposals to modernise medical disciplinary law. The then existing disciplinary norm namely, performing acts which undermine confidence in the status of the medical profession should be replaced by another, namely failing to provide requisite care for a person requesting the assistance of an expert with regard to his or her state of health. As concerns the lodging of a complaint, the right to do so should be exclusively assigned to the Health Inspectorate.[16]

### II. Disciplinary Norms

*118.* Physicians may be held disciplinarily liable for not acceding to one of the following norms. First, any act or omission contrary to the care that a professional should exercise in that capacity with regard to: (1) a person with regard to whose state of health he provides assistance or his assistance has been invoked; (2) a person who, in distress, needs assistance to his state of health; or (3) the closest relations of the persons referred to in (1) or (2) (Article 47.1a IHCP Act). Second, any act or omission than those referred to under Article 47.1a, contrary to what befits a proper professional (Article 47.1b). The second norm originally regarded any act or omission that was conflicting with the interest of good practice in individual healthcare. The law of 11 July 2018 (*see* paragraph 95) has replaced this norm which has now a broader field of application.

*119.* The first disciplinary norm is mainly directed at an already existing relation between a physician and a patient and his/her closest relatives but also regards the situation of an unconscious patient where such a relation does not exist (yet). The second norm does not regard the relation between a physician and a patient but more in general regards relations with colleagues and health insurers or undermining public trust by unprofessional behaviour in the media. Also, the behaviour of a physician in the private sphere can be sanctioned in light of this norm.

---

16. Ministerie van Volksgezondheid en Milieuhygiëne, *Rapport van de Staatscommissie Medische Beroepsuitoefening* (Staatsuitgeverij 1973) with an English summary at pp. 142–144.

*120.* These norms have been deliberately formulated in a broad way in order to capture the respect of norms such as the rights of the patient, good practices, guidelines and protocols. The Dutch disciplinary system aims at quality improvement by correcting and, in severe cases restricting professional behaviour. Disciplinary case law is published anonymously (*see* paragraph 120) and this has given rise to a rich database of disciplinary decisions regarding varying themes, such as euthanasia on a patient with advanced dementia (*see* paragraph 373), rights of the patients, medical confidentiality and so on.

## III. Disciplinary Boards

*121.* In disciplinary law, the disciplinary jurisprudence is the competence of the regional disciplinary boards; in appeal, the central disciplinary board is competent (Article 47.3 IHCP Act).

*122.* There are five regional disciplinary boards, each consisting of two lawyers, one of whom acts as president of the board and three physicians. In November 2020, a bill was pending in the Second Chamber in order to reduce the number of regional disciplinary boards from five to three. The central disciplinary board consists of two lawyers, one of whom acts as president of the central disciplinary board and three physicians (Articles 55 and 56 IHCP Act). The central disciplinary board is established in The Hague (Article 53.2).

## IV. Disciplinary Sanctions

*123.* A disciplinary board can impose one of the following disciplinary sanctions: (a) a warning; (b) a reprimand; (c) a fine not exceeding EUR 4,500; (d) a suspension of the registration for one year at the most; (e) a partial prohibition to practise (f) a cancellation of the entry in the register; and (g) the binding of special conditions to practise the profession for which the professional is entered in the register (Article 48.1) The sanctions referred to in c and d, d and e, and e and g may be imposed simultaneously (Article 48.3). The consequences of a suspension of the registration and a striking off the register are that the physician concerned may not (temporarily) use the title of a physician nor practice a reserved procedure. Also, licensure as a medical specialist will (temporarily) expire. According to the circumstances, it is possible to restore the registration of the person concerned. A partial prohibition has no consequence for the registration but regards the legal authority to practise certain procedures. Disciplinary sanctions that imply a limitation or a prohibition to practice are mentioned in the register. From 1 July 2012 until 1 April 2019, a reprimand and a fine were also mentioned in the register in order to enable patients to be better informed of a physician. From the onset, this policy has led to debate between politicians, patient representatives and the DMA. During the parliamentary preparation of the law of 11 July 2018, a majority in the Dutch House of

Representatives voted against disclosure of reprimands, leaving disclosure of reprimands a discretion of the disciplinary board when deemed appropriate or necessary.[17]

## V. Procedural Aspects

*124.* A disciplinary procedure before a regional disciplinary board against a physician starts upon a written complaint of among others, a directly interested person or the Health Inspectorate (Article 65.1 IHCP Act). In practice, the complainant is, most of the times, a patient or his or her closest relatives. Article 55a.1 provides that the minister takes care of the appointment of disciplinary complaint officers who may advise the complainant on how to formulate his complaint and change it. This provision has been added to the IHCP Act by the law of 11 July 2018. It aims at directing complaints that are of minor importance to the internal complaint procedure provided for in the Quality, Complaints and Disputes Act (QCDHC Act) (*see* paragraph 124) and to formulate complaints directed to a disciplinary board more clearly in order to increase the chances that such a board might make a meaningful decision. However, it is up to the complainant to decide which procedure will be followed.[18] An amicable settlement may be sought at the preliminary hearings (Article 65.3 and 65.4 IHCP Act). A study of the facts often brings to light a failure in communication. The Act allows for public sessions of the boards unless there are important objections (Article 70 IHCP Act). The position of the plaintiff has been strengthened by the fact that he may be represented by a proxy and may be acted for by a lawyer (Article 65 IHCP Act) as well as the fact that the plaintiff may be present in court during the hearing of the case and may give evidence (Article 67 IHCP Act). The complaints must be filed within ten years after the act or omission (Article 65.5 IHCP Act). The complete process, from filing a complaint to the judgment, usually takes between one and two years. Article 70 provides that a regional disciplinary board may decide that its decision shall anonymously be made public in the State Journal, journals or newspapers.

## VI. Measures on Account of Incompetence

*125.* Apart from the disciplinary jurisprudence which provides measures for professional reprehensible behaviour, the IHCP Act also provides for the possibility to impose the following measures on account of incompetence as a consequence of mental or physical disease or by abuse of alcohol or drugs (Article 80): a restriction of qualification under certain conditions; a partial disqualification and a cancellation of the entry in the register. The board for medical supervision in The Hague is

17. B. Laarman et al., 'How Do Doctors in the Netherlands Perceive the Impact of Disciplinary Procedures and Disclosure of Disciplinary Measures on Their Professional Practice, Health and Career Opportunities? A Questionnaire among Medical Doctors Who Received a Disciplinary Measure', *BMJ Open*, 9 (2019) e023576, 6–7.

18. J. Legemaate, 'Gezondheidsrecht', *Tijdschrift voor Consumentenrecht en Handelspraktijken* (2020) 86.

authorised to impose these measures. The board consists of two lawyers and three physicians. Only the Health Inspectorate may present a case to the board. An appeal against a decision of the board for medical supervision can be lodged with the central disciplinary board by the professional concerned as well as by the Health inspector who presented the case.

## §2. Professional Liability

### I. Introduction

*126.* The expression 'professional liability' as used here connotes the responsibility in general of the physician in the exercise of his or her profession. In addition to civil liability, this embraces obligations enjoined by the criminal and disciplinary laws (*see* for the latter paragraph 115).

*127.* The professional liability of a physician is, with the exception of the disciplinary liability, not governed by special laws. This means that both the civil liability and the criminal liability of the physician for damage or injury caused by improper performance of the duties entailed in the discharge of his professional functions are governed by the general rules of civil and criminal law as to (professional) liability.

*128.* An exception to this rule is the regulation in the Medical Treatment Agreements Act which has been incorporated into Book 7 (Special Contracts) of the Dutch Civil Code, concerning joint or central liability of hospitals in the case of an error made by a hospital-employed professional (*see* paragraph 147).

*129.* First, the issue of civil liability will be dealt with, then the more specific issue of hospital liability and, finally, the issue of criminal law liability.

*130.* Although there is an increase in the number of cases of professional liability of physicians, on the whole, this number is small. Causes of this increase are said to be the increase in medical activities in absolute numbers, the increased awareness of patients and the fair amount of attention paid by the media to healthcare, accidents and near-accidents. The fact that the number of legal proceedings is only small originates, on the one hand, from the excellence of the social welfare provision: patients can only claim compensation for that part of their damage that is not yet covered by salary arrangements, social insurance or private compensatory schemes,[19] and on the other hand, from the fact that the greater part of liability actions is concluded with the withdrawal of the complaint by the injured party

19. I. Giesen and E. Engelhard, 'Medical Liability in the Netherlands', in B.A. Koch (ed.), *Medical Liability in Europe: A Comparison of Selected Jurisdictions* (Berlin, De Gruyter, 2011) 363.

because of the lengthy nature of such proceedings. This aside, a considerable number of damage claims is concluded with a settlement out of court. Insurance companies are, for that matter, rather reluctant to offer information, which does not facilitate an insight into the nature of professional errors.

## II. Civil Liability

### A. *Classification of Physician's Liability*

*131.* If a physician causes injury to a patient by his/her treatment, he/she may be sued on the grounds of default (contract law) or tort (tort law). Default consists in the failure to fulfil a contract; a patient is commonly assumed to enter into a medical treatment contract or agreement with his/her physician on the basis of which he/she can sue the doctor for default at the latter's failure to fulfil the contract. Default compels the guilty party to compensate the claimant for the damage sustained, unless the guilty party cannot be blamed for the failure, nor can he/she be held accountable under the law, a legal transaction or the prevailing social views. Default is defined as the violation of the privacy of a third party, as well as an action or omission in conflict with a legal obligation, or with what is deemed socially proper by common law; all of these, barring the existence of justification. The offender may be held accountable for default if he carries the blame for this or another action for which he can be held accountable under the law or prevailing social views.

*132.* Whether a claim is founded on contract law or tort law is hardly of any consequence under Dutch law. The standard of care and the burden of proof are the same (*see* paragraph 139).[20]

### B. *Contents of the Physician's Duty (Standard of Care)*

*133.* In case law on the contractual liability and on tortious liability of physicians, the criterion of the 'reasonably able and reasonably acting' professional has been adopted to describe the general standard of care that is expected of all professions and not only physicians.[21] Applied to physicians, the criterion is the way a reasonably competent physician ought to act in ordinary circumstances, which is an idealised criterion. It is of no importance whether the doctor deems himself to have acted reasonably. The criterion of the 'reasonably able and reasonably acting' physician was first formulated by the Dutch Supreme Court in a judgment of 9 November 1990 as follows: 'The Court of Appeal has used as a standard measurement the

---

20. *Ibid.*, 387.
21. B. Laarman and A. Akkermans, *Compensation Schemes for Damage Caused by Healthcare and Alternatives to Court Proceedings in the Netherlands*: *The Netherlands National Report to the 20th General Congress of the International Academy of Comparative Law* (Fukuoka, Japan, 22–28 Jul. 2018) 2.

meticulousness to be expected from a reasonably competent and reasonably acting medical specialist. This standard measurement is correct.'[22]

*134.* Later on, this standard has been incorporated in Article 7:453 Dutch Civil Code, entitled 'level of care'. This Article reads as follows: 'In providing the medical treatment, a healthcare provider must observe the standards of a prudent care provider and, in doing so, he/she has to act in conformity with the responsibilities laid upon him/her by the professional standard for care providers among which the quality standard referred to in Article 1z of the Care Insurance Act that defines a quality standard "as a guideline, a module, a norm, a care standard or the description of an organisation that 1) regards the entire care process or part of it, 2) determines what is necessary to deliver quality care in the perspective of the client and 3) according to Article 66b of the Care Insurance Act has been recorded in a public register".'[23] Article 7:453 Civil Code has been amended by Article IV of the Act of 9 September 2020 amending the QCDHC Act.[24] The reference to the Care Insurance Act has been replaced by a reference to the professional standards and quality standard in Article 1.1. QCDHC Act. Moreover, in Article 7:453, a new paragraph is added, providing that Article 2a.1 and 2a.2 QCDHC Act is also applicable to healthcare providers accordingly (*see* paragraph 227). This part of the Act of 9 September 2020 has not yet entered into force.

*135.* For physicians, the professional standard consists of the state of the art of medical practice as reflected in professional guidelines, standards, protocols and scientific publications. Case law is also an important source.

*136.* In judging whether the criterion of 'a reasonably competent physician' has been met, the opinion of experts is of major importance. In a judgment of the Supreme Court of 30 November 1976,[25] a ruling of the Amsterdam Court was quashed on the grounds of inadequate justification by the Court for its deviation from the experts' judgment. The Advocate General said in his summing-up: 'the correctness or reasonableness of the perception of the physician-defendant can hardly be judged in another way than by the opinion of other physicians who are experts in the field of question. Their opinion will be used by the judge as a criterion in answering the question whether the physician involved acted in a responsible way'.

*137.* The obligation a physician enters into with a patient is usually regarded as an obligation of means (effort), not as an obligation of result. This means that a physician has to make all reasonable efforts to obtain a certain result; the result itself needs not to be guaranteed. If a certain treatment fails or has unsatisfactory results, the injured party – if he holds the physician liable for an obligation of means – will

22. Supreme Court, 9 Nov. 1990, *NJ* 1990, 26; ECLI:NL:HR:1990:AC1103.
23. Translation partially based on ww.dutchcivillaw.com; *see also* E. Hondius and A. van Hooft, 'The New Dutch Law on Medical Services', *Netherlands International Law Review,* XLIII (1996) 5.6 Appendix: Dutch Medical Services Act 1994.
24. *State Journal* (2020), 346.
25. Supreme Court, 30 Nov. 1976, *NJ* (1977), 195.

have to prove that the physician failed to make an effort expected of a reasonably competent physician in similar circumstances. This is no easy task.

*138.* In a small number of cases, an obligation of result is the issue at stake. Examples are the pulling of a tooth, extirpation of an inflamed appendix, supplying the patient with adequate information and amputate the right leg and not the wrong one. In these cases, it is easier for an injured party to prove default, as the absence of the desired result is all he has to prove. To escape a liability charge, the physician will have to prove the absence of result to be due to circumstances beyond his/her control.

*139.* More often than not, the distinction between an obligation of means and an obligation of result is hard to make. A cure cannot always be guaranteed, but the dispensing of correct medication can be. When a physician makes a solemn promise to procure a certain result without mentioning the possible complications, an obligation of result is assumed to exist. The so-called informed consent plays a significant part in this. A patient can only deliberately decide to consent to a certain form of treatment if he is well informed about the advantages and the disadvantages of the treatment.

### *C. The Basis of Liability and Burden of Proof*

#### 1. Fault

*140.* Fault is the main basis of a claim for malpractice either in contract or in tort. Deviation from the professional standard is to be considered as a fault. In liability cases, the person to allege is, as a rule, the one to prove. The onus of proof of a physician's failing in effort or performance, or of his culpable default, rests on the patient claiming damages on the grounds of default or tort. The Supreme Court, however, states that the physician is required to supply adequate factual information to motivate his objection to the patient's statements in order to supply the patient with leads for evidence, if necessary. A simple denial will not be accepted but will have to be substantiated, for instance, by the provision of documentation like the patient's medical file.[26]

*141.* In itself, this does not reverse the burden of proof, although the result may be the same. According to Hondius and van Hooft, this 'comes close to a reversal of the burden of proof'.[27] The applicable standard is whether the information provided by the physician provides the patient with sufficient data to substantiate his

26. Supreme Court, 20 Nov. 1987 ECLI:NL:HR:1987:ADOO58, cited in B. Laarman and A. Akkermans, *Compensation Schemes for Damage Caused by Healthcare and Alternatives to Court Proceedings in the Netherlands: The Netherlands National Report to the 20th General Congress of the International Academy of Comparative Law* (Fukuoka, Japan, 22–28 Jul. 2018) 6, n. 30.
27. E. Hondius and A. van Hooft, 'The New Dutch Law on Medical Services', *Netherlands International Law Review*, XLIII (1996) 6.

claim. When the physician fails to meet this standard, the judge can place the burden of proof upon the physician.[28] This may ease the patient's onus of proof. The judge sometimes reverses the onus of proof. This seems to have been a recurring event in recent years, which apparently somewhat improves the patient's position as far as the onus of proof is concerned.

## 2. Damages

*142.* A patient is only entitled to recover damages with respect to negligent medical treatment if he/she has actually suffered damage. In principle, all the damage he/she suffered has to be compensated.

*143.* The 'loss of a chance' doctrine is used as an instrument to compensate patients in the event that a causal link between fault and physical damage cannot be established. The Supreme Court has recently accepted this doctrine in a case against a physician, and it is widely accepted in medical liability cases.[29] Laarman and Akkermans cite the following example: 'when in the absence of a timely intervention in a birth process, the new born child is suffering perinatal asphyxia, that might also have occurred if there would have been a timely intervention, the court might ask the medical expert's opinion about the chance of avoiding damage to the child's brain when the gynaecologist would have acted according to his professional standard, and when that chance is sufficiently substantial, might award damages for loss of that chance'.[30]

*144.* A first important step in the gradual acceptance of the loss of a chance doctrine was the judgment of the District Court of Amsterdam of 15 December 1993 and the judgment on appeal of the Amsterdam Court of Appeal on 4 January 1996.[31] Both judgments have been summarised as follows by Giesen and Engelhard: 'The plaintiff's one-month-old daughter was referred to the hospital by the family physician after several small spontaneous bleedings were discovered. The doctor consulted there, the defendant, examined her but did not find conclusive signs of a brain hemorrhage, as was feared. He decided that Ruth could go home and should come back the next morning for an extensive examination. The same

28. Supreme Court 18 Feb. 1994, *NJ* 1994, 368; Supreme Court, 13 Jan. 1995, ECLI:NL:HR:1994:ZC1269; Supreme Court, 15 Dec. 2006, ECLI:NL:HR:2006:AZ1083, all cited in B. Laarman and A. Akkermans, *Compensation Schemes for Damage Caused by Healthcare and Alternatives to Court Proceedings in the Netherlands: The Netherlands National Report to the 20th General Congress of the International Academy of Comparative Law* (Fukuoka, Japan, 22–28 Jul. 2018) 6, n. 32.
29. Supreme Court, 27 Oct. 2017, ECLI:NL:HR:2017:2786, cited in B. Laarman and A. Akkermans, *Compensation Schemes for Damage Caused by Healthcare and Alternatives to Court Proceedings in the Netherlands: The Netherlands National Report to the 20th General Congress of the International Academy of Comparative Law* (Fukuoka, Japan, 22–28 Jul. 2018) 7, n. 35.
30. *Ibid.*, 7.
31. Court of Appeal Amsterdam 4 Jan. 1996, *NJ* 1997, 213 cited in I. Giesen and E. Engelhard, 'Medical Liability in the Netherlands', in B.A. Koch (ed.), *Medical Liability in Europe: A Comparison of Selected Jurisdictions* (Berlin, De Gruyter, 2011) 380.

evening around 8.00 pm, the claimant went back to the hospital again. The doctor on duty concluded there was no need for further examinations at that point in time. The next morning Ruth was examined again. A large brain hemorrhage on the left side was discovered; Ruth was placed on the intensive care ward immediately and underwent brain surgery that same day. Ruth parents' started a civil procedure claiming medical faults were made (they claimed that a more extensive examination should have been undertaken immediately; Ruth should not have been sent home) and these faults caused or at least contributed to the disabilities that Ruth consequently suffered from. The doctors claimed that Ruth's late admission into the hospital did not cause the damage. Since the bleeding had already been going on for some time, there would have been residual damage in any case, even if there had been an early diagnosis. Experts had concluded this as well.'

*145.* The District Court concluded that not admitting Ruth when she visited the hospital the second time, at 8.00 pm in the evening, was a medical error. With regard to the question of whether this fault led to more residual damage for Ruth than it would have occurred if she had been admitted earlier, the court concluded the following, based on the report by the medical experts: 'the fault had led to the loss of a chance for Ruth at a better end result, given adequate medical treatment. That this chance was nil or negligibly small was not decided by the experts, nor raised by defendants. The court did not, however, agree with the plaintiffs' claim that the chance of complete recovery was lost as well. Considering the above, the court found that the damage, being the lost chance of reaching a better result of treatment, was 25%. For this percentage, the defendants were liable for Ruth's damage. The Court of Appeal had to consider, *inter alia*, objections raised against the decision by the District Court that the chance of complete recovery had not been lost. It decided that although the chance of complete recovery could not be excluded with 100% certainty, the chance was extremely large that even with an early diagnosis, residual damage would have remained. It also ruled that the District Court was right in holding that the percentage of damage due to the late admittance into the hospital had to be put at 25%'. And both authors conclude: 'One can thus safely say that the loss of chance approach has been accepted in the Netherlands.'

## 3. Causation

*146.* The injured party also has to prove that the damage is a direct result of the physician's (non-)performance. A judgment of the Breda Court shows that even if a medical error admittedly has been made, strict requirements are to be met in the proving of causality between error and alleged damage.[32] Moreover, the patient will have to cooperate in an examination to establish causality, if necessary. This is disadvantageous to the patient, the more so when the examination is of a stressful and/or invasive nature.

32. Court of Breda 28 May 1993, Summary Proceedings (*KG*) 236.

*147.* There is not a lot of case law that deals explicitly with the question of whether a condition *sine qua non* relation is needed or required to establish liability because this is accepted in general as one of the cornerstones of liability law.[33]

### D. Aspects of Vicarious Liability

#### 1. Liability of Hospitals for the Acts of Their Medical Staff

*148.* Thanks to the so-called joint or central liability approach, if the patient received treatment based on the medical services contract as provided for in Article 7:446–7:468 Dutch Civil Code (which is the default rule), he/she can sue not only his/her physician in person but also the hospital. Article 7:462-1 states that if in the implementation (performance) of the medical treatment agreement, activities are performed in a hospital which is not a party to that agreement, the hospital shall bear joint liability for any failure to comply with the medical treatment agreement as if it was a party to that agreement itself. By a 'hospital', it is understood an institution or a department thereof that under Article 5 of the Admission of Care Institutions Act is licensed or admitted as a hospital, nursing home or mental institution, an academic hospital or an abortion clinic within the meaning of the Termination of Pregnancy Act (Article 7:462.2 Civil Code).

#### 2. Physician's Liability for Medical Activity of Other Persons (Strict Liability)

*149.* Article 6:76 of the Dutch Civil Code states that if the debtor to an obligation (which may include physicians that act upon a medical services contract) used other persons in order to fulfil this obligation, he shall be liable for their acts or omissions in a similar way as for his own behaviour. According to Giesen and Engelhard, it is not clear how far the scope of that Article reaches in the medical sphere: does it mean that a physician can be held liable for the faulty analysis of a pathologist? The literature seems divided on this.[34]

### E. Limitation or Exclusion of Liability

*150.* Article 7: 463 Dutch Civil Code stipulates that the liability of a physician or, in the case referred to in Article 7:462, of a hospital cannot be limited or excluded.

33. I. Giesen and E. Engelhard, 'Medical Liability in the Netherlands', in B.A. Koch (ed.), *Medical Liability in Europe: A Comparison of Selected Jurisdictions* (Berlin, De Gruyter, 2011) 375.
34. *Ibid.*, 385–386.

### III. Criminal Liability

*151.* When a physician has made a serious professional error, he can be prosecuted by a criminal court on the basis of Article 307 Criminal Code (culpable homicide) as well as on the basis of Article 308, Criminal Code (grievous bodily harm). The Public Prosecutor decides whether to prosecute or not. This will only be done on reasonable suspicion of culpability and the certainty of proof of causality between the physician's actions and the occurrence of death or grievous bodily harm. If these requirements are not fulfilled, there will be no conviction, so rendering prosecution futile. The culpability referred to in Articles 307 and 308 Criminal Code is more or less of gross negligence, omission and inattentiveness; what it is not, is slight negligence or non-observance of extreme carefulness.

*152.* Since 1976, criminal conviction of legal persons, such as hospitals insofar as they are run by a legal person, has been made possible. In 1987, a hospital was convicted of culpable homicide as a result of insufficient care taken of the safety of the anaesthetics equipment in use at the hospital.[35]

*153.* The right to institute criminal proceedings for most crimes which physicians might commit is precluded after six years by reason of lapse of time (Articles 300, 307–309 Criminal Code). The term begins on the day following the one of perpetration, with some specified exceptions. The term expires at the institution of proceedings, provided that the prosecuted person has been informed or has been served a writ (Article 72 Criminal Code).

*154.* Specific criminal liability for abortion, euthanasia, assisting in suicide, medical secrecy, etc., is dealt with in Part II.

## §3. Quality Assurance

*155.* On the basis of Article 22 of the Constitution, the Dutch Government has to take measures to promote public health; in other words, the public is entitled to good healthcare. This is the case when the quality, the functional availability, the geographical accessibility and the financial attainability of healthcare are guaranteed. Quality refers to, among others, the education and actions of medical professionals, the level of care provided by individuals and institutions, as well as to the means used. Quality can be guaranteed in various ways: both private organisations, citizens and the government can play their parts (*see* paragraphs 218 et seq.).

## §4. Medical Ethics Committees

*156.* In intramural care, medical-ethical committees play a prominent role in a variety of ways. The number of tasks are the preparation of policy, consultation in

35. Court Leeuwarden 23 Dec. 1987, *NJ* 1988, 981.

the occasional difficult case, development and evaluation of research. Besides these tasks, medical-ethical committees often pass judgment on other medical-ethical matters, such as the continuation or discontinuation of treatment of disabled premature babies. The composition of these committees will vary from hospital to hospital. No legal rules exist yet.

*157.* In the Netherlands, there is no national bioethics council as such. This task has been left to committees of the Health Council that deal with bioethical issues and always consist of members from several professions, such as medicine, law, bioethics, psychology and sociology. Such a committee describes the scientific evidence, reflects on the several arguments for and against the use of the new development and formulates advice to the government.[36]

*158.* In January 2016, the permanent committee on ethics and law of the Health Council was installed. The committee issues solicited and unsolicited advisory reports on subjects in the field of health ethics and health law. In addition, and where necessary, it supports other Health Council committees where important ethical and legal problems arise. A number of committee members represent the Health Council in the Centre for Ethics and Health, a joint venture of the Health Council and the Council for Health and Society.[37]

*159.* *See* paragraph 475 for medical research ethics committees.

36. E. Borst-Eilers, 'The Role of Public Debate and Politics in the Implementation of the Convention', in J.K.M. Gevers et al. (ed.), *Health Law, Human Rights and the Biomedicine Convention: Essays in Honour of Henriette Roscam Abbing* (Leiden, Martinus Nijhoff Publishers, 2005) 251–252.
37. www.gezondheidsraad.nl/en.

# Part II. The Physician: Patient Relationship

## Chapter 1. General Description

### §1. Rights and Duties of Patients and Physicians

*160.* Rights of patients are mainly laid down in the Medical Treatment Agreement Act and the QCDHC Act. Both Acts are largely complementary, although there are also important differences with regard to the field of application.

#### I. The Medical Treatment Agreement Act

*161.* The rights and duties of patients and physicians are in the first place regulated by the Act of 17 November 1994 amending the Civil Code and other legislation in connection with the incorporation of provisions concerning the agreement to provide medical treatment (The Medical Treatment Agreement Act) This Act has been incorporated in Book 7, Title 7, Subchapter 5 (Medical Treatment Agreement) of the Civil Code.[38] The Act of 17 November 1994 has been amended by among others an Act of 22 December 2005 with regard to the retention period of the medical record[39] (*see* paragraph 192) and more importantly by an Act of 5 June 2019 modifying Book 7 of the Civil Code and different other laws to ameliorate patient-centred care and regulating the right to access the medical file of a deceased patient.[40] The Act of 5 June 2019 entered into force on 1 January 2020.

*162.* The intention of the Medical Treatment Agreement Act is to strengthen the legal position of the patient by clarifying his or her rights in relation to the healthcare provider. This strengthening was considered necessary because of the dependent and therefore, intrinsic weaker position. The strengthening of the legal position of the weaker partner in a civil agreement by specifying the contents of this contract is in line with the tradition of Dutch law. Legislation of an administrative nature was considered as an alternative but was rejected because of interfering too strongly in the physician-patient relationship. An obvious advantage of the civil law approach is that the patient has a direct claim on the physician to respect his rights

38. *State Journal* (1994), 837.
39. *State Journal* (2006), 29.
40. *State Journal* (2019), 224.

and has means of enforcing this respect at his own initiative and does not have to rely on the initiatives of the State to enforce respect for the rights of patients.[41]

### A. *Scope of Application*

#### 1. Medical Treatment Agreement

*163.* A medical treatment agreement is an agreement under which a natural or legal person ('the care provider') engages him/herself in the course of his/her medical professional practice or medical business towards another ('the principal') to carry out (perform) medical actions which directly affect the principal personally or a specific third party (Article 7:446-1 Civil Code).

#### 2. Patient

*164.* The person who is directly affected by the medical actions is referred to as 'the patient' (Article 7:446-1 Civil Code).

#### 3. Medical Actions

*165.* The term 'medical actions' means: (a) all activities – including examinations and providing medical consults – directly affecting a person and intended to cure him/her of a disease, to protect him/her from a disease, to assess his/her state of health or to render obstetric assistance; (b) actions other than those referred to under point (a) which directly affect a person and which are carried out by a physician or dentist acting in that capacity (Article 7:446-2 Civil Code).

*166.* Medical actions also include the attendant care and nursing of the patient and the provision in any other way for the latter's direct benefit of the material facilities under which such actions may be carried out (Article 7:446-3 Civil Code).

*167.* Originally, Article 7:446-4 Civil Code provided that medical actions did not include actions in the field of pharmacy within the meaning of the Medicines Act if performed by a freely established pharmacist within the meaning of that Act while such actions performed by a hospital pharmacist or a dispensing GP did. Meanwhile, this provision has been deleted by the Act of 15 March 2007 amending the Medicine's Act and section 5, title 5 of book 7 Civil Code.[42] Freely established pharmacists had been excluded from the Medical Treatment Agreement Act because in the early nineties the protection offered to the clients of such a pharmacist were considered to be protected sufficiently by the Medicine's Act while the legal relation

41. L.F. Markenstein, 'The Codification in the Netherlands of the Principal Rights of Patients: A Critical Review', *European Journal Health Law*, 2 (1995) 34.
42. *State Journal* (2007), 92.

was regulated by the purchase agreement rules in the Civil Code. However, to the extent that freely established pharmacists had become providers of pharmaceutical care and not only merely purchasers of medicinal products but the Medical Treatment Agreement Act also had to be amended.

*168.* Actions to assess a person's state of health or to provide medical supervision do not constitute a medical treatment agreement if carried out on the instructions of a person by others in connection with determining debt-claims or obligations, eligibility for acceptance by an insurer or access to a facility, or suitability for a course of training, employment or the performance of certain work (Article 7:446-5 Civil Code). Such activities are nevertheless also regulated by the Civil Code and also by the Medical Examinations Act (*see* paragraph 246).

### *B. The Right to Information*

*169.* The physician informs the patient in a clear way having regard his or her ability to comprehend and discusses timely with the patient the intended examination and intended treatment and of developments related to the examination, the treatment and the state of health of the patient (Article 7:448-1 Civil Code). The requirement of information 'in a clear way' is generally understood to mean that the information must be sufficiently understandable for the patient.[43] The words 'having regard his or her ability to comprehend and discusses timely' have been added by the Act of 5 June 2019 in order to stimulate a dialogue between the patient and the physician and not just informing the patient. Already before this amendment, the patient's right to information included a right to receive answers to questions: if the patient is asking for more information, the physician has to respond to this request unless that would be unreasonable.[44]

*170.* In complying with this obligation, the physician will be guided by what the patient reasonably needs to know with respect to: (a) the nature and purpose of the envisaged examination, the proposed treatment or the medical actions to be carried out; (b) the to-be-expected consequences and the risks for the health of the patient of the envisaged examination, the proposed treatment, the medical actions to be carried out and of not treating the patient; (c) other possible methods of examination or treatments to be carried out or not by other care providers; (d) the state of the patient's health and what is to be expected in this respect as far as it concerns the field of possible methods of examination or treatments; and (e) the term in which the possible methods of examination or treatments can be carried out and their expected duration (Article 7:448-2 Civil Code). Also, Article 7:448-2 has been amended by the Act of 5 June 2019. Article 7:448-2(e) is completely new, while the other parts of it are more detailed. These changes have been inspired by the shared

43. I. Giesen and E. Engelhard, 'Medical Liability in the Netherlands', in B.A. Koch (ed.), *Medical Liability in Europe: A Comparison of Selected Jurisdictions* (Berlin, De Gruyter, 2011) 389.
44. C. Ploem, 'Handling Unsolicited Findings in Clinical Care: A Legal Perspective', *European Journal Health Law,* 21 (2014) 497.

decision-making model. It is generally accepted that this list is not limitative and that depending upon the circumstances also information with regard to the costs of treatment or the experience of the physician has to be provided.[45]

*171.* Article 7:448-3 obliges the physician to inform himself regarding the situation and the needs of the patient, to invite the patient to ask questions and to inform the patient in writing or electronically when the patient requests this. This provision has also been inserted in the Medical Treatment Agreement Act by the Act of 5 June 2019.

*172.* Regarding the risks, not all possible risks have to be mentioned, but the so-called common, foreseeable risks.[46] According to Janssen, the norm for the extent of disclosure of risks can, in general, be labelled as the reasonable (or prudent) patient standard: what does a reasonable person in the circumstances of the case need to know in order to make a sufficiently informed decision about the proposed intervention. However, also the circumstances of the individual case/patient are relevant for the range of risk disclosure.[47] From the jurisprudence, it follows that the question of whether there is a duty to disclose a specific risk relates both to its probability and the seriousness of the consequences when it materialises. A duty to disclose is more likely to exist when the probability is higher, and the complication has more serious consequences for the patient. If an intervention is not therapeutically indicated (for instance, cosmetic surgery), the physician has an increased duty to disclose risks compared to therapeutic interventions.[48]

*173.* Although there is a clear link between the right to information and the right to give informed consent, the duty to inform imposed on the physician also covers information that is not required to give informed consent but that the patient nevertheless should know in order to make informed decisions, such as information concerning possible side-effects of the prescribed medication[49] or in the case of a terminal and untreatable illness, requesting euthanasia of making up a will.

*174.* The physician may only withhold the above-mentioned information from the patient as far as providing it would clearly cause serious harm to the patient (the so-called therapeutic exception).[50] If the interest of the patient requires so, the physician must give the information to a person other than the patient. The information

45. J. Legemaate, 'Gezondheidsrecht', *Tijdschrift voor Consumentenrecht en handelspraktijken* (2020) 83.
46. I. Giesen and E. Engelhard, 'Medical Liability in the Netherlands', in B.A. Koch (ed.), *Medical Liability in Europe: A Comparison of Selected Jurisdictions* (Berlin, De Gruyter, 2011) 389.
47. A.J.G.M. Janssen, 'Informing Patients about Small Risks: A Comparative Approach', *European Journal Health Law,* 13 (2006) 161 and 163.
48. *Ibid.,* 164–165.
49. I. Giesen and E. Engelhard, 'Medical Liability in the Netherlands', in B.A. Koch (ed.), *Medical Liability in Europe: A Comparison of Selected Jurisdictions* (Berlin, De Gruyter, 2011) 389.
50. L.F. Markenstein, 'The Codification in the Netherlands of the Principal Rights of Patients: A Critical Review', *European Journal Health Law,* 2 (1995) 38.

shall be provided to the patient when there is no longer any danger of causing serious harm. The physician shall not use the authority to withhold information without consulting another care provider on the matter (Article 7:448-4 Civil Code). This requirement should guarantee a more or less objective interpretation of the criterion of 'serious harm'. A parliamentary proposal to delete the therapeutic exception because it is an infringement of the patient's right to self-determination did not obtain a majority.[51] The jurisprudence on this particular issue is scarce, but from a decision of the regional disciplinary board of Amsterdam, it can be derived that a less prosperous course of the healing process or insecurity about the prognosis is in itself an insufficient reason for invoking the therapeutic exception.[52]

*175.* Article 7:448 Civil Code does not provide explicitly that the physician is required to check that the patient has understood the information. However, this obligation has been accepted in the jurisprudence in certain cases, for instance, when the patient is in a very bad condition or is under the influence of medication.[53]

*176.* The right to information regarding one's state of health also implies the right to be informed regarding medical errors. The professional responsibility of the physician requires that possible harm to patients is prevented and that the consequences of already caused damage are as far as possible limited. By not or not timely informing the patient regarding errors and their consequences, damage may be caused or made worse.[54]

### *C. The Right Not to Know*

*177.* If the patient has stated that he does not want to be informed, the information shall not be provided, except where the interests of the patient in not receiving information are outweighed by the detrimental effects that failure to provide information might have an impact on him or on others (Article 7:449 Civil Code). The inclusion of harm to the patient could open the door to paternalistic use. Limiting the possibility of an exception to situations of 'harm to others' would be preferable, according to Markenstein.[55] From a judgment of the Supreme Court, it can be concluded that a patient's request not to obtain the result of a (mandatory) HIV test should be respected.[56]

---

51. *Ibid.,* 38.
52. Regional Disciplinary Board 6 Sep. 1993 cited by C. Ploem, 'Handling Unsolicited Findings in Clinical Care: A Legal Perspective', *European Journal Health Law,* 21 (2014) 498.
53. H.J.J. Leenen et al., *Handboek Gezondheidsrecht* (Den Haag, Boom, 2017) 109–110.
54. *Ibid.,* 110–112.
55. L.F. Markenstein, 'The Codification in the Netherlands of the Principal Rights of Patients: A Critical Review', *European Journal Health Law,* 2 (1995) 38.
56. ECLI:NL:HR:2003:AL8442 cited in C. Ploem, 'Handling Unsolicited Findings in Clinical Care: A Legal Perspective', *European Journal Health Law,* 21 (2014) 499.

*178.* The right not to know was deliberately incorporated in the Act to stress that the right to information does not automatically imply a duty to receive it; if this were the case, an individual's right to self-determination would be violated. It is the patient's responsibility to express a wish not to know certain information. According to Ploem, he/she may have various reasons such as avoiding problems in finding life insurance or work or preferring not to be informed about an incurable disease or inevitable suffering.[57]

### *D. The Right to Give Consent*

#### 1. General Remark

*179.* A distinction is usually made between consent to enter into an agreement for medical treatment and consent to the medical treatment itself. Explicit consent is required for an agreement for medical treatment, which must be distinguished from the various separate, medical actions. Consent once granted does not imply consent to each and every medical action; the separate actions require consent as well.

#### 2. Necessary Consent of the Patient

*180.* The consent of the patient is required for actions to be performed in the implementation (performance) of the medical treatment agreement (Article 7:450-1 Civil Code). Prior to any medical action based on the agreement, the physician needs patient consent.[58]

#### 3. Written Consent upon Request of the Patient for Invasive Actions

*181.* Upon the request of the patient, the physician shall, in any event, put down in writing the consent given by the patient for medical actions of an invasive nature (Article 7:451 Civil Code).

#### 4. Presumed Consent for Non-invasive Actions

*182.* A consent that is required pursuant to Article 7:450 Civil Code is presumed to have been given if the action in question is not of an invasive nature (Article 7:466-2 Civil Code). Presumed consent may also be deduced from a person's behaviour (in which case one preferably uses the expression implicit or tacit consent because the will of the patient is known through his/her behaviour which is not the

57. *Ibid.*, 498.
58. I. Giesen and E. Engelhard, 'Medical Liability in the Netherlands', in B.A. Koch (ed.), *Medical Liability in Europe: A Comparison of Selected Jurisdictions* (Berlin, De Gruyter, 2011) 389.

case for presumed consent): if a patient visits a physician to have a bleeding wound treated, the physician may deduce consent for treatment from the patient's behaviour. A physician should not presume consent too easily. If he does so, he will have to furnish proof of consent. A much-criticised decision of the central disciplinary board concerned a case in which sheer passiveness was considered as presumed consent. The central disciplinary board argued that 'if a patient consents to the taking of a blood sample without being interested in what exactly is going to be examined, no separate consent is needed for each part of the examination'. Actual cooperation at the taking of the blood sample does not acquit the physician of the obligation to give information and ask for consent, (in this case an HIV test) according to Roscam Abbing.[59]

*183.* The question of which medical procedures are 'non-invasive' and which are 'invasive' can give rise to a debate. For instance, testing for HIV is in itself neither invasive nor complicated. But the consequences of the results are such that nevertheless explicit consent for this kind of procedure is required at the request of the patient.[60] A layperson will sooner consider a procedure being invasive than a physician.

## 5. Exceptions

*184.* When the 'therapeutic exception' has been invoked (*see* paragraph 172), no consent is required. One could argue that consent may be presumed in these circumstances, but this is considered artificial.[61]

*185.* Neither is consent required in the case of an emergency and where there is no time to request the consent of the legal representative (*see* paragraphs 202 et seq.) of an unconscious patient. If immediate carrying out of action is clearly necessary to prevent serious harm to the patient, the action may be carried out without the consent of the legal representative (Article 7:466-1 Civil Code). An instance here could be when during an operation, the need arises to perform a follow-up operation, which has not been consented to (the so-called extended operation). Relevant considerations here are the severity and emergency of the unforeseen situation and the inconvenience of a separate operation. Here, as elsewhere, reasonableness and fairness are the criteria for a physician's actions: what would a patient in sound mind have wanted?

59. Central Disciplinary Board, 25 Aug. 1988, *Tijdschrift voor Gezondheidsrecht* (1988) 498–500 with a critical annotation of H.D.C. Roscam Abbing.
60. L.F. Markenstein, 'The Codification in the Netherlands of the Principal Rights of Patients: A Critical Review', *European Journal Health Law,* 2 (1995) 37.
61. H.J.J. Leenen et seq., *Handboek Gezondheidsrecht* (Den Haag, Boom, 2017) 118.

6. Sanctions

*186.* Consent to treatment serves as the legal justification of the physician's intervention. Without it, there is, generally speaking, a situation of maltreatment for which the physician can be prosecuted. Civil law procedures are another option to sue a physician on the grounds of default or tort. The furnishing of proof, in particular fault and causality, will confront the patient with considerable problems; the patient will have to state and prove that an action has been carried out without his consent unless the burden of proof lies elsewhere because of any special regulation or the demands of reasonableness and fairness (Article 177 Civil Legal Procedure Code). In order to alleviate the patient's burden of proof to some degree, the physician's accountability is stressed. In disciplinary terms, the absence of consent results in 'damaging the trust in the medical profession'.

*E. The Right to Advance Refusal of a Treatment*

*187.* In the event that an adult patient cannot be regarded as being capable of making a reasonable appreciation of his interests in the matter, the physician and the legal representative of the incapacitated patient shall comply with the apparent opinion of the patient expressed in writing while he was still capable of making a reasonable appreciation of his interests and containing a refusal to give his consent as referred to in Article 7:450-1 Civil Code.

*188.* The physician may nevertheless deviate from this statement if he thinks there are well-founded reasons for doing so (Article 7:450-3 Civil Code).

*189.* It has taken a lot of pressure from the Dutch Parliament to have this provision incorporated in the Medical Treatment Agreement Act. Against the wishes of the government, and at the last moment, an amendment has been approved by a majority in Parliament. The main issue was the value that should be attached to a written advance refusal. For the government, the amendment added little to the then already accepted principle of informed consent, while in the view of the Parliament, the amendment was necessary to end the uncertainty that surrounded advance refusals in daily life.[62]

*190.* According to Markenstein, this provision 'is a compromise and has a very limited scope'. Physicians should use their power to deviate from the advance

62. H. Nys, 'Emerging Legislation in Europe on the Legal Status of Advance Directives and Medical Decision-Making with Respect to an Incompetent Patient ("Living-Wills")', *European Journal Health Law,* 4 (1997) 185.

refusal only in situations in which the statement is apparently unspecific and/or outdated. In situations in which the significance of the statement leaves too much margin for interpretation, the physician ought to consult with the relatives of the patient.[63]

### *F. The Right to Withdraw Consent*

*191.* The Medical Treatment Agreement Act does not explicitly mention the right to withdraw consent. However, this right is generally recognised. The physician has to inform the patient regarding the consequences of the withdrawal of consent.[64]

### *G. Rights Related to the Patient's Medical Record*

#### 1. The Right to a File and to Add Documents

*192.* The physician has to maintain a file related to the treatment of the patient. He shall use the file to record data concerning the health of the patient and the actions performed on him. The physician adds other data to the file containing information which is regarded to be necessary for the purpose of providing the patient with the standard of care of a prudent physician (Article 7:454-1 Civil Code). A physician was disciplinarily sanctioned with a reprimand for not adequately informing a patient regarding a complication that had occurred and for not mentioning this complication in the patient's medical file. Moreover, the file did not make clear that the patient had previously been informed with regard to the possible occurrence of complications during the surgical procedure she had to undergo.[65]

*193.* If requested, the physician adds to the file a declaration made by the patient (Article 7:454-2 Civil Code), as amended by the Act of 5 June 2019 in order to enlarge the right of the patient to add a declaration. Previously, such a declaration could only be made with regard to documents already contained in the file. However, patients have no right to amend or correct the data in the file.[66]

*194.* Without prejudice to the provisions of Article 7:455 Civil Code (*see* next paragraph), the physician keeps the documents in the file for twenty years from the date on which the latest change in the file took place or for as long as reasonably follows from the care of a prudent care provider (Article 7:454-3 Civil Code as amended by the Act of 5 June 2019). The latter might be the case for genetic data.

63. L.F. Markenstein, 'The Codification in the Netherlands of the Principal Rights of Patients: A Critical Review', *European Journal Health Law*, 2 (1995) 37.
64. H.J.J. Leenen et seq., *Handboek Gezondheidsrecht* (Den Haag, Boom, 2017) 119.
65. Regional disciplinary board The Hague, 28 Jan. 2020, ECLI:NL:TGZRGR:2020:30.
66. L.F. Markenstein, 'The Codification in the Netherlands of the Principal Rights of Patients: A Critical Review', *European Journal Health Law*, 2 (1995) 39.

In the very first version of Article 7:455, the retention period was only ten years, and this was, in general, considered too short to assess what data might still be needed in the future.[67] Later on, it became fifteen years, and now it is twenty years.

## 2. The Right to Destruction of the File

*195.* The physician shall destroy the documents which he keeps pursuant to Article 7:454 Civil Code within three months after he has received a written or electronic request to this effect from the patient. This does not apply as far as the request of the patient concerns documents of which it is likely that their preservation is of considerable importance for another person than the patient or as far as a statutory provision made by or pursuant to law opposes against such destruction (Article 7:455 Civil Code).

## 3. The Right to Access and the Right to a Copy

*196.* If requested, the physician shall provide the patient with access to and copies of the documents referred to in Article 7:454 Civil Code. Access to and copies of the documents shall not be provided insofar as this is necessary to protect the privacy of persons other than the patient. The care provider may charge a reasonable fee for providing the copies (Article 7:456 Civil Code). The right to access does not encompass the so-called personal notes of the physician.[68]

*197.* The right to access medical files is almost unrestricted. There is no so-called therapeutic exception (*see* paragraph 172) provided for in Article 7:456 Civil Code. By requesting access to his/her file, a patient can obtain knowledge of information which was previously withheld from him/her on the basis of the therapeutic exception. This has been a deliberate choice of the legislator.[69] Would a physician nevertheless decide to restrict a patient's access right, the only legal basis could be provided by an appeal on 'force majeure'.[70]

*198.* In its original version, the Medical Treatment Agreement Act did not provide for a right to access by the closest relatives of a deceased patient. During the parliamentary discussions of the bill, the government did not see the need to make such a provision, referring to the exception based on the patient's presumed consent

67. W. Dondorp, J. Legemaate and H. van de Klippe, 'The Retention of Medical Records: Dutch Health Council Report in Favour of Future Change', *European Journal Health Law,* 11 (2004) 273–282. In this Report the Health Council already pleaded to prolong the then existing period of ten years to thirty.
68. H.J.J. Leenen et al., *Handboek Gezondheidsrecht* (Den Haag, Boom, 2017) 168.
69. L.F. Markenstein, 'The Codification in the Netherlands of the Principal Rights of Patients: A Critical Review', *European Journal Health Law,* 2 (1995) 39.
70. C. Ploem, 'Handling Unsolicited Findings in Clinical Care: A Legal Perspective', *European Journal Health Law,* 21 (2014) 498.

as accepted in case law and in the legal doctrine. This exception was considered sufficient to meet the relatives' interests involved in access to medical records of the deceased.[71] In addition to the concept of presumed consent, the exception based on the so-called important interests had increasingly been applied by the courts in cases where the relatives claimed access to medical records of the deceased.[72] The Act of 5 June 2019 has inserted two new articles in the Civil Code, Article 458a and 458b with regard to the right of access to and a copy of the data in the file of a deceased patient. Article 458a.1 Civil Code stipulates that notwithstanding Article 457.1 (*see* paragraph 201), a physician grants on request access to or copy of the data in the medical file of a deceased patient to: (a) a person to whom the patient when alive has given consent, provided this consent is laid down in writing or electronically; (b) a relative or a person who has received information with regard to an incident as referred to in Article 10.3 QCDHC Act (*see* paragraph 230); (c) everyone who has a weighty interest and makes it acceptable that this interest may be harmed and that access to or copy of the file is necessary to the protection of this interest. According to Article 458a.2, a physician provides notwithstanding Article 457.1, to the person who exercised authority over a patient who died before the age of sixteen, on request access to or copy of the data in the medical file of this patient unless this violates the care of a good care provider. According to Article 458a.3, data may only be provided on the basis of Article 458a to the extent that they relate to the reason why access is granted. According to Article 458a.4, no data may be provided on the basis of Article 458a when it has been determined in writing or electronically that the deceased patient who had reached the age of 12 years and was able to evaluate his interests, did not wish access or when this access would violate the personal life of another.

*199.* According to Article 8:27 of the Compulsory Mental Healthcare Act (*see* paragraph 342), the relatives of a deceased patient against whom a measure of compulsory care has been taken, have a right to access to or copy of the file of the deceased patient upon their request to the extent that the privacy of third persons is not harmed and provided that the patient had given written consent or that the relatives have a weighty interest in this respect.

*200.* Article 458b Civil Code provides that when access or copy is requested on the basis of Article 458a.1c because of a suspected medical fault and the physician does not agree to provide access or copy, this physician has to provide access or copy to an independent physician appointed by the applicant. This independent physician evaluates whether the refusal to provide access or copy is justified. If the independent physician concludes that the refusal is not justified, the physician is obliged to provide access or copy.

---

71. L.M.H. Bongers, 'Disclosure of Medical Data to Relatives after the Patient's Death: Recent Developments with Respect to Relatives' Entitlements in the Netherlands', *European Journal Health Law,* 11 (2011) 257 and 261–262.
72. *Ibid.*, 266.

*H. The Right to Protection of Secrecy*

*201.* The physician ensures that persons other than the patient are not provided with information about the patient or with access to copies of the data referred to in Article 7:454 Civil Code without the patient's consent. Information or access to copies of data shall be provided only as far as no other person's privacy is infringed thereby. Information or access to copies of documents may be provided regardless of the restrictions referred to in the preceding sentences if this is required by or pursuant to an Act of Parliament (Article 7:457-1 Civil Code).

*202.* 'Persons other than the patient' do not include those persons who are directly involved in the implementation (performance) of the medical treatment agreement, nor persons who act as a substitute (locum) for the physician, insofar the provision of information or access to copies of data is necessary for the activities to be performed by them in that context (Article 7:457-2 Civil Code).

*203.* Nor do 'persons other than the patient' include those persons whose consent is required pursuant to Article 7:450 and 7:465 Civil Code (legal representative of the incapacitated patient – *see* paragraphs 202 et seq.) in connection with the implementation (performance) of the medical treatment agreement. If by providing information or access to copies of data, the physician cannot be regarded to be acting in accordance with what is required of a prudent physician, he shall refrain from acting this way (Article 7:457.3 Civil Code).

*I. The Right to Privacy*

*204.* The actions performed by the physician in the framework of the medical treatment agreement shall not be observed (watched) by any individual other than the patient unless the patient has given permission for doing so (Article 7:459-1 Civil Code).

*205.* 'Individuals other than the patient' shall not include those persons whose professional assistance is required to carry out the actions in question (Article 7:459-2 Civil Code). The individuals whose consent for the actions is required under Article 7:450 and 7:465 Civil Code shall not be included either. If by allowing the actions to be observed (watched), the care provider cannot be regarded to be acting in accordance with what is required of a prudent care provider, he shall not permit such observation (Article 7:459-3 Civil Code).

### *J. The Right to Representation in the Event of Incompetence*

#### 1. The Incapacitated Patient Is Placed under Protective Mentorship for Adults (Article 1:450–1:462 Civil Code) (Legal Representative)

*206.* If an adult due to his/her physical or mental condition is temporarily or permanently unable or hindered to look after his/her own non-financial interests, the district court may order a protective mentorship on his/her behalf (Article 1:450-1 Civil Code). A protective mentorship may also be ordered if it is to be expected that an adult within a foreseeable period will get in a situation, as meant in paragraph 1 (Article 1:450-3 Civil Code). A protective mentorship order on behalf of an adult may be requested by the adult himself, his spouse, registered partner or other life companion, one of his blood relatives in the direct line or in the collateral line up to and including the fourth degree, the person who pursuant to Article 1:253s or 1:253t Civil Code exercises authority over the person involved, his legal guardian exercising guardianship over him as a minor, his guardian exercising guardianship over him as an adult or his legal administrator as meant in Title 19 of Book 1 of the Civil Code. In the situation referred to in Article 1:450-3, a request for a protective mentorship order may be filed only by the involved adult himself (Article 1:451-1 Civil Code).

*207.* The court that orders a protective mentorship appoints at the same time or as soon thereafter a legal mentor. The court shall ascertain if the person to be appointed is prepared to exercise the right of protective mentorship (Article 1:452-1 Civil Code). When appointing a legal mentor, the court shall follow the explicit preferences of the involved adult, unless there are profound reasons to object to the appointment proposed by him (Article 1:452-3 Civil Code). If the involved adult is married or registered under a registered partnership or maintains another close personal relationship with a life companion, then preferably his spouse, registered partner or that other life companion is to be appointed as legal mentor, unless paragraph 3 has been applied. If the preceding sentence is not applicable, then preferably one of his parents, children, brothers or sisters is to be appointed as legal mentor. When the involved adult later enters into a marriage or registered partnership or finds a life companion with whom he/she starts to maintain a close personal relationship, then each of these persons may request the court to be appointed as legal mentor in replacement of the earlier appointed legal mentor (Article 1:452-4).

*208.* During the existence of the protective mentorship, the involved adult has no legal capacity to perform juridical acts in matters concerning his care, nursing, treatment and the provision of assistance and support unless the law or a treaty implicates otherwise (Article 1:453-1).

### 2. The Incapacitated Patient Is Not Placed under Protective Mentorship

#### a. Representation by an Appointed Representative

*209.* If a patient who has reached the age of majority and who cannot be regarded as being capable of making a reasonable appreciation of his interests in the matter, is not placed under adult guardianship (which is rather exceptional and is not discussed here) or under protective mentorship (*see* paragraph 202), the physician has to fulfil the obligations to the patient arising from the Medical Treatment Agreement Act towards the person who is authorised in writing to act on the patient's behalf (Article 7:465-3 Civil Code) (the so-called personal or appointed representative). This person can be considered as 'the prolongation of the mind' of the patient.[73] The representative does not become a party to the medical treatment agreement.[74]

#### b. Representation by a Not-Appointed Representative

*210.* If there is no appointed representative or if this representative does not act, the obligations shall be fulfilled towards the spouse, the registered partner or other life companion of the patient unless this person refuses this, or if there is no spouse, registered partner or other life companion, towards a parent, child, brother, sister, grandparent or grandchild of the patient unless that person refuses (Article 7:465-3 Civil Code as amended by the Act of 5 June 2019). This sequence is hierarchical.[75] The physician has to fulfil his obligations towards only one representative which means that in some cases (for instance, two parents or more than one brother or sister), the physician will have to make a choice.[76]

#### c. Obligations of the Physician and the Representative

*211.* The physician shall fulfil his obligations towards the patient's representative unless this is incompatible with the standards of a prudent physician (Article 7:465-4 Civil Code).

*212.* The representative shall exercise the duty of care of a prudent legal representative. He/she shall involve the patient as much as possible in the fulfilment of his/her duties (Article 7.465-5 Civil Code).

*213.* Where the patient objects to an action of a far-reaching nature for which his or her representative has given his/her consent, this action may be performed only if it is clearly necessary to prevent serious harm to the patient's health (Article 7.465-6 Civil Code).

---

73. H.J.J. Leenen et al., *Handboek Gezondheidsrecht* (Den Haag, Boom, 2017) 131.
74. District Court Rotterdam, 4 Nov. 2009, ECLI:NL: RBROT:BK3477, Stichting Medisch Centrum Rijnmond Zuid.
75. L.F. Markenstein, 'The Codification in the Netherlands of the Principal Rights of Patients: A Critical Review', *European Journal Health Law,* 2 (1995) 41.
76. H.J.J. Leenen et al., *Handboek Gezondheidsrecht* (Den Haag, Boom, 2017) 132.

*214.* Markenstein calls the lack of clear criteria to determine whether an adult is (in) competent or not in a given situation 'a weak point of the regulation'. The development of such criteria is left to healthcare providers in practice.[77]

## *K. Obligations of the Patient*

*215.* The patient shall to the best of his/her knowledge give the physician the information and cooperation which the physician reasonably requires for the implementation (performance) of the medical treatment agreement (Article 7:452 Civil Code). Both obligations have been criticised because they do not fit well in a services agreement.[78]

*216.* In its advice on 'Good Patientship', the Council for Health and Society stated that there is a need for 'Good Patientship'. In the Council's view, Good Patientship implies the acceptance of responsibility under three headings: (1) adherence to generally accepted standards of interpersonal behaviour: patients should show care practitioners respect; this means that they should not be aggressive, should not make unreasonable demands and should keep their appointments; (2) fulfilment of financial obligations: patients should take out appropriate medical insurance and should pay the associated premiums and personal contributions on time; and (3) cooperation with treatment: patients should keep their care practitioners properly informed, talk issues over with them and participate in the formulation of treatment decisions; patients should also follow the instructions, advice and lifestyle guidance they are given.[79]

*217.* According to the Council, there are various widely accepted ways in which fulfilment of responsibilities of the first two kinds already can be – and is – encouraged. For example, many care establishments have football-style systems of yellow and red cards, which are used to keep aggressive or over-assertive patients in line. The principle of no-show charges for patients who fail to keep appointments without a valid reason is also well established, and people who fail to take out insurance or pay their premiums are liable to face financial penalties. Enforcing the acceptance of the patient's responsibilities under the third heading is another matter. Little scope exists for making people cooperate with treatment, even though such cooperation has the potential to yield greater public health and efficiency benefits than the fulfilment of the other responsibilities described above.

*218.* Finally, the Council gave the following guidance: Good Patientship can be encouraged by promoting (cost-) awareness among the general public (the patient population) and by providing incentives for healthy lifestyle decisions. Care practitioners should do more to call patients to account for irresponsible behaviour and

77. L.F. Markenstein, 'The Codification in the Netherlands of the Principal Rights of Patients: A Critical Review', *European Journal Health Law,* 2 (1995) 41.
78. H.J.J. Leenen et al., *Handboek Gezondheidsrecht* (Den Haag, Boom, 2017) 103.
79. Council for Health and Society, *Good Patientship*, 20 Mar. 2010 (summary).

should define boundaries where necessary. They should make greater use of existing options, such as downgrading treatment goals in cases where patients habitually fail to cooperate. If they are to pursue such policies, care practitioners need to believe that they have support. To this end, the development of non-compliance protocols can be advantageous.

*219.* The imposition of financial sanctions through the health insurance system is inadvisable. Although such measures might ease the pressure on solidarity (by showing people that their fellow citizens pay for the problems they cause), they are unlikely to bring about the desired behavioural changes. If the government were to impose such measures, serious opposition could be expected, not only from patients but also from care practitioners and insurers. The Council would like to see more public debate about personal responsibility in relation to health. Its chief benefit would be a clearer definition of (the enforceability of) patients' personal responsibilities, and of the boundaries of the services that care practitioners may be expected to provide.

### *L. Termination of the Medical Treatment Agreement*

*220.* The physician shall not terminate the medical treatment agreement unless there are compelling reasons for doing so (Article 7:460 Civil Code). Compelling reasons are for instance: a serious disturbance of the relation between physician and patient; a complete refusal of cooperation by the patient; the appearance of sexual attraction between them both; and also when the patient moves to an address far away from the professional address of the physician.[80]

### *M. Mandatory Law*

*221.* Parties may not derogate to the detriment of the patient from the provisions of the Medical Treatment Agreement Act (Article 7:468 Civil Code).

## II. The Quality, Complaints and Disputes in Healthcare Act

### *A. Introduction*

*222.* Already in 2005, the Netherlands Patients' and Consumers' Federation[81] proposed to replace the Medical Treatment Agreement Act by one, all integrating Healthcare Consumer Act. The ongoing healthcare reform made patients a major health market party, enabling patients to make independent and rational choices. The patient was increasingly considered a consumer. According to the Federation, patients' rights were too fragmented, creating uncertainty as to exactly what the

80. H.J.J. Leenen et al., *Handboek Gezondheidsrecht* (Den Haag, Boom, 2017) 139.
81. In Dutch *Nederlandse Patiënten Consumenten Federatie (NPCF).*

patient's entitlements are, what the statutory basis of those entitlements is and the extent to which the various statutory provisions reinforce or compromise one another. Furthermore, new developments and insights are yet to be translated into rights and obligations. Hence, the proposal of the Federation was received with mixed feelings, to say the least. Academic health lawyers, such as Prof. Dute and Prof. Legemaate, reacted rather critically, although Prof. Van Wijmen had already in 1997 suggested to bring all kinds of care delivery relations into one law.

*223.* The then Minister of Health, however, asked the then Council of Public Health and Care (now, the Council for Health and Society) whether it shared these concerns and, if so, whether it felt that a care consumers Act could make an effective contribution to the consolidation of the care consumer's legal position. The Council's investigations focused on the statutory basis for the rights that are most important in the context of enabling individual patients to act as care consumers. The rights in question are the right to freedom of choice, the right to information, the right to appropriate care and the right to complain.[82]

*224.* Although the legal position of the individual patient is generally secure, the Council's research did reveal a number of shortcomings. These mainly surround the right to comparative decision-support information, which is not adequately protected. While the Healthcare Market Regulation Act did address this issue, the relevant provisions did not have sufficient force. The patient cannot derive from the Act any right to comparative information regarding the quality and outcomes of care provided for particular conditions, even though such information is critically important in this context.

*225.* Another problem signalled by the Council concerned the inaccessibility of patients' rights, in particular, the right to appropriate care. A serious matter according to the Council: if it is not clear what a patient is entitled to expect from a care provider or health insurer in a particular situation, the patient's right not only to appropriate care but also to freedom of choice and to complain are significantly curtailed.

*226.* Nevertheless, the Council did not regard an integrated care consumers Act as the best solution to the problems it has identified. Such an Act would need to address a wide variety of issues, which do not lend themselves to accommodation within a common legal framework. Hence, the Act would need to occupy a distinct legal position, complicating harmonisation with the Civil Code. The latter strikes a balance between provisions that allow for contract freedom and provisions that serve to protect vulnerable parties, such as consumers and patients. Removing from the Civil Code, those provisions that afford patient protection would be more likely to weaken the patient's legal position than reinforce it.

*227.* Notwithstanding the rather negative reactions, the Minister of Health continued to prepare one integral care consumers Act. In May 2008, the then Minister

82. Council for Health and Society, *A Healthcare Consumers Act,* 9 Nov. 2006.

and State Secretary of Health, Welfare and Sports presented their intentions to revise the patients' rights legislation. Overall, these intentions were inspired by the government's wish to strengthen the individual and collective position of the client in the healthcare system.[83] In this so-called May letter, it was proposed to enlarge the field of application of the rights of patients included in the Medical Treatment Agreement Act to the domains of nursery, care and assistance. The patient was not anymore referred to as (care) consumer but 'somehow neutral' as a client. This client would receive seven so-called basic rights (apart from the already existing 'classic' patients' rights): the rights to available/accessible care; the right to choice and choice-information; the right to quality and safety; the right to reinforcement of his position regarding the care provider; the right to coordination of care between care providers; the right to a good complaints procedure and the right to co-decision and good governance. Whereas the Medical Treatment Agreements Act formulates the rights of the patients as duties of the care provider, the client would receive rights directly. This would make, as was suggested, the clients' rights directly enforceable. Again, academic health lawyers such as Prof. Gevers and Ten Hoopen reacted critically.

*228.* On 12 March 2009, a draft of the bill of the Clients' Rights Care Act was circulated for consultation. In its quality as President of the Dutch Association of Health Law, Prof. Legemaate reacted very critically and was disappointed.[84] In July 2009, the bill was nevertheless sent to the Council of State. The opinion of the Council was 'highly critical':[85] the bill had to be reconsidered entirely. Remarkable is the critical remark concerning the use of the notion 'client' to refer to the patient. According to the Council, the notion expresses only the market-related aspects of the physician-patient relationship and not the other aspects, in particular, mutual trust.

*229.* On 7 June 2010, the Clients' Rights Care bill was introduced in the Parliament. The bill contained some of the so-called basic rights of the client mentioned in the so-called May letter: the right to good care (Articles 5–12), the right to treatment of complaints and disputes (Articles 27–30) and the right to co-decision (Articles 31–38). Most of the other basic rights mentioned in the May letter had not been integrated into the bill, although some of them were reflected in Article 13 (right to choice-information) and in the provisions concerning good governance (Articles 39–41), availability and transparency of the supply of care (Articles 42–45) and financial provisions (Articles 46–57). The right to coordination of care had disappeared. The field of application of the Medical Treatment Agreement Act was enlarged to nursery and care (assistance not being mentioned anymore).

83. L.M.H. Bongers, 'Disclosure of Medical Data to Relatives after the Patient's Death: Recent Developments with Respect to Relatives' Entitlements in the Netherlands', *European Journal Health Law,* 11 (2011) 270.
84. J. Legemaate, 'Low Trust in de gezondheidszorg', *Tijdschrift voor gezondheidsrecht* (2009) 353 (Low Trust in Healthcare).
85. L.M.H. Bongers, 'Disclosure of Medical Data to Relatives after the Patient's Death: Recent Developments with Respect to Relatives' Entitlements in the Netherlands', *European Journal Health Law,* 11 (2011) 272.

*230.* In February 2013, the successor of the previous Minister of Health concluded that the Clients' Rights Care bill had received little support and proposed to regulate some of these rights in an entirely new Act that would exist next to the Medical Treatment Agreement Act. This Act has become the QCDHC Act of 7 October 2015. It entered into force on 1 January 2017. This Act applies to all care providers, from large institutions like hospitals to independent care professionals like GPs and physiotherapists.[86] The QCDHC Act is applicable independent of the existence of a medical treatment agreement: once care is provided, the Act applies.

### *B. The Right to Good Care*

*231.* Article 2.1. QCDHC Act obliges every care provider (which also includes physicians) to offer good care. Article 2.2. QCDHC Act defines 'good care' as care of high quality and high level that: (a) in any case is safe, efficient, effective and client-focused, delivered timely and tuned to the real needs of the client; and (b) is delivered in conformity with the responsibility that rests upon the providers, having regard their professional standard; and (c) where the rights of the client are carefully respected, and the client is treated with respect. According to Legemaate, although this provision contains nothing new, it does no harm to make this explicit.[87] Article I of the Act of 9 September 2020 amending the QCDHC Act (*see* paragraph 135) had added Article 2a in the latter Act. It states that to the extent that a part of a professional standard has potentially substantial financial consequences for the collective healthcare expenses, healthcare providers have only to act in accordance with this part to the extent that this standard is a quality standard. Article 2a QCDHC Act entered retroactively into force on 5 July 2018.

*232.* According to Article 2.3 QCDHC Act, a so-called alternative care provider (defined in Article 1.1. QCDHC Act as a non-registered care provider who delivers healthcare as defined in the IHCP Act – *see* paragraph 99) may only provide care that, except in a case of urgency, does not cause harm or a serious chance of harm to the health of the client while carefully respecting the rights of the client and treating the client with respect.

### *C. The Right to Choice-Information*

*233.* In order to enable the client to make a well-considered choice among different providers, a physician informs the client on his/her request about the healthcare he/she provides, among others the tariffs of this healthcare, its quality and the experiences of clients with it. The physician also informs the client regarding the scientifically evidenced effectiveness or not of this healthcare and the waiting time (Article 10.1 and 10.2 QCDHC Act). Compared with the Medical Treatment Agreement Act, both provisions reinforce the physicians' duty to inform.

---

86. www.government.nl/topics/quality-of-healthcare/healthcare-quality-complaints.
87. J. Legemaate, 'De Wkkgz over kwaliteit van zorg', *Tijdschrift voor Gezondheidsrecht* (2016) 54.

### D. *The Right to be Informed of Incidents*

*234.* A physician informs the client, a representative of the client or a relative of the client in case he/she has died without delay of nature and the course of incidents in the delivery of healthcare to the client that has or may have noticeable consequences for him/her. The physician also makes a notice of nature and the course of the incident in the client's file, as well as of the time on which the incident has occurred and the names of those involved in the incident. The physician informs the client about the possibilities to lift or limit the consequences of the incident (Article 10.3 QCDHC Act). No definition of incident is given.

### E. *The Right to an Effective and Low-Threshold Complaints and Disputes Procedure*

#### 1. Complaints

*235.* Every physician has to dispose of a written procedure aimed at effective and low-threshold handling of complaints regarding him/her and that fulfils the conditions provided for in Article 13 (Article 13.1 QCDHC Act). The procedure is determined in agreement with a representative organisation of clients (Article 13.2 QCDHC Act) or, if applicable, a clients' council (Article 13.3 QCDHC Act). The physician communicates the procedure and its possible amendments to clients and their representatives (Article 13.4 QCDHC Act).

*236.* A client, a relative of a deceased client or the representative of a client can submit a written complaint regarding the behaviour of a physician in the course of the delivery of healthcare. When a physician refuses to consider someone as the representative of a client, this person can also submit a written complaint (Article 14 QCDHC Act).

*237.* The physician indicates one or more competent persons (called 'patient contact person' or 'patient's confidential advisor')[88] who on request give(s) advice to the complainant and support him/her in formulating the complaint and in exploring the possibilities to solve the complaint. The physician guarantees the independence of the person(s) and does not cause a disadvantage to him/her (Article 15 QCDHC Act).

*238.* Each complaint has to be examined in a careful way. The handling of a complaint is directed to reach a solution that satisfies both the complainant and the physician. The complainant is kept informed about the progress in the handling of the complaint (Article 16 QCDHC Act).

88. B. Laarman and A. Akkermans, *Compensation Schemes for Damage Caused by Healthcare and Alternatives to Court Proceedings in the Netherlands: The Netherlands National Report to the 20th General Congress of the International Academy of Comparative Law* (Fukuoka, Japan, 22–28 Jul. 2018) 13.

*239.* As soon as possible and not later than six weeks (to be prolonged with another four weeks by the physician if necessary) after the submission of the complaint, the complainant receives a written and motivated statement of the physician containing the 'conclusion'[89] of the handling of the claim, the decision taken by the physician and the timeframe within which measures to be taken will effectively be realised (Article 17 QCDHC Act). According to the parliamentary history of the Act,[90] there is some room for manoeuvre, as this written 'conclusion' does not necessarily amount to a final judgment; if circumstances require so, it can suffice to explain that more time is needed and to indicate the steps that will be taken to reach a final conclusion. The short timeframe of six weeks serves to ensure that healthcare providers do respond to complaints, according to Laarman and Akkermans.

## 2. Disputes

*240.* Every physician has to join an independent healthcare disputes tribunal[91] that has to be licensed by the minister. The physician communicates the possibility to submit a dispute before such a tribunal to clients and their representatives (Article 18 QCDHC Act). The Act contains only general requirements for the tribunals, leaving the operational details to the healthcare sector. This resulted in a list of requirements drawn up by a national group of representatives of healthcare institutions, patients' organisations and medical liability insurers on the basis of which requirements for thirty-one tribunals have been established, divided over different healthcare sectors.[92]

*241.* The president of a tribunal will be a lawyer – often a judge or an otherwise experienced adjudicator – and the members have to be nominated by healthcare providers or patients' organisations.[93]

*242.* The task of a healthcare disputes tribunal consists of settling disputes regarding the behaviour of a physician towards a client in the course of the delivery of healthcare (Article 19.1 QCDHC Act). The tribunal is competent to settle disputes by binding advice, including the binding award of damages up to EUR 25,000 (Article 20 QCDHC Act).

*243.* A dispute with a physician can be submitted in writing to a tribunal by a client, a relative of a deceased client or a representative of a client if: (a) the rules for dealing with a complaint have been violated; (b) the communication referred to in Article 17 QCDHC Act (*see* paragraph 239) does not answer in a satisfactory way the complaint; or (c) it cannot reasonably be expected from the client that, given the circumstances, he directs his complaint to the physician (Article 21.1 QCDHC Act).

89. *Ibid.*, 14.
90. *Ibid.*
91. *Ibid.*
92. *Ibid.*
93. *Ibid.*

*244.* A tribunal takes a decision within six months after the dispute has been submitted (Article 22.1 QCDHC Act). The decisions of a dispute tribunal are to be binding and cannot be appealed.[94]

## III. The Act Containing Additional Dispositions Regarding the Treatment of Personal Data in the Care Sector

*245.* The Act of 10 April 2008 containing additional dispositions regarding the treatment of personal data in the care sector offers the client more possibilities to have control over his electronic file.[95] Part of this Act it the so-called Act on Client Rights during electronic processing of data.[96]

*246.* A healthcare provider (among which a physician) can make data of a client only available in an electronic exchange system with the explicit consent of the client (Article 15a.1 Act) containing additional dispositions regarding the treatment of personal data in the care sector.

*247.* A healthcare provider makes data of a client only available in an electronic exchange system in as far as the consultation of these data by another healthcare provider will not infringe the privacy of another person than the client (Article 15a.3). The healthcare provider informs the client about the electronic exchange system, the way to exercise his rights and the operation of the exchange system. When new categories of healthcare providers join the system or when the operation of this system is substantially modified, the healthcare provider informs the client about these modifications and the possibility to adapt or withdraw his/her consent (Article 15c). If the client requests access to a copy of his file or his data that the healthcare provider makes available through an electronic exchange system, the healthcare provider allows access with regular intervals. Access and copy are provided for free (Articles 15d.1 and 15d.3). Notwithstanding Article 15 GDPR (General Data Protection Regulation) (*see* paragraphs 285–287) a copy as referred to in Article 15d.1 contains on request of the client who has made available through the exchange system which information and on which data and who has accessed the system or requested which information on which data (Article 15e). Article 15d and Article 15e entered into force on 1 July 2020 by the single Article of the Decree of 10 June 2020.[97] According to the note of explanation to this Decree, Article 15d is more specific than Article 15 GDPR and supplements it.[98] Article 15d.2 contains specific rules concerning the exchange of data concerning self-medication. This

94. *Ibid.*, 15.
95. J. Nouwt, 'Naar een Recht op Elektronische Inzage in het Medisch Dossier', *Privacy en Informatie* (2016) 247–249 (related to a previous version); *see* more in general C. Ploem and S. Gevers, 'Introduction of a National Electronic Patient Record in the Netherlands: Some Legal Issues', *European Journal Health Law,* 18 (2011) 191–204.
96. *State Journal* (2017), 279.
97. *State Journal* (2020), 178.
98. *Ibid.*

right of the client is not regulated in the GDPR and also supplements the GDPR.[99] On request of the client, a pharmacist who delivers medication gives him direct access to his medication data and also on request makes this data available to other healthcare providers through the electronic exchange system. According to the note of explanation, Article 15e imposes an obligation to logging while the GDPR does not provide this explicitly.[100]

## IV. Implementation of the Cross-Border Healthcare Directive

### *A. National Contact Point*

*248.* The Cross-Border Healthcare Directive obliges the Member States to establish national contact points to give information to patients who intend to receive cross-border care. In the Dutch healthcare system, health insurers control a great deal of information. This explains why the Dutch Healthcare Insurance Board has been appointed by the Minister of Health, Welfare and Sport to perform the task of the national contact point.[101]

### *B. The Right to Receive Choice-Information*

*249.* Article 38.1 of the Healthcare Market Regulation Act obliges healthcare providers to make information available about the characteristics of the services they provide in such a way that these data are easily comparable for consumers. This information concerns at least the tariffs and the quality of the services provided.[102]

## V. The Medical Examinations Act

*250.* Medical examinations are regulated by the Act of 5 July 1997 with a view to strengthening the legal position of those undergoing medical examinations (Medical Examinations Act).[103] It came into force on 1 January 1998.

*251.* During the parliamentary preparation of the Medical Examinations Act, the legislator took into consideration that some rights of the medical examinee were already regulated by the Medical Treatment Agreement Act. This Act is not only

99. *Ibid.*
100. *Ibid.*
101. L.M.H. Bongers and D.M.R. Townend, 'The Implementation of the Directive on the Application of Patients' Rights in Cross-Border Healthcare in the Netherlands', *European Journal Health Law,* 21 (2014) 71.
102. *Ibid.,* 73.
103. *State Journal* (1997), 365.

applicable on the 'classic' relationship between a physician and a patient but by analogy also on a medical examination in the scope of private insurance or employment (Article 7:464-1 Civil Code).[104]

*252.* The Medical Examinations Act is a framework Act, leaving it to the parties concerned to implement further details (Article 9). In 2003, a protocol on medical examinations for insurance purposes came into force; it was amended in 2012.

*253.* A medical examination means enquiring about someone's status of health and carrying out medical investigation in order to obtain among others employment of an insurance (Article 1a). A person who is subjected to a medical examination is a medical examinee (Article 1b).

*254.* According to Article 2.1, medical examinations have to be limited with respect to their nature, contents and size to the purpose for which they are carried out (purpose limitation). The data acquired may only be used for this purpose (Article 2.2).

*255.* In the course of a medical examination, no questions may be asked, and no investigations may be carried out that disproportionally infringe upon the personal life of the examinee (Article 3.1.). In any case, no medical investigation may be carried out, the interest of which is disproportionate to the risks for the examinee or that brings with it an unreasonable heavy burden for the examinee (Article 3.2). Notwithstanding Article 3, Article 6 allows under certain conditions an HIV test before underwriting an insurance agreement.

*256.* According to Article 11, an examinee may refuse to collaborate to the carrying out of a medical examination or a part of it that infringes the Medical Examinations Act.

## VI. The Legal Duty to Help

*257.* Strictly speaking, Dutch law knows no obligation of assistance for doctors and other medical professionals. There are, however, a number of situations in which an obligation of assistance could be said to exist.

*258.* Article 255 Criminal Code provides that any person who intentionally puts or leaves in a helpless condition a person for whose maintenance, care or nursing he is responsible pursuant to the law or agreement shall be liable to a term of imprisonment not exceeding two years or a fine of the fourth category. This Article itself is not meant for healthcare exclusively, even if its application to healthcare is self-evident. Article 255 refers to the obligation of nursing and care, which makes it applicable to hospital staff, district nurses, ambulance personnel, et al. It is a matter

104. S. Defloor, 'The Medically Examined Applicant for Private Insurance and His/Her Right to Informed Consent: A Comparative Analysis', *European Journal Health Law,* 18 (2011) 329.

of debate whether this Article includes the physician who provokes a condition of helplessness for the patient by neglecting to carry out medical actions. Authors generally hold the view that Article 255 does apply when necessary medical assistance is withheld, even though this has hardly ever led to prosecution.

*259.* Article 450 Criminal Code provides that any person who witnesses the immediate mortal danger of another person and who fails to render or procure such aid and assistance even as he is capable of rendering or procuring where there is no reasonable expectation of danger to himself or others is liable to a term of detention not exceeding three months or a fine of the second category. The condition to be punishable is the death of the person in need as a direct consequence of the negligence. This article is not exclusively applicable to physicians. Article 450 is of minimal importance as it does not apply to a physician being sent for in an emergency. It only applies to those present at the scene of mortal danger. If a physician happens to be passing the scene of an emergency, this Article does not apply.

*260.* There are no recent disciplinary recent judgments on assistance in emergencies. A 1973 decision of the central disciplinary board leads to the conclusion that in judging reprehensible behaviour in emergencies, the distance between the physician and the patient involved in an accident is of vital importance. The conclusion of the board was that, in principle, a physician should go to the scene of an accident if so requested.[105] This obligation did not apply when the physician came to the conclusion that his presence was not strictly necessary, having regard to the available information. Nor is there an obligation when the physician considers another person to be more qualified to give assistance.

## VII. Protection of the Health Data and Genetic Data of the Patient

*261.* The processing of data concerning health and genetic data is governed by Regulation (EU) 2016/679 of the European Parliament and of the Council of 27 April 2016 on the protection of natural persons with regard to the processing of personal data and on the free movement of such data, and repealing Directive 95/46/EC (GDPR).[106] It entered into force on 24 May 2016 (Article 99.1) and has become applicable since 25 May 2018 (Article 99.2).

*262.* The GDPR replaces the Personal Data Protection Act. The Regulation is directly binding but leaves the Member States for some issues to make national choices. The Act of 16 May 2018 has implemented the GDPR (The Implementation Act). It entered into force on 25 May 2018.[107] It preserves as far as possible the rules of the previous Personal Data Protection Act unless this is made impossible in light of the Regulation.

---

105. Central disciplinary board 22 Nov. 1973, *Medisch Contact* (1974) 803–804.
106. *OJ* 2016, L 119.
107. *State Journal* (2018), 145.

*A. Field of Application*

*263.* The GDPR applies to the processing of personal data wholly or partially by automated means and to the processing other than by automated means of personal data which form part of a filing system or are intended to form part of a filing system (Article 2.1).

*264.* Processing means any operation or set of operations which is performed on personal data or on sets of personal data, whether or not by automated means, such as collection, recording, organisation, structuring, storage, adaptation or alteration, retrieval, consultation, use, disclosure by transmission, dissemination or otherwise making available, alignment or combination, restriction, erasure or destruction (Article 4(2)).

*265.* Personal data means any information relating to an identified or identifiable natural person ('data subject'); an identifiable natural person is one who can be identified, directly or indirectly, in particular, by reference to an identifier such as a name, an identification number, location data, an online identifier or to one or more factors specific to the physical, physiological, genetic, mental, economic, cultural or social identity of that natural person (Article 4(1)).

*266.* Filing system means any structured set of personal data which are accessible according to specific criteria, whether centralised, decentralised or dispersed on a functional or geographical basis (Article 4(4)).

*267.* The GDPR does not apply to the personal data of deceased persons. Member States may provide for rules regarding the processing of personal data of deceased persons (*see* Recital 27 in the Preamble).

*B. Processing of Data Concerning Health and Genetic Data*

1. Prohibition of Processing of Data Concerning Health and Genetic Data

*268.* The processing of 'special categories of personal data' is prohibited by Article 9.1. GDPR and by Article 22.1 Implementation Act Recital 10 in the Preamble in the Regulation refers to such data as 'sensitive data'. The special categories of personal data are personal data revealing racial or ethnic origin, political opinions, religious or philosophical beliefs, or trade union membership, genetic data, biometric data for the purpose of uniquely identifying a natural person, data concerning health or data concerning a natural person's sex life or sexual orientation (Article 9.1. GDPR).

*269.* Data concerning health means personal data related to the physical or mental health of a natural person, including the provision of healthcare services, which reveal information about his or her health status (Article 4(15)). According to Recital 35 in the Preamble, this information relates to the past, current or future physical or mental health status of the data subject and includes information about the natural person collected in the course of the registration for, or the provision of, healthcare services as referred to in the Cross-Border Healthcare Directive to that natural person; a number, symbol or particular assigned to a natural person to uniquely identify the natural person for health purposes; information derived from the testing or examination of a body part or bodily substance, including from genetic data and biological samples; and any information on, for example, a disease, disability, disease risk, medical history, clinical treatment or the physiological or biomedical state of the data subject independent of its source, for example, from a physician or other health professional, a hospital, a medical device or an in vitro diagnostic test.

*270.* Genetic data means personal data relating to the inherited or acquired genetic characteristics of a natural person which give unique information about the physiology or the health of that natural person and which result, in particular, from an analysis of a biological sample from the natural person in question (Article 4(13)), (in particular chromosomal, deoxyribonucleic acid or ribonucleic acid analysis, or from the analysis of another element enabling equivalent information to be obtained) (*see* Recital 34 in the Preamble).

## 2. Derogation from the Prohibition on Processing of Data Regarding Health and Genetic Data

### a. Compliance with the Principles Relating to Processing of Personal Data

*271.* When processing personal data, the following principles always have to be respected: the principles of lawfulness, fairness and transparency (Article 5.1a); the principle of purpose limitation (Article 5.1b); the principle of data minimisation (Article 5.1c); the principle of accuracy (Article 5.1d); the principle of storage limitation (Article 5.1e) and the principle of integrity and confidentiality (Article 5.1f).

*272.* Moreover, the controller is responsible for and able to demonstrate compliance with these principles (principle of accountability, Article 5.2.). Controller means the natural or legal person, public authority, agency or other body which, alone or jointly with others, determines the purposes and means of the processing of personal data (Article 4(7)).

### b. One of the Following Justifications Applies

#### The Data Subject Has Given Explicit Consent

*273.* Data regarding health or genetic data may be processed for one or more specified purposes if the data subject has given explicit consent, except where EU law or Member State law provides that the prohibition to process such data may not be lifted by the data subject (Article 9.2a GDPR and Article 22.2a Implementation

Act). The GDPR does not define 'explicit' consent, nor is it explained in the Preamble (also Recital 51 in the Preamble merely refers to explicit consent). Also, the Implementation Act does not define explicit consent.

*274.* Consent for processing of non-special categories of personal data (Article 6.1a) is defined as any freely given, specific, informed and unambiguous indication of the data subject's wishes by which he/she, by a statement or by clear affirmative action, signifies agreement to the processing of personal data relating to him or her (Article 4(11)).

*275.* Article 7 GDPR defines the conditions for consent. The controller has to be able to demonstrate that the data subject has consented to the processing of his or her data (Article 7.1). If the data subject's consent is given in the context of a written declaration which also concerns other matters, the request for consent has to be presented in a manner which is clearly distinguishable from the other matters, in an intelligible and easily accessible form, using clear and plain language. Any part of such a declaration which constitutes an infringement of the GDPR is not binding (Article 7.2).

*276.* The data subject has the right to withdraw his or her consent at any time. The withdrawal of consent does not affect the lawfulness of processing based on consent before its withdrawal. Prior to giving consent, the data subject has to be informed thereof. It has to be as easy to withdraw as to give consent (Article 7.3).

### Necessity to Protect the Vital Interests of the Data Subject or of Another Natural Person

*277.* Data regarding health or genetic data may be processed in order to protect the vital interests of the data subject or of another natural person where the data subject is physically or legally incapable of giving consent (Article 9.2b GDPR and Article 22.2b Implementation Act). A vital interest is an interest 'which is essential for the life'. Processing of personal data based on the vital interest of another natural person should, in principle, take place only where the processing cannot be manifestly based on another legal basis (*see* Recital 46 in the Preamble).[108]

### Necessary for Reasons of Substantial Public Interest

*278.* Data regarding health or genetic data may be processed when this is necessary for reasons of substantial public interest, on the basis of Union or Member

108. The concept of 'vital interest' was already present in the text of Directive 95/46/EC. The Article 29 Working Party has provided clarifications on the concept of 'vital interests' in its Opinion 06/2014 on the notion of legitimate interests of the data controller (WP 217). The national data protection authorities are as of May 2018 responsible for monitoring and enforcing the provisions of the General Data Protection Regulation. Questions regarding the application of the 'vital interest' legal basis in a specific case should in the first place addressed to them; *see* answer given by Ms Jourova on behalf of the Commission on 11 Jan. 2018 to a Parliamentary question by R. Sulik on 11 Oct. 2012, E-006389-2017.

State law which has to be proportionate to the aim pursued, respect the essence of the right to data protection and provide for suitable and specific measures to safeguard the fundamental rights and the interests of the data subject (Article 9.2g). According to Recital 52 in the Preamble, one of the reasons of substantial public interest is health security, monitoring and alert purposes, the prevention or control of communicable diseases and other serious threats to health. And the Recital continues: 'Such a derogation may be made for health purposes, including public health and the management of health-care services, especially in order to ensure the quality and cost-effectiveness of the procedures used for settling claims for benefits and services in the health insurance system.' Having regard to Article 9.2g GDPR, Article 28.1 Implementation Act provides that the prohibition to process genetic data is not applicable when the processing takes place with regard to the person from whom these data have been obtained. In all other cases then referred to in Article 28.1, the prohibition to process genetic data is according to Article 28.2 exclusively not applicable if: (a) a weighty medical interest prevails, or (b) the processing is necessary for scientific research that serves a general interest or for the purpose of statistics if: (i) the person concerned has given explicit consent, and (ii) guarantees have been provided in order not to harm disproportionally the privacy of the person concerned. According to Article 28.3, the consent referred to in Article 28.2 is not required when asking the explicit consent is impossible or requires a disproportionate effort.

### Necessary for Legal Claims

*279.* Data regarding health or genetic data may be processed when this is necessary for the establishment, exercise or defence of legal claims (Article 9.2f GDPR and Article 22.2e Implementation Act). The sharing of health data of a patient by a hospital without the consent of the patient with an external expert in order to defend itself against a malpractice claim by the patient has been considered justified on the basis of this ground.[109] Article 9.2f is only applicable in case of legal claims and not on extrajudicial procedures.[110]

### Necessary for Health-Related Purposes

*280.* Data regarding health or genetic data may be processed when this is necessary for the purposes of preventive or occupational medicine, for the assessment of the working capacity of the employee, medical diagnosis, the provision of health or social care or treatment or the management of health or social care systems and services on the basis of Union or Member State law or pursuant to contract with a health professional and subject to the conditions and safeguards referred to in Article 9.3 (Article 9.2h). Recital 53 in the Preamble calls this the processing for health-related purposes. This Recital specifies that such processing should be necessary to achieve those purposes for the benefit of natural persons and society as a

109. District Court Amsterdam, 18 Mar. 2020, ECLI:NL:RBAMS:2020:2200: 4.5, *X v. Stichting VUMC Amsterdam*.
110. District Court Rotterdam, 10 Apr. 2020, ECLI:NL.RBROT:2020:3430.

whole, in particular in the context of the management of health or social care services and systems, including processing by the management and central national health authorities of such data for the purpose of quality control, management information and the general national and local supervision of the health or social care system, and ensuring continuity of health or social care and cross-border healthcare or health security, monitoring and alert purposes '( … ) based on Union or Member State law which has to meet an objective of public interest ( … )'. Having regard to Article 9.2h GDPR, the prohibition to process data regarding health is according to Article 30.3a Implementation Act not applicable if healthcare providers, healthcare institutions or social care institutions process data regarding health when this is necessary in order to diligently treat or care the person concerned or to manage their institution or professional practice. When Article 30.3a is applied, the data regarding health may according to Article 30.4 Implementation Act only be processed by persons who are legally obliged to respect secrecy.

*281.* Article 9.3 requires that the data are processed by or under the responsibility of a professional subject to the obligation of professional secrecy under Union or Member State law or rules established by competent national bodies or by another person also subject to an obligation of secrecy under Union or Member State law or rules established by competent national bodies.

**Necessary for Reasons of Public Interest in the Area of Public Health**

*282.* Data regarding health or genetic data may be processed if it is necessary for reasons of public interest in the area of public health, such as protecting against serious cross-border threats to health or ensuring high standards of quality and safety of healthcare and of medicinal products or medical devices, on the basis of Union or Member State law which provides for suitable and specific measures to safeguard the rights and freedoms of the data subject, in particular professional secrecy (Article 9.2i). Recital 54 in the Preamble emphasises that in such a case, the processing is possible without the consent of the data subject. This is remarkable because this is also the case in the situation mentioned in the previous jurisdiction. Public health should be interpreted as defined in Regulation (EC) No. 1338/2008 of the European Parliament and of the Council on Community Statistics on Public Health and Health and Safety at Work[111] namely all elements related to health, such as health status, including morbidity and disability, the determinants having an effect on that health status, healthcare needs, resources allocated to healthcare, the provision of, and universal access to, healthcare as well as healthcare expenditure and financing, and the causes of mortality (Recital 54 in the Preamble).

*283.* Such processing of data concerning health for reasons of public interest should not result in personal data being processed for other purposes by third parties such as employers or insurance and banking companies (Recital 54 in the Preamble).

111. *OJ* 2008, L 354.

*284.* There seems to exist an overlap between Article 9.2g and Article 9.2i, having regarded the explanations given in the Recitals accompanying both provisions. Obviously, the difference is between substantial public interest (Article 9.2g) and substantial interest (Article 9.2i) but where to draw the line and what the consequences are, remain vague.

c. Comply with Member States' Further Conditions

*285.* Member States may maintain or introduce further conditions, including limitations, with regard to the processing of genetic data, biometric data or data concerning health (Article 9.4). However, this should not hamper the free flow of personal data within the Union when those conditions apply to cross-border processing of such data (*see* Recital 53 in the Preamble).

## *C. Rights of the Data Subject*

### 1. The Right to the Protection of Personal Data

*286.* The GDPR protects fundamental rights and freedoms of natural persons and, in particular, their right to the protection of personal data (Article 1.2). Such data must be processed fairly for specified purposes and on the basis of the consent of the person concerned or some other legitimate basis laid down by law. Everyone has the right of access to data which has been collected concerning him or her, and the right to have it rectified (Article 8.2). Compliance with these rules shall be subject to control by an independent authority (Article 8.3).

### 2. Information to be Provided Where Personal Data Are Collected from the Data Subject

*287.* Where personal data relating to a data subject are collected from the data subject, the controller has, at the time when personal data are obtained, to provide the data subject with all of the following information: the identity and the contact details of the controller and, where applicable, of the controller's representative; the contact details of the data protection officer, where applicable; the purposes of the processing for which the personal data are intended, as well as the legal basis for the processing; the recipients or categories of recipients of the personal data, if any (Article 13.1a, 13.1b, 13.1c, and 13.1e).

*288.* In addition to this information, the controller has, at the time when personal data are obtained, to provide the data subject with the following further information necessary to ensure fair and transparent processing: the period for which the personal data will be stored, or if that is not possible, the criteria used to determine that period; the existence of the right to request from the controller access to and rectification or erasure of personal data or restriction of processing concerning the data subject or to object to processing as well as the right to data portability; where the processing is based on Article 9.2a, the existence of the right to withdraw consent at any time, without affecting the lawfulness of processing based on consent before its withdrawal; the right to lodge a complaint with a supervisory authority; whether the provision of personal data is a statutory or contractual requirement, or a requirement necessary to enter into a contract, as well as whether the data subject is obliged to provide the personal data and of the possible consequences of failure to provide such data; the existence of automated decision-making, including profiling, referred to in Article 22(1) and 22(4) and, at least in those cases, meaningful information about the logic involved, as well as the significance and the envisaged consequences of such processing for the data subject (Article 13.2).

*289.* Where the controller intends to further process the personal data for a purpose other than that for which the personal data were collected, the controller has to provide the data subject prior to that further processing with information on that other purpose and with any further relevant information as referred to in Article 13.2 (Article 13.3).

*290.* Article 13.1, 13.2 and 13.3 do not apply where and insofar as the data subject already has the information (Article 13.4).

### 3. The Right of Access by the Data Subject

*291.* The data subject has the right to obtain from the controller confirmation as to whether or not personal data concerning him or her are being processed, and, where that is the case, access to the personal data and the following information: the purposes of the processing; the categories of personal data concerned; the recipients or categories of recipients to whom the personal data have been or will be disclosed, in particular recipients in third countries or international organisations; where possible, the envisaged period for which the personal data will be stored, or, if not possible, the criteria used to determine that period; the existence of the right to request from the controller rectification or erasure of personal data or restriction of processing of personal data concerning the data subject or to object to such processing; the right to lodge a complaint with a supervisory authority; where the personal data are not collected from the data subject, any available information as to their source; the existence of automated decision-making, including profiling, referred to in Article 22.1 and 22.4 and, at least in those cases, meaningful information about the logic involved, as well as the significance and the envisaged consequences of such processing for the data subject (Article 15.1).

*292.* The controller provides a copy of the personal data undergoing processing. For any further copies requested by the data subject, the controller may charge a reasonable fee based on administrative costs (*see also* Article 12.5 and below, paragraph 316). Where the data subject makes the request by electronic means, and unless otherwise requested by the data subject, the information is provided in a commonly used electronic form (Article 15.3). The right to obtain a copy referred to in Article 15.3 should not adversely affect the rights and freedoms of others (Article 15.4).

*293.* A data subject has the right of access to personal data which have been collected concerning him or her, and to exercise that right easily and at reasonable intervals, in order to be aware of, and verify, the lawfulness of the processing. According to Recital 63 in the Preamble, this right includes the right for data subjects to have access to data concerning their health, for example, the data in their medical records containing information such as diagnoses, examination results, assessments by treating physicians and any treatment or interventions provided.

## 4. Right to Rectification

*294.* The data subject has the right to obtain from the controller without undue delay the rectification of inaccurate personal data concerning him or her. Taking into account the purposes of the processing, the data subject has the right to have incomplete personal data completed, including by means of providing a supplementary statement (Article 16).

*295.* The controller has to communicate any rectification to each recipient to whom the personal data have been disclosed unless this proves impossible or involves disproportionate effort. The controller has to inform the data subject about those recipients if the data subject requests it (Article 19).

## 5. Restricted Right to Erasure of Personal Data Regarding Health of Genetic Data ('Right to Be Forgotten')

*296.* The data subject has the right to obtain from the controller the erasure of personal data concerning him or her without undue delay, and the controller has an obligation to erase personal data without undue delay where one of the following grounds applies:

(a) the personal data are no longer necessary in relation to the purposes for which they were collected or otherwise processed;
(b) the data subject withdraws consent on which the processing is based according to Article 9.2a and where there is no other legal ground for the processing;
(c) the data subject objects to the processing pursuant to Article 21.1, and there are no overriding legitimate grounds for the processing or the data subject objects to the processing pursuant to Article 21.2;
(d) the personal data have been unlawfully processed;
(e) the personal data have to be erased for compliance with a legal obligation in the Union or Member State law to which the controller is subject;

(f) the personal data have been collected in relation to the offer of information society services referred to in Article 8(1).

*297.* However, the right to erasure does not apply to the extent that processing of data regarding health and genetic data is necessary for reasons of public health in accordance with Article 9.2h (processing is necessary for health-related purposes), with Article 9.2i (processing is necessary for reasons of public interest in the area of public health) as well as Article 9.3 (processing under the responsibility of a professional subject to the obligation of professional secrecy) (Article 17.3c).

*298.* More, in general, the right to erasure is not applicable, also with regard to data regarding health and genetic data, to the extent that their processing is necessary for exercising the right of freedom of expression and information and for the establishment, exercise or defence of legal claims (Article 17.3a and 17.3e).

*299.* On the other hand, the right to erasure is applicable if data regarding health or genetic data have been processed with the explicit consent of the data subject based on Article 9.2a.

*300.* The controller has to communicate any erasure of personal data to each recipient to whom the personal data have been disclosed unless this proves impossible or involves disproportionate effort. The controller has to inform the data subject about those recipients if the data subject requests it (Article 19).

## 6. Right to Restriction of Processing

*301.* Restriction of processing means the marking of stored personal data with the aim of limiting their processing in the future (Article 4(4)).

*302.* The data subject has the right to obtain from the controller restriction of processing, where one of the following applies:

(a) the accuracy of the personal data is contested by the data subject, for a period enabling the controller to verify the accuracy of the personal data;
(b) the processing is unlawful, and the data subject opposes the erasure of the personal data and requests the restriction of their use instead;
(c) the controller no longer needs the personal data for the purposes of the processing, but they are required by the data subject for the establishment, exercise or defence of legal claims;
(d) the data subject has objected to processing pursuant to Article 21.1 pending the verification whether the legitimate grounds of the controller override those of the data subject (Article 18.1).

*303.* Where processing has been restricted, the personal data should, with the exception of storage, only be processed with the data subject's consent or for the establishment, exercise or defence of legal claims or for the protection of the rights of another natural or legal person or for reasons of important public interest of the Union or of a Member State (Article 18.2). A data subject who has obtained restriction of processing has to be informed by the controller before the restriction of processing is lifted (Article 18.3).

*304.* The controller has to communicate any restriction of processing to each recipient to whom the personal data have been disclosed unless this proves impossible or involves disproportionate effort. The controller has to inform the data subject about those recipients if the data subject requests it (Article 19).

*305.* Methods to restrict the processing of personal data could include, *inter alia*, temporarily moving the selected data to another processing system, making the selected personal data unavailable to users, or temporarily removing published data from a website. In automated filing systems, the restriction of processing should, in principle, be ensured by technical means in such a manner that the personal data are not subject to further processing operations and cannot be changed. The fact that the processing of personal data is restricted should be clearly indicated in the system (*see* Recital 67 in the Preamble).

### 7. Restricted Right to Portability of Data Regarding Health or Genetic Data

*306.* The data subject has the right to receive the personal data concerning him or her, which he/she has provided to a controller, in a structured, commonly used and machine-readable format and has the right to transmit those data to another controller without hindrance from the controller to which the personal data have been provided, when the processing is carried out by automated means. When it concerns data regarding health or genetic data, this so-called right to portability only applies when these data have been processed upon explicit consent (*see* Article 9.2a) (Article 20.1) and not in the other situations mentioned in Article 9.2a (*see also* Recital 68 in the Preamble: 'It should not apply where processing is based on a legal ground other than consent.').

*307.* In exercising his or her right to data portability, the data subject has the right to have the personal data transmitted directly from one controller to another, where technically feasible (Article 20.2). The right to portability of data may not adversely affect the rights and freedoms of others (Article 20.4).

### 8. Right Not to be Subject to Automated Individual Decision-Making, Including Profiling

*308.* The data subject has the right not to be subject to a decision based solely on automated processing, including profiling, which produces legal effects concerning him or her or similarly significantly affecting him or her (Article 22.1). Profiling means any form of automated processing of personal data consisting of the use of personal data to evaluate certain personal aspects relating to a natural person, in particular, to analyse or predict aspects concerning that natural person's performance at work, economic situation, health, personal preferences, interests, reliability, behaviour, location or movements (Article 4(4)). However, the data subject may be subject to such a decision when it is based on (*inter alia*) the data subject's explicit consent (Article 22.2). However, data regarding health and genetic data are excluded from this possibility unless the decision is based on such data regarding health or genetic data processed after the explicit consent of the data subject (*see* Article 9.2a) or the processing of which is necessary for reasons of substantial public interest (*see* Article 9.2g) (Article 22.3).

## 9. Right to Transparent Information and Communication Concerning Rights of the Data Subject

*309.* The controller takes appropriate measures to provide any information referred to in Articles 13 and 14 and any communication under Articles 15–22 and 34 relating to processing the data subject in a concise, transparent, intelligible and easily accessible form, using clear and plain language, in particular for any information addressed specifically to a child. The information is provided in writing, or by other means, including, where appropriate, by electronic means. When requested by the data subject, the information may be provided orally, provided that the identity of the data subject is proven by other means (Article 12.1). The controller facilitates the exercise of the data subject rights under Articles 15–22 (Article 12.2).

*310.* The controller provides information on action taken on a request under Articles 15–22 to the data subject without undue delay and in any event within one month of receipt of the request. That period may be extended by two further months where necessary, taking into account the complexity and number of the requests. The controller informs the data subject of any such extension within one month of receipt of the request, together with the reasons for the delay. Where the data subject makes the request by electronic form means, the information has to be provided by electronic means where possible, unless otherwise requested by the data subject (Article 12.3). If the controller does not take action on the request of the data subject, he has to inform the data subject without delay and at the latest within one month of receipt of the request of the reasons for not taking action and on the possibility of lodging a complaint with a supervisory authority and seeking a judicial remedy (Article 12.4).

## 10. Right to Lodge a Complaint and to an Effective Judicial Remedy

*311.* Without prejudice to any other administrative or judicial remedy, every data subject has the right to lodge a complaint with a supervisory authority, in particular in the Member State of his or her habitual residence, place of work or place of the alleged infringement if the data subject considers that the processing of personal data relating to him or her infringes the GDPR. The supervisory authority with which the complaint has been lodged has to inform the complainant on the progress and the outcome of the complaint, including the possibility of a judicial remedy pursuant to Article 78 (Article 77).

*312.* Without prejudice to any other administrative or non-judicial remedy, each data subject has the right to an effective judicial remedy where the supervisory authority which is competent does not handle a complaint or does not inform the data subject within three months on the progress or outcome of the complaint lodged pursuant to Article 77. Proceedings against a supervisory authority are to be brought before the courts of the Member State where the supervisory authority is established (Article 78.2 and 78.3).

*313.* Without prejudice to any available administrative or non-judicial remedy, including the right to lodge a complaint with a supervisory authority pursuant to Article 77, each data subject has the right to an effective judicial remedy against a controller or a processor where he/she considers that his or her rights under the GDPR have been infringed as a result of the processing of his or her personal data in non-compliance with the GDPR. Such proceedings are to be brought before the courts of the Member State where the controller or processor has an establishment. Alternatively, such proceedings may be brought before the courts of the Member State where the data subject has his or her habitual residence unless the controller or processor is a public authority of a Member State acting in the exercise of its public powers (Article 79).

### 11. Right to Be Represented

*314.* The data subject has the right to mandate a not-for-profit body, organisation or association which has been properly constituted in accordance with the law of a Member State has statutory objectives which are in the public interest and which is active in the field of the protection of data subjects' rights and freedoms with regard to the protection of their personal data to lodge the complaint on his or her behalf, to exercise the rights referred to in Articles 77, 78 and 79 on his or her behalf, and to exercise the right to receive compensation referred to in Article 82 on his or her behalf where provided for by Member State law (Article 80.1).

### 12. Right to Compensation and Liability

*315.* Any person who has suffered material or non-material damage as a result of an infringement of the GDPR has the right to receive compensation from the controller or processor for the damage suffered. Any controller involved in processing is liable for the damage caused by processing which infringes the GDPR. A processor is liable for the damage caused by processing only where it has not complied with obligations of the GDPR specifically directed to processors or where it has acted outside or contrary to lawful instructions of the controller. A controller or processor is exempt from liability if it proves that it is not in any way responsible for the event giving rise to the damage. Where more than one controller or processor, or both a controller and a processor, are involved in the same processing and where they are responsible for any damage caused by processing, each controller or processor is held liable for the entire damage in order to ensure effective compensation of the data subject (Article 82.1–82.4).

### *D. Modalities for the Exercise of the Rights of the Data Subject*

*316.* Information provided under Articles 13 and 14 and any communication and any actions taken under Articles 15–22 and 34 are provided free of charge (*see also* Article 15.3, above paragraph 286). Where requests from a data subject are manifestly unfounded or excessive, in particular, because of their repetitive character, the controller may either: charge a reasonable fee taking into account the administrative costs of providing the information or communication or taking the action requested; or refuse to act on the request. The controller bears the burden of demonstrating the manifestly unfounded or excessive character of the request (Article 12.5).

*317.* Where the controller has reasonable doubts concerning the identity of the natural person making the request referred to in Articles 15–21, the controller may request the provision of additional information necessary to confirm the identity of the data subject (Article 12.6).

*318.* The information to be provided to data subjects pursuant to Articles 13 and 14 may be provided in combination with standardised icons in order to give in an easily visible, intelligible and clearly legible manner a meaningful overview of the intended processing. Where the icons are presented electronically, they have to be machine-readable (Article 12.7). The Commission is empowered to adopt delegated acts in accordance with Article 92 for the purpose of determining the information to be presented by the icons and the procedures for providing standardised icons (Article 12.8).

### *E. Data Protection by Design and by Default*

*319.* Taking into account the state of the art, the cost of implementation and the nature, scope, context and purposes of processing as well as the risks of varying likelihood and severity for rights and freedoms of natural persons posed by the processing, the controller implements, both at the time of the determination of the means for processing and at the time of the processing itself, appropriate technical and organisational measures, such as pseudonymisation, which are designed to implement data protection principles, such as data minimisation, in an effective manner and to integrate the necessary safeguards into the processing in order to meet the requirements of this Regulation and protect the rights of data subjects (Article 25.1).

*320.* Pseudonymisation means the processing of personal data in such a manner that the personal data can no longer be attributed to a specific data subject without the use of additional information, provided that such additional information is kept separately and is subject to technical and organisational measures to ensure that the personal data are not attributed to an identified or identifiable natural person (Article 4(5)). The likelihood and severity of the risk to the rights and freedoms of the data subject should be determined by reference to the nature, scope, context and purposes of the processing. Risk should be evaluated on the basis of an objective assessment, by which it is established whether data processing operations involve a risk or a high risk (*see* Recital 76 in the Preamble).

*321.* The controller has to implement appropriate technical and organisational measures for ensuring that, by default, only personal data which are necessary for each specific purpose of the processing are processed. That obligation applies to the amount of personal data collected, the extent of their processing, the period of their storage and their accessibility. In particular, such measures have to ensure that by default, personal data are not made accessible without the individual's intervention to an indefinite number of natural persons (Article 25.2).

### *F. Communication of a Personal Data Breach to the Data Subject*

*322.* Personal data breach means a breach of security leading to the accidental or unlawful destruction, loss, alteration, unauthorised disclosure of, or access to, personal data transmitted, stored or otherwise processed (Article 4(12)).

*323.* When the personal data breach is likely to result in a high risk to the rights and freedoms of natural persons, the controller has to communicate the personal data breach to the data subject without undue delay (Article 34.1). This communication to the data subject describes in clear and plain language the nature of the personal data breach and contains at least the following information and measures: the name and contact details of the data protection officer or other contact point where more information can be obtained, the likely consequences of the personal data breach and the measures taken or proposed to be taken by the controller to address the personal data breach, including, where appropriate, measures to mitigate its possible adverse effects (Article 34.2).

*324.* The communication to the data subject is not required if any of the following conditions are met: (a) the controller has implemented appropriate technical and organisational protection measures, and those measures were applied to the personal data affected by the personal data breach, in particular, those that render the personal data unintelligible to any person who is not authorised to access it, such as encryption; (b) the controller has taken subsequent measures which ensure that the high risk to the rights and freedoms of data subjects is no longer likely to materialise; (c) it would involve a disproportionate effort. In such a case, there has instead to be a public communication or similar measure whereby the data subjects are informed in an equally effective manner (Article 34.3).

### *G. Data Protection Impact Assessment*

*325.* Directive 95/46/EC provided for a general obligation to notify the processing of personal data to the supervisory authorities. While that obligation produced administrative and financial burdens, it did not, in all cases, contribute to improving the protection of personal data. Such indiscriminate general notification obligations have therefore been abolished and replaced by effective procedures and mechanisms which focus instead on those types of processing operations which are likely to result in a high risk to the rights and freedoms of natural persons by virtue of their nature, scope, context and purposes. Such types of processing operations may be those which in particular involve using new technologies or are of a new kind and where no data protection impact assessment has been carried out before by the controller, or where they become necessary in the light of the time that has elapsed since the initial processing (*see* Recital 89 in the Preamble).

*326.* Where a type of processing, in particular, using new technologies, and taking into account the nature, scope, context and purposes of the processing, is likely to result in a high risk to the rights and freedoms of natural persons, the controller has, prior to the processing, to carry out an assessment of the impact of the envisaged processing operations on the protection of personal data. A single assessment may address a set of similar processing operations that present similar high risks (Article 35.1).

### *H. Designation of a Data Protection Officer When Data Regarding Health or Genetic Data are Processed on a Large-Scale*

*327.* The controller and the processor have to designate a data protection officer in any case where the core activities of the controller or the processor consist of processing on a large-scale data regarding health or genetic data (Article 37.1c). Large-scale processing operations aim to process a considerable amount of personal data at regional, national or supranational level and which could affect a large number of data subjects and which are likely to result in a high risk. The processing of personal data is not considered to be on a large-scale if the processing concerns personal data from patients by an individual physician or other healthcare professional. In such cases, a data protection officer is not mandatory (analogues to Recital 91 of the Preamble).

## VIII. Duty of Medical Secrecy

### *A. General Principle*

*328.* One of the most important legal obligations owed by a physician to a patient is to keep secrecy over the confidentialities revealed by a patient to a physician. Article 272 of the Criminal Code contains the legal basis for this obligation:

'Any person who intentionally violates any secret which he knows or has reasonable cause to suspect he is obliged to keep by reason of his office, profession or a statutory requirement, or his former office or profession, shall be liable to a term of imprisonment not exceeding one year or a fine of the fourth category.' A broad interpretation of the application of the duty of medical secrecy is indicated.[112]

*329.* The duty of medical secrecy is a right of the patient and does not apply towards the patient him or herself.

### B. *Exceptions*

#### 1. Privilege of Non-disclosure in Court

*330.* Those persons who have a duty of secrecy by reason of their position, profession or office may also assert privilege when called to testify or answer certain questions, but only in regard of information entrusted to them in their aforementioned capacity (Article 218 Code Criminal Procedure). The privilege of non-disclosure does not entail the right of non-appearance as a witness in a Court of law.

#### 2. Statutory Obligations to Disclose Confidential Information

*331.* The duty of medical secrecy is not absolute; first and foremost, it can be lifted by law. The general legal basis is Article 42 of the Criminal code: 'Any person who commits an offence in carrying out a statutory requirement shall not be criminally liable.'[113] One example is Article 2 of the Control of Contagious Diseases and Detection of Causes of Disease Act. Under this Act, the physician is obliged to inform the State Inspector of Public Health of the occurrence of certain contagious diseases. The obligatory notification of suspicious/inexplicable death of a minor for the purpose of having a death review performed (autopsy) that became effective as of 1 October 2012 is another example.[114] Another example is Article 4.3 of the Disposal of the Dead Act, which states that a physician is obliged to issue a death certificate when he is convinced that death has been caused by a natural cause. There is, however, no mandatory duty to report child abuse or domestic violence.[115]

112. H.J.J. Leenen et al., *Handboek Gezondheidsrecht* (Den Haag, Boom, 2017) 141.
113. *Ibid.*, 149.
114. H. Roscam Abbing, 'Medical Confidentiality and Patient Safety: Reporting Procedures', *European Journal Health Law,* 21 (2014) 252 who adds in note 19: 'soon after the introduction of the procedure, it was considered unworkable'; *see also* T. Vansweevelt, 'Liabilities of a Physician Confronted with Child Abuse', *European Journal Health Law,* 20 (2013) 275.
115. H. Roscam Abbing, 'Medical Confidentiality and Patient Safety: Reporting Procedures', *European Journal Health Law,* 21 (2014) 253.

### 3. Conflict of Duties

*332.* Also, without a legal prescription or the consent of the patient (*see* paragraphs 331 and 334), a physician may, under certain circumstances, reveal information covered by the duty of secrecy. Article 40 of the Criminal Code forms the legal basis for what is commonly referred to as a conflict of duties: 'Any person who commits an offence under the compulsion of an irresistible force shall not be criminally liable.'[116] A possible application of the conflict of duties doctrine may occur when a physician is informed of the intention of a patient to kill someone ('duty to warn').

*333.* In 2012, 'a general right to breach confidentiality' was introduced into the General Data Protection Act for cases where sharing of information would be of vital importance while asking consent is not possible. This regards situations of an immediate or threatening danger for the life or health of the person concerned or a third party. An example is serious cases of child abuse (*see also* paragraph 331). This 'general right to breach confidentiality' can be seen as a general codification of the conflict of duties doctrine.[117] The General Data Protection Act is no longer applicable.

### 4. Consent of the Patient

*334.* Consent of the patient, either explicit or implicit, gives the physician the right to speak. Specifically, at proceedings at which the physician appears as a witness, he may speak with the patient's consent, but he is not obliged to do so.

### 5. Issuing Medical Certificates to Third Parties

*335.* The physician has to be extremely careful with providing information to a third party, which, in principle, requires the patient's consent. The issuing of medical certificates has regularly been an issue at disciplinary boards. From their decisions, the following can be concluded: first, the physician issuing a medical certificate must exercise due caution. Before issuing a certificate, he must conduct sufficient examinations of his/her own. Second, the certificate may not contain any statement outside the physician's field of competence.

## IX. Medical Fees

*336.* The patient owes the physician payment, except insofar as the latter receives payment for his work by virtue of or pursuant to statutory provisions or on

116. H.J.J. Leenen et al., *Handboek Gezondheidsrecht* (Den Haag, Boom, 2017) 150.
117. H. Roscam Abbing, 'Medical Confidentiality and Patient Safety: Reporting Procedures', *European Journal Health Law,* 21 (2014) 253.

some other basis as provided for in the medical treatment agreement (Article 7:461 Civil Code).

# Chapter 2. The Physician: Patient Relationship in Specific Terms

## §1. The Minor Patient

### I. The Patient Has Not Yet Reached the Age of Twelve Years

*337.* If the patient has not yet reached the age of 12 years, the physicians shall fulfil the obligations to the patients arising from the Medical Treatment Agreement Act in respect of either the parents who exercise parental responsibility (authority) over the patient or the patient's legal guardian (Article 7:465-1 Civil Code). Conflicts between parents are settled by the judge (Article 1:256-1 Civil Code). The physician shall fulfil his obligations towards the minor's parents or guardian unless this is incompatible with the standards of a prudent physician (Article 7:465-4 Civil Code).

### II. The Patient is at Least Twelve Years but Not Yet Sixteen Years

*338.* In this case, the 'double consent' rule applies. First, his or her consent is, in principle, always required according to the general rule in Article 7:450.1 Civil Code (*see* paragraph 178). If the minor refuses to give consent for an activity, it cannot be performed. However, also the consent of his/her parents exercising parental responsibility (authority) over him/her or of his/her legal guardian is, in principle, required (Article 7:450-2 Civil Code). In the so-called *David* case, it has been decided that a minor of 12 years old who suffered from medulloblastoma (a malignant brain tumour of childhood) could refuse the continuation of chemotherapy and radiotherapy against the will of his father.[118] According to Article 7:450 Civil Code, a psychologist has to ask for the consent of both (divorced) parents of a minor of 15 years. Psychological treatment is a major intervention, and the consent of the mother to it should not have been presumed. The psychologist was reprimanded.[119]

*339.* However, the activity may be performed without the consent of the parents or the legal guardian if the treatment is clearly necessary in order to avoid serious harm to the patient or if the minor, after careful consideration, still wants the actions to be performed after the required consent has been refused by the parents (Article 7:450-2 Civil Code).

118. District Court Noord Holland, 12 May 2017, ECLI:NL:RBNHO:2017:3955, confirmed in appeal by Court Amsterdam, 11 Jul. 2017, ECLI:NL.GHAMS:2017:2688; B. Blankenburg et.al., 'Access to Justice voor 12- tot 16 jarigen bij niet nakoming van de geneeskundige behandelingsovereenkomst?', *Tijdschrift voor Jeugdrecht,* 2 (2020) 94–100.

119. Regional disciplinary board Eindhoven, 6 Nov. 2020, ECLI:NL:TGZEIN:2020:54.

### III. The Patient Has Reached the Age of Sixteen Years

*340.* Article 1:234 Civil Code provides that minors have, in principle, no legal competence. However, the Medical Treatment Agreement Act stipulates that a minor who has reached the age of 16 years has the legal capacity to enter into a medical treatment agreement for him/herself and to perform juridical acts that immediately relate to that agreement (Article 7:447-1 Civil Code). Such a minor is liable for obligations arising from such a medical treatment agreement, without prejudice to the duty of his parents to meet the costs of care and upbringing (Article 7:447-2 Civil Code).

*341.* In the event that a patient of the age of 16 years or older cannot be regarded as being capable of making a reasonable appreciation of his interests in the matter, the physician and the representative of this patient shall follow the patient's clear opinion as expressed in writing while he/she was still capable of making a reasonable assessment of his/her interests and containing a refusal to give his/her consent. The physician may nevertheless deviate from this statement if he/she thinks there are well-founded reasons for doing so (Article 7.450.3 Civil Code).

## §2. The Mental Patient and Involuntary Admission and Treatment

### I. The Legal Framework

*342.* The Act of 29 October 1992[120] which was called in a rather euphemistic way an Act on the Special Admission in a Psychiatric Hospital, contained rules governing the involuntary admission in such a hospital. From 1 January 2020 onwards, this Act has been withdrawn (Article 16:2) and replaced by two Acts: the Act of 24 January 2018 containing rules to provide compulsory care to persons suffering from a mental illness disease (The Compulsory Mental Healthcare Act; in Dutch: Wvggz)[121] and the Act of 24 January 2018 on Care and Compulsion for Psychogeriatric and Intellectually Disabled Patients Act (The Care and Coercion Act).[122] These two groups of patients (psychiatric patients and those suffering from an intellectual disability or dementia) have different problems and interests. The creation of two separate pieces of legislation aims to take better care of the needs of each category and better protect their legal status.[123]

120. *State Journal* (1992), 669.
121. *State Journal* (2018), 37.
122. *State Journal* (2018), 38.
123. https://www.government.nl/topics/mental-health-services.

## II. The Compulsory Mental Healthcare Act

### A. *Definition of Compulsory Care*

*343.* Compulsory care is the care that notwithstanding the resistance of the patient or his legal representative may be provided following: (a) a compulsory care authorisation; (b) a crisis measure; (c) an authorisation to continue a crisis measure; (d) a decision to provide temporary compulsory care preceding a crisis measure; or (e) a decision to provide temporary compulsory care. In the following, the two most important measures, the compulsory care authorisation and the crisis measure will be dealt with (Article 3:1). Compulsory care consists of: (a) the compulsory administration of fluid, food or medication, performing medical examinations or other medical interventions and applying compulsory therapeutic measures in order to treat a mental illness or a somatic illness that is related to a mental illness; (b) the restriction of the freedom of movement; (c) locking a person in; (d) exercising supervision over a person; (e) searching a person's clothing or body; (f) searching a person's residence or accommodation for behaviour-affecting substances or dangerous objects; (g) monitoring for the presence of behaviour-affecting substances; (h) restricting the freedom to determine one's own life in a way that the person concerned has to act or to refrain from acting, among which the use of means to communicate; (i) limiting the freedom to receive a visit, compulsory admission in accommodation and deprivation of freedom in a place that is equipped for a temporary stay (Article 3:2.2).

### B. *Criteria for Compulsory Care*

*344.* Compulsory care may only be considered as a last resort when there are no possibilities anymore to provide care on a voluntary basis (Article 2:2.1). If the behaviour of a person, as a consequence of a mental illness not being a psychogeriatric or intellectual disability causes serious disadvantage, compulsory care in the sense of Article 3:1 (*see* paragraph 353) may be provided as a last resort if: (a) there are no possibilities to provide care on a voluntary basis; (b) there are no less onerous alternatives having the same aimed effect; (c) the compulsory care is having regard to the aimed purpose, proportional; and (d) it is reasonable to expect that the compulsory care will be effective (Article 3:3). Serious disadvantage is defined as: (a) the prevalence of or a serious risk to danger of life, serious physical harm, serious mental, material, immaterial or financial harm, serious neglect or social loss, serious disturbed development of the person concerned or others; (b) a threat for the security of the person concerned whether or not he is under the influence of someone else; (c) the situation that the person concerned provokes by his dangerous behaviour aggression of others; or (d) the situation that the safety of persons or goods, in general, is in danger (Article 1:1.2).

*345.* Compulsory care may be provided: (a) to avert a crisis situation, (b) to avert serious disadvantage, (c) to stabilise the mental health condition of the subject, (d) to restore the mental illness of the subject in a way that he regains his autonomy as much as possible, or (e) to stabilise or to restore the physical health condition of the subject when his/her behaviour causes him/her serious harm as a consequence of his mental illness (Article 3:4).

### C. *The Self-Binding Declaration*

*346.* A person 16 years or older who is able to make a reasonable appreciation of his interests with regard to the treatment of his mental illness, may commit himself to treatment in a so-called self-binding declaration (Article 4:1.1). In this way, the patient retains as much control as possible during the entire period of compulsory care. Other means in this respect are the care card (Article 5:12) and the care plan (Article 5:13-15).[124] The subject and the person responsible for care draft a self-binding declaration in which it is described: (a) under which circumstances compulsory care has to be provided in order to avert serious disadvantage; (b) the care and the compulsory care that may be provided and the maximal duration of the compulsory care; (c) the circumstances following which the compulsory care is to be ended; (d) the validity term of the self-binding declaration; and (e) the relatives who have to be contacted when the circumstances referred to under (a) occur having regard to the continuity of care (Article 4:1.2). The self-binding declaration is accompanied by a care plan (Article 4:1.3). If the subject is older than 12 but not 16 years old, the responsible for care involves the legal representative in the drafting of the self-binding declaration (Article 4:1.3). The responsible for care refers to the possibility that a relative or a patient advocate gives assistance while drafting a self-binding declaration (Article 4:1.5). A patient advocate gives assistance and advice on request in the drafting of a self-binding declaration (Article 4:1.6). An independent physician writes a declaration testifying that the subject is able to make a reasonable appreciation of his interest as to the matter involved (Article 4:1.7). The subject, the responsible for care and the medical director (being a psychiatrist at a mental healthcare institution)[125] date and sign the self-binding declaration. The medical director delivers the self-binding declaration to the subject and a validated copy to, among others, the legal representative and the public prosecutor (Article 4.2). The self-binding declaration may be modified or withdrawn (Article 4:3).

### D. *The Compulsory Care Authorisation*

*347.* The initiative to order a compulsory care authorisation is taken by the public prosecutor on his own initiative or upon request, and to this effect, he instructs a medical director. The medical director seeks a medical declaration made up by a psychiatrist. This psychiatrist may not have provided care to the subject during at least one year (Article 5:7 and Article 5:8). The medical declaration of the psychiatrist has to contain: (a) his conclusion regarding the symptoms and a diagnosis of the mental illness, (b) the relation between the mental illness and the behaviour of

124. What is the compulsory mental healthcare Act? www.dwangindezorg.nl/wvggz/english-version.
125. What is a care authorisation? www.dwangindezorg.nl/wvggz/english-version.

the subject that causes the serious harm, and (c) the necessary care in order to avert the serious harm (Article 5:9.1). The medical director delivers the medical declaration of the psychiatrist to the public prosecutor. The public prosecutor does not start a procedure to obtain a compulsory care authorisation if it appears from the psychiatrist's declaration that there is no mental illness or that the behaviour caused by the mental illness does not cause serious harm or that compulsory care is not necessary to avert the serious harm (Article 5:11.1-2). If the public prosecutor decides that the conditions for compulsory care are fulfilled he immediately submits a request for a compulsory care authorisation to the competent court (Article 5:17.1-2). The decision on the request is taken by a judge. No appeal is possible against a decision to grant a compulsory care authorisation (Article 6:1 and Article 6:3). The maximal duration of a compulsory care authorisation is two years (Article 6.5). It can be renewed (Article 6.6.).

*348.* A request of the public prosecutor for a compulsory care authorisation in order to administer compulsory medication (a contraceptive) to a young woman was allowed by the judge.[126]

### *E. The Crisis Measure*

*349.* A crisis measure can be ordered by the Mayor regarding a person residing in his commune if: (a) there is an immediate threat to serious harm, (b) and a serious presumption that the behaviour of the subject as a consequence of a mental illness is causing this threat to serious harm, (c) and the crisis measure may lift the serious threat, (d) and the situation is so serious that a compulsory care authorisation cannot be waited for, and (e) there is opposition of the person concerned or his legal representative (Article 7:1.1). A psychiatrist has confirmed in a medical declaration that the conditions required by Article 7:1.1 are fulfilled (Article 7:1.3a). In his decision, the major mentions, among others, the care that is necessary to avert the crisis situation and the possibility to appeal his decision before a judge (Article 7:2a and 7:2d). In advance of the decision regarding a crisis measure, compulsory care may already be provided during a short period if it may be reasonably be supposed that such a measure will be taken. For example, medication may be administered to calm down the subject.[127] This period may not last for longer than eighteen hours. Such a decision may be taken by a person responsible for ambulance transport or by a care provider who has been providing care to the subject on a voluntary basis (Article 7:3). The Mayor determines the duration of the crisis measure that may not be longer than three days (Article 7:4). If according to the public prosecutor, the circumstances that justified the crisis measure are still present, he may request for an authorisation to continue the crisis measure (Article 7:7.1). The decision on this request is taken by a judge within three days. No appeal is possible against this decision (Article 7:8.3 and 7:8.5). The authorisation to continue a crisis

126. District Court Noord Holland, 20 Oct. 2020, ECLI:NL:RBNNE:2020:3684.
127. Crisis measure, www.dwangindezorg.nl/wvggz/english-version.

measure has a duration of a maximum of three weeks (Article 7:9). If necessary, the public prosecutor may request for a compulsory care authorisation subsequently to a crisis measure (Article 7:11).

### *F. Temporary Compulsory Care in Case of Emergency*

*350.* The care responsible may, in case of opposition by the subject or the legal representative, decide to provide compulsory care that is not envisaged in the crisis measure, the authorisation to continue a crisis measure or the compulsory care authorisation to the extent that this is necessary to avert an emergency having regard to: (a) a serious danger, (b) the safety within the accommodation where care or compulsory care is provided, (c) the protection and the rights of others, or (d) the prevention of criminal acts (Article 8:11). The duration of such a measure is limited to a maximum of three days (Article 8:12.1).

### *G. Right to Complain and Compensation of Damage*

*351.* The person concerned, his legal representative or a relative of the person concerned may file a written and motivated complaint before the complaint commission to which the care provider is adhered to. This commission may suspend a decision against which a complaint has been filed. The commission has to take a final decision within fourteen days. If the commission decides to admit the complaint, it nullifies the contested decision partially or wholly. The commission may also order to take a new decision. A decision of the complaints commission can be appealed before the judge (Article 10:7). Together with a request to nullify a decision addressed to the complaint commission or the judge, compensation of damage can also be requested. The complaint commission or the judge may allow compensation of damage in fairness (Article 10:11).

### *H. The Patient Advocate*

*352.* Article 11:1 provides for a so-called patient advocate who has the responsibility to give advice and assistance to a person for whom a request for a compulsory care authorisation or a crisis measure is prepared or for whom a care authorisation or a crisis measure has been taken, with regard to; (a) the drafting of a self-binding declaration, (b) the preparation of a crisis measure, an authorisation to continue a crisis measure, (c) the performance of a crisis measure or an authorisation to continue a crisis measure or a care authorisation, (d) the termination of such measures, a complaint procedure and questions or complaints regarding care. The patient advocate gives advice and assistance concerning the performance of the rights of the person concerned (Article 11:2).

## III. The Care and Coercion Act

### A. *Definition of Coerced Care*

*353.* Coerced care is care resisted by the client or his legal representative and that consists of: (a) the compulsory administration of fluid, food or medication, performing medical examinations or other medical interventions and applying compulsory therapeutic measures in order to treat a psychogeriatric condition, an intellectual disability or a related mental illness or a combination of such as well as to treat a somatic illness that is related to a condition, disability or illness; (b) the restriction of the freedom of movement; (c) locking a person in; (d) exercising supervision over a person; (e) searching a person's clothing or body; (f) searching a person's residence or accommodation for behaviour-affecting substances or dangerous objects; (g) monitoring for the presence of behaviour-affecting substances; (h) restricting the freedom to determine one's own life in a way that the person concerned has to act or to refrain from acting, among which the use of means to communicate; and (i) limiting the freedom to receive visitors (Article 2:1).[128] In the explanatory notes to the bill, the legislator states that the difference between (b) and (c) is that the latter involves the person being secluded or separated in an appropriate space. It was consciously decided not to specify the other categories of coerced care in any further detail and to leave this to the caregivers to interpret.[129] A client is a person who according to a statement made up by a physician with relevant expertise is in need of care because of a psychogeriatric condition or an intellectual disability (Article 1:1c).

### B. *Rights of the Client*

*354.* Clients who are older than 16 years decide themselves on the care that is provided to them and the rights and the duties formulated in this Act. Clients between 12 and 16 years take such decisions together with their parent(s) or their guardian. For clients less than 12 years, such decisions are taken by their parent(s) or their guardian (Article 3:1). Representatives only take decisions for a client to the extent they are competent to act as a legal representative or to the extent that an experienced physician who is not involved in the care to this client has determined in accordance with prevailing guidelines that the client is not able to reasonably assess his/her interests with regard to the decision that has to be taken regarding him/her (Article 3:2).

*355.* The care provider appoints for every client a care responsible who drafts, approves, executes, evaluates and if necessary, modifies a care plan for this client (Article 5:1-2). Care may only be provided on the basis of a care plan (Article 6:1). The care responsible tries to obtain the consent of the client or the representative

128. B. Frederiks et al., 'Reporting of Use of Coercive Measures from a Dutch Perspective', *Advances in Mental Health and Intellectual Disabilities,* 11 (2017) 68.
129. *Ibid.*, 67.

regarding the care plan, taking into account as much as possible the wishes and the preferences of the client. A copy of the written expression of will and preferences of the client or the representative is added to the care plan. If it is not possible to take into account this expression of will, the care responsible informs the client or the representative in a written and motivated statement (Article 7:3). The care responsible may add to the care plan involuntary care as a last resort if: (a) the behaviour of the client as a consequence of the psychogeriatric condition or intellectual disability causes serious disadvantage; (b) the involuntary care is necessary to prevent or avert the serious disadvantage; (c) the involuntary care is suitable to prevent or avert the serious disadvantage; and (d) there are no less intrusive alternatives to prevent or avert the serious disadvantage (Article 10.2). Involuntary care is only incorporated in the care plan after consultation with at least one other expert in another discipline than the care responsible and if the latter is not a physician, a physician not involved in the care to the client (Article 10.3). During this consultation are discussed: (a) the possible serious disadvantage to the client; (b) the cause of the behaviour from which the serious disadvantage may originate; (c) the role interactions between the client and his environment may play in the emergence of the serious disadvantage; (d) the possibilities for voluntary care in order to avoid involuntary care; (e) the adverse effects of involuntary care balanced against the serious disadvantage that has to be averted; and (f) the term during which the involuntary care has to be incorporated in the care plan, having regard that this term should be as short as possible and maximum three months (Article 10:3 and 10:4). Based on the conclusions of the consultation referred to in Article 10:3, the care responsible adapts the care plan and describes in it the serious disadvantage for which it is indicated to provide coerced care and what kind of coerced care may be provided; which care provider or categories of care providers are competent to provide this coerced care; if applicable, the duration or frequency of the coerced care; the term during which coerced care may be applied and the way this term will be cut back (Article 10:8).

*356.* If the client or his representative resists to the implementation of the care plan, it is only implemented when it has been established according to Article 13 that this is necessary to prevent serious disadvantage (Article 12:1). The care provider only provides the planned coerced care if the care provider before the first provision of such care and with the consent of the care responsible came to a conclusion that: (a) the serious disadvantage described in the care plan has occurred, (b) the coerced care is necessary to prevent or avert this serious disadvantage; (c) the coerced care is effective to avert or prevent the serious disadvantage and is proportional; (d) there are no less intrusive alternatives; and (e) monitoring is available (Article 13:1). Before providing the coerced care, the care responsible informs the legal representative and the client unless informing the client would raise serious objections. If the situation is so urgent that giving information is not possible, the care responsible gives the information as soon as possible afterwards (Article 13:2). To foster the quality of care and the intelligibility for the client and the representative, the care responsible maintains a file. Notwithstanding Article 7:454-1 Civil Code (*see* paragraph 190), this file contains the care plan and all decisions concerning this plan (Article 16).

### *C. Involuntary Admission and Stay in an Accommodation*

*357.* An involuntary admission, a stay or a prolonged stay of a client are only possible after a judicial authorisation in a registered accommodation. The admission, stay and prolonged stay are involuntary if: (a) the client of 12 years or older or his parents resist; (b) the representative resists; or (c) the parents disagree. The judge may authorise an involuntary admission: (a) if the behaviour of the client as a consequence of a psychogeriatric condition or an intellectual disability or as a consequence of a related mental illness or a combination of such causes serious disadvantage; (b) the admission, stay or prolongation are necessary to prevent or avert serious disadvantage; (c) the admission, stay or prolongation are suited to prevent or avert serious disadvantage; and (d) there are no less intrusive possibilities to prevent or avert the serious disadvantage. If a client has been admitted and stays voluntary in accommodation but afterwards resists care in a way that providing client-centred care is impossible, the continuation of the stay is considered being involuntary (Article 24). Notwithstanding Article 24, an involuntary admission in a registered accommodation without judicial authorisation is possible by a decision of the Mayor (Article 29).

## §3. The Dying Patient

### I. Euthanasia and Physician-Assisted Suicide

*358.* With the Review Procedures for the Termination of Life on Request and Assisted Suicide and Amendment of the Criminal Code and the Burial and Cremation Act (hereinafter the 'Euthanasia Act') euthanasia and physician-assisted suicide became, although a criminal act, justified if performed under certain conditions and requirements.[130]

### *A. Historical Background*

*359.* Before the Euthanasia Act came into effect on 1 April 2002, the legal acceptance of euthanasia and physician-assisted suicide was based on jurisprudence and the doctrine of 'force majeure' (or 'general defence of necessity'). Article 40 Criminal Code states that a person who commits an offence as the result of a force he could not be expected to resist is not criminally liable. In 1984, in *Schoonheim,*[131] the Supreme Court opened up the possibility of a successful appeal to Article 40 for physicians. *Schoonheim* was a GP who had administered euthanasia to a 95-year-old woman in a very poor medical condition, on her explicit and repeated request. The Supreme Court argued that since it was the physician's duty not only to preserve life (and to obey the law) but also to relieve suffering and to respect the

130. *See* for an unofficial English translation *European Journal Health Law,* 8(2001) 183–191.
131. Supreme Court 27 Nov. 1987, *NJ* (1985), 106.

patient's wishes, a conflict of duties might arise. Since no one else can face such a conflict of legal and medical-ethical duties, only physicians can appeal to Article 40 Criminal Code.

*360.* Since 1984, the conditions under which physicians can appeal to 'force majeure' have been set out in a number of criminal and disciplinary cases. Physicians who performed euthanasia or physician-assisted suicide had (and still have) to observe these so-called criteria of due care. Those who did were – in accordance with prosecutorial policy – not prosecuted by the public prosecutor.

*361.* In 1994, following nationwide research into end-of-life-decisions by physicians, political debate resulted in a change in statute law. Due to a change in the Burial and Cremation Act, the so-called notification procedure – euthanasia was introduced. According to this procedure, physicians who had performed euthanasia or physician-assisted suicide, had to complete a form (in which the criteria of due care were listed) and report to the public prosecutor. On its part, the Assembly of Prosecutors General adopted the policy of not prosecuting physicians who had duly reported after having performed euthanasia or physician-assisted suicide in accordance with the requirements of due care.[132]

*362.* The second nationwide study of end-of-life-decisions by physicians showed that, although the number of notifications to the authorities had increased, the majority of cases were still going unreported. Evaluation of the notification procedure showed that physicians were disinclined to report cases of euthanasia and physician-assisted suicide to the authorities, mainly out of fear of direct contact with the judicial system.[133]

*363.* In order to stimulate physicians to report cases of euthanasia and physician-assisted suicide, the notification procedure was adapted by a ministerial decree in May 1998. Five regional review boards for the termination of life on request and assisted suicide, each consisting of an ethicist, a physician and a legal expert, were set up and started working in November 1998. According to the new procedure, the public prosecutor notified these boards. They then reviewed the reported act of euthanasia or physician-assisted suicide and forwarded their findings to the public prosecutor.

132. J.M. Cuperus-Bosma, G. van Der Wal and P.J. van Der Maas, 'Physician-Assisted Death: Policy-Making by the Assembly of Prosecutors General in the Netherlands', *European Journal Health Law,* 4 (1997) 225–238.

133. G. van Der Wal and P.J. van Der Maas, *Euthanasie en Andere Medische Beslissingen rond het Levenseinde* (Den Haag, SDU Uitgevers, 1996).

### B. *Definition of Euthanasia and Physician-Assisted Suicide*

#### 1. Euthanasia

*364.* Surprisingly, the notion of euthanasia does not appear in the so-called Euthanasia Act. Instead, it uses the expression 'termination of life on request'. No definition is given.

#### 2. Assisted Suicide

*365.* Assisted suicide is defined as intentionally helping another person to commit suicide or providing him with the means to do so as referred to in Article 294.2 of the Criminal Code (Article 1b Euthanasia Act).

### C. *Criteria of Due Care*

*366.* According to Article 293.1 of the Criminal Code, any person who terminates the life of another person at that other person's express and earnest request shall be liable to a term of imprisonment not exceeding twelve years or a fine of the fifth category. According to Article 293.2, this offence shall not be punishable if it is committed by a physician who meets the criteria of due care referred to in Article 2 of the Euthanasia Act.

*367.* According to Article 294.2 of the Criminal Code, any person who intentionally assists in the suicide of a person or provides him/her with the means thereto shall, if suicide follows, be liable to a term of imprisonment not exceeding three years or a fine of the fourth category. Article 293.2 (*see* previous paragraph) shall apply *mutatis mutandis*.

*368.* The due care criteria referred to in Article 293.2 of the Criminal Code are stipulated in Article 2.1. of the Euthanasia Act. The attending physician must:

(a) Be satisfied that the patient has made a voluntary and well-considered request for euthanasia or physician-assisted suicide. The Act does not require a written request, an oral request suffices.
(b) Be satisfied that the patient's suffering is unbearable and that there is no prospect of improvement (hopeless). There has been some debate regarding this requirement. What does unbearable and hopeless suffering mean? In the *Schoonheim case*, it was decided that it meant 'increasing loss of personal dignity' and 'the prospect of an undignified death'. Ten years later, in the *Chabot case*,[134] the Supreme Court decided that suffering did not need to be somatic. Furthermore, the patient did not need to be terminally ill.

134. Supreme Court 21 Jun. 1994, *NJ* (1994), 656.

(c) Have informed the patient about his/her situation and further prospects.
(d) Have come to a conclusion, together with the patient, that there is no other reasonable alternative in the light of the patient's suffering situation.
(e) Have consulted at least one other, independent physician who must have seen the patient and given a written opinion on whether the due care criteria set out in (a) to (d) have been fulfilled. The Act is more restrictive than the jurisprudence was prior to 1 April 2002; the other physician consulted did not have to see the patient himself. A conversation with his colleague was all that was required. Nowadays, the independent physician consulted will also have to examine the patient.
(f) Have terminated the patient's life or provided assistance to suicide with due medical care and attention.

A crucial aspect of the Euthanasia Act is that it, to a large extent, consists of 'open norms'. Answering questions like 'what is unbearable suffering' or 'what is a voluntary and well-considered request' is left to the interpretation of physicians.[135]

*D. Advance Directive Requesting Euthanasia*

*369.* If a patient aged 16 or over who is no longer capable of expressing his/her will, but before reaching this state was deemed capable of making a reasonable appraisal of his/her own interests, has made a written declaration that his/her life be terminated, the attending physician may comply with this request. The due care criteria referred to in Article 2.1 shall apply accordingly (Article 2.2).

*370.* While the due care criteria in Article 2.1. are largely based on jurisprudence, Article 2.2. contains a completely new provision.[136] According to the parliamentary documents, such a written advance directive requesting euthanasia has the same legal value as an oral or written request of a competent patient. No additional requirements are prescribed by the Euthanasia Act for advance directives requesting euthanasia, except that they should be made up in writing. This follows from the last sentence in Article 2.2. that states that the due care criteria referred to in Article 2.1. 'shall apply *mutatis mutandis*'. An advance request has the same status as an oral request for euthanasia.

*371.* The Parliamentary documents make it clear that the legislator used the words '*mutatis mutandis*' to indicate that the due care criteria 'apply as much as possible to the given situation'. With regard to the due criterion under (a), the physician can assume that the patient's request was voluntary and well-considered

135. M. de Boer et al., 'Pressure in Dealing with Requests for Euthanasia of Assisted Suicide: Experiences of General Practitioners', *Journal of Medical Ethics,* 45 (2019) 425; T. Quill, 'Dutch Practice of Euthanasia and Assisted Suicide: A Glimpse at the Edges of the Practice', *Journal of Medical Ethics,* 44 (2018) 297–298.
136. P. Mevis et al., 'Advance Directives Requesting Euthanasia in the Netherlands: Do They Enable Euthanasia for Patients Who Lack Mental Capacity?', *Journal of Medical Law and Ethics,* 4 (2016) 127.

unless he has reason to believe otherwise, according to the Parliamentary documents. However this does not provide an answer to the question of how to apply the other due care criteria in case of a written advance directive: do they apply in full, or can they be altered to apply to the specific situation? For example, how should physicians apply the requirement of unbearable suffering if the patient (as is the case in an advanced stage of dementia) does not seem to be suffering?[137] Hence, physicians struggle with the question of whether an advance directive in writing can replace an oral or a written request. As a consequence, they are very reluctant to actually carry out euthanasia on patients lacking capacity on the basis of an advance directive. For them, it is of utmost importance that patients confirm until the very last moment that they are suffering unbearably and choose to end their life.[138]

*372*. The first prosecution of a physician since the Euthanasia Act ended in acquittal.[139] The facts of the case have been described extensively in the judgment of the district court of The Hague.[140] On 11 September 2012, the gerontologist diagnosed the patient with dementia, type Alzheimer. On 2 October 2012, the gerontologist informed the patient about this. On 20 October 2012, the patient signed a request for euthanasia that conformed to the model of the Dutch association for voluntary termination of life. To the request for euthanasia, the patient also added a handwritten and signed the so-called dementia clause of the same date. On that same day, she signed a power of attorney regarding medical decision-making, in which she appointed her husband as her authorised representative and her daughter as substitute authorised representative. On 28 November 2012, the patient visited her GP with her husband where the request for euthanasia and the dementia clauses were discussed. The request for euthanasia was regularly confirmed with her GP. On 13 January 2015, the patient signed a revised dementia clause related to the request for euthanasia. This clause read as follows, as far as was relevant for the case: '*I want to exercise the legal right to have voluntary euthanasia performed on me when I am slightly mentally competent and no longer able to live at home with my husband. I definitely do not want to be placed in an institution for demented elderly persons. I want a dignified parting from my husband and my cherished loved ones. My mother was nursed for 12 years in an institution for demented persons before she died, so I have first hand experience of what it's like. So I know what I am talking about. I really do not want to go through this. It has seriously traumatised me and caused the entire family a lot of grief.*' From July 2015 onwards, the condition of the patient deteriorated, and she started going to the day care one day a week to relieve her husband in the care for her. From December 2015, the patient went to the day care five days a week. On 3 March 2016, the patient was admitted to the nursing home where the physician who later performed euthanasia was practising as a nursing home doctor (geriatric specialist). Her husband discussed the request for euthanasia, the dementia clause of 2012 and the revised dementia clause of 2015 with the nursing

137. *Ibid.,* 130–131.
138. *Ibid.,* 139.
139. E.C.A. Asscher and S. van de Vathorst, 'First Prosecution of a Dutch Doctor Since the Euthanasia Act of 2002: What Does the Verdict Mean?', *Journal of Medical Ethics,* 46 (2020) 71.
140. District Court The Hague, 11 Nov. 2019, ECLI:NL.RBDHA:2019:10650, para. 4.4.1. Actual background (English version).

home physician. This physician started her examination whether euthanasia was possible on the basis of the request for euthanasia and the dementia clause. According to the medical file of the patient, the physician has had contact with the patient several times and observed her several times for a longer period. The patient was also filmed (with authorisation of the husband and the daughter) to record her behaviour. Furthermore, the physician reviewed the GP's medical file of the patient, including among others, reports of the patients' gerontologist. The physician also consulted the GP of the patient, the nursing staff of the nursing home, the husband and the daughter, the patients' psychologist and a consultant of the 'end-of-life clinic'. On 29 March 2016, this consultant had contact with the patient and observed her and concluded based on this that the patient had no awareness of the illness and was not mentally competent. The consultant also checked the due care criteria for euthanasia with the physician. Furthermore, the physician consulted two SCEN physicians independently of each other. From the medical file of the patient, containing observations of the nursing staff and the physician, the following image of the patient came across. During the larger part of the day, the patient showed signs of agitation, unrest, stress, anxiousness, sorrow, anger and panic. She cried a lot, often said that she found it horrible and that it was breaking her down and said every day (up to twenty times a day) that she wanted to die. Her day and night rhythm was disrupted, and she wandered over the hallways almost daily, also at night. She banged on the windows and doors until her hands hurt. She accosted random people believing that they were acquaintances. This often led to conflicts with fellow residents. There was also a physical loss of dignity by large dependency and incontinence. In their written overview of the life cycle of the patient, the husband and the daughter independently described that they saw the patient suffer in the nursing home. Both the SCEN physicians had had contact with the patient on different moments in April 2016 and had observed her and independently came to the conclusion that the request for euthanasia of the patient complied with the legal criteria for due care. On 22 April 2016, in The Hague, the accused physician terminated the life of the patient by administering medicine for euthanasia. At that moment, the patient was for one year and three months not competent anymore to confirm her request. Before performing euthanasia, the physician sedated her mixing a sedative in her coffee, in order to avoid confusion and (apparent) resistance. The patient was restrained by her family during the further performance of the euthanasia.[141]

*373.* As required, the nursing home physician notified the euthanasia to the municipal forensic pathologist (*see* paragraph 381) after which the competent regional euthanasia review committee (*see* paragraph 382) assessed whether the legal conditions had been met. According to the review committee, there was no unequivocal voluntary and well-considered request by the patient as there was no actual request at the time of euthanasia and the advance request was not clear. The

141. E.C.A. Asscher and S. van de Vathorst, 'First Prosecution of a Dutch Doctor Since the Euthanasia Act of 2002: What Does the Verdict Mean', *Journal of Medical Ethics*, 46 (2020) 72; Letter to the Second Chamber regarding the judgment of the Supreme Court on euthanasia in case of advanced dementia by the Minister of Public Health, 2 Jul. 2020, 2.

case was referred to the Healthcare Inspectorate and the Public Prosecutor for further investigation following which the Inspectorate filed a complaint before the regional disciplinary board of The Hague. This board agreed with the decision of the regional review committee that the advance request did not fulfil the legal requirements. The physician was reprimanded.[142] The physician appealed to the Central Disciplinary Board. This Board found that the physician did not meet the due care criteria set by Article 2, §1(a) and (f) Euthanasia Act. The Board also evaluated the euthanasia in light of the guidelines for professional conduct, established by the DMA and the Euthanasia Code issued by the regional review committees. These guidelines state that the physician, before performing euthanasia, should attempt to discuss an actual wish with the patient. This is not a requirement in the Euthanasia Act itself. In this case, the physician argued that she had not discussed an actual wish as she believed the patient would not understand this and would only cause unduly stress. The Central Disciplinary Board imposed her the sanction of a warning (the least severe disciplinary sanction).[143] The court considered this sanction appropriate because the physician had done extensive examination and consultation before she came to the conclusions and because she had been open and transparent about her actions and the reasons she had for them.[144]

*374.* According to the Public Prosecutor, the physician had violated an important due diligence requirement for euthanasia because of which this was no longer a case of justified euthanasia but voluntary manslaughter. Furthermore, the case brought important judicial issues to the fore about the interpretation of Article 2.1. and 2.2. Euthanasia Act. For the sake of legal certainty for physicians and patients, it was important to provide clarity.[145] The public prosecutor submitted to the court the following question: 'Does the physician have an obligation to verify the actual present wish to live or to die of an incapacitated profoundly dementing patient to qualify this as a well-considered request?' which had not been answered by the disciplinary board. The district court recognised the major societal importance of legal certainty for physicians and patients, which benefits from a clear judgment of the court about the points of law that were raised. The court declared the criminal prosecution of the physician admissible.[146]

*375.* In its introduction, the district court remarked that it was very well aware that euthanasia and assisting in suicide are very sensitive topics and that, whether or not motivated by religious, moral, ethical and/or professional convictions, there are very diverging views on this issue in society. This was even more so when, as in the present case, it was about the termination of the life of a patient with dementia in an advanced stage. These diverging views existed until the present day, despite the

142. Regional disciplinary board The Hague, 24 Jul. 2018, ECLI:NL:TGZRSGR:2018:165.
143. Central Disciplinary Board, 19 Mar. 2019, ECLI:NL:TGZCTG:2019:68. This decision has been annulled by the Supreme Court on 21 Apr. 2020, ECLI:HR:NL:2020:713.
144. E.C.A. Asscher and S. van de Vathorst, 'First Prosecution of a Dutch Doctor Since the Euthanasia Act of 2002: What Does the Verdict Mean', *Journal of Medical Ethics*, 46 (2020) 72–73.
145. District Court The Hague, 11 Nov. 2019, ECLI:NL.RBDHA:2019:10650, para. 3.2. The position of the public prosecutor (English version).
146. *Ibid.*, para. 3.3. The opinion of the court.

Euthanasia Act. This Act does not preclude euthanasia on persons with dementia. However, this Act also does not imply that anybody who asks for it also has a right to euthanasia or assistance to suicide. Neither does this Act imply that a physician is obliged or can be obliged to respond to a request for euthanasia or assistance to suicide. In the present case, the court had to decide if the patient had the explicit and serious wish to have her life terminated. If this question is answered by a 'no', the court has to decide about the alternative charge of voluntary manslaughter or unlawful manslaughter. If this question is answered by a 'yes', the court has to consider if the accused had complied with all the criteria of due care set by the Euthanasia Act when the life was terminated. If the accused had complied with all these criteria, this should lead to the judgment that this was not a criminal offence.[147]

The court was of the opinion that the accused, based on the findings of the GP, the gerontologist, the two SCEN physicians, the husband, the daughter and her own findings as an appropriately qualified physician had rightly concluded that the patient was mentally competent at the time she drafted the request for euthanasia and the dementia clauses and that those statements unambiguously expressed the serious, well-considered and enduring wish of the patient for termination of life in case of admittance to a nursing home because of very advanced dementia. And the court concluded that on 22 April 2016 in The Hague, the accused as a geriatric specialist intentionally ended the life of the patient at her explicit and serious wish by administering medication for euthanasia. The court also concluded that the accused after careful consideration and taking into account all the relevant circumstances could have concluded that there was a voluntary and well-considered request. On this basis, the accused had obtained and could have obtained the conviction that the request was voluntarily and well-considered and communicated when the patient was still capable of a reasonable assessment of her interests in this regard. The court concluded that this due care requirement had been complied with.[148] Finally, the court judged that the accused had complied with all due care criteria laid down in Article 2.1 Euthanasia Act and discharged the accused of criminal prosecution.[149]

*376.* The Public Prosecutor decided to take the case before the Supreme Court in order to give the court the opportunity to answer some legal questions.[150] On 21 April 2020, the Supreme Court decided on this request.[151] The most important question was whether a physician in a situation where advanced dementia brings with it that the patient is no longer able to express his will might give effect to an advance request for euthanasia made up by this patient according to Article 2.2. Euthanasia Act provided that the other conditions are all respected. The Supreme Court answered this question in principle positively.[152] In other words, only when the patient with advanced dementia is no longer capable of forming and expressing a will concerning the termination of life, a physician may perform euthanasia on the basis of an advance request. The Euthanasia Act does not provide a term after which

147. *Ibid.,* para. 4.1. Introduction.
148. *Ibid.,* para. 5.3.2.
149. *Ibid.,* para. 5.3.7.
150. Opinion P.G. Silvis, 17 Dec. 2019, ECLI:NL:PHR:2019:1338.
151. Supreme Court, 21 Apr. 2020, ECLI:NL:2020:712.
152. *Ibid.,* para. 4.3.1.

the validity of such a request expires and also the Supreme Court did not pay attention to this. In this particular case, the advance request was not older than fifteen months. If it is, however, not possible to ascertain whether or not the patient is still able to form and express a will concerning the termination of life, the advance request cannot replace an actual request for euthanasia.[153] It is the responsibility of the physician to evaluate whether the patient is no longer able to form and to express a will concerning the termination of life. The single circumstance that the patient is still capable of uttering words does not preclude the physician from concluding that this is not the case anymore and to perform euthanasia on the basis of the advance request.[154]

*377.* According to Article 2.2. Euthanasia Act, the due care criteria apply 'accordingly' in case of an advance request (*see* paragraph 359). The Supreme Court referred to the parliamentary preparations of the Euthanasia Act, which state that this means 'as much as factually is possible'. From this follows that the contents and the significance of the due care criteria in the given situation in certain respects have to be interpreted, especially in light of the fact that the circumstances in which the advance request was made may differ substantially from those in which possibly have to be given effect to this request. This difference is, among others, the consequence of the fact that dementia is advancing as time proceeds and may drastically change the person and the personality of the patient.[155] With regard to the unbearable suffering condition (Article 2.1.b), the Supreme Court recalled that during the parliamentary preparations, the question of whether a patient with very advanced dementia suffers unbearably had been extensively discussed. This question can only be answered on a case-by-case basis by the physician, which always requires a very difficult weighing up. If there are no clear signs of actual unbearable suffering, the fact that the patient has in his advance request considered his future advanced dementia as unbearable is not sufficient to conclude that he is actually suffering unbearably. A concrete and careful evaluation of the actual situation is always required. All utterances of the patient, verbal or not, may play a role in this evaluation.[156] In its summary and final conclusion, the Supreme Court considered that the physician has to take account of the possible irrational and unpredictable behaviour of the patient, which may be an indication to administer medication beforehand.[157] The Supreme Court dismissed the appeal.

*378.* The president of the regional euthanasia review boards announced on 20 November 2020 that the so-called Euthanasia Code will be modified as a consequence of the judgment of the Supreme Court. One of the changes would imply that a physician may, just before performing euthanasia on a patient with advance dementia, administer a tranquiliser, e.g., in the coffee or apple sauce, because the

153. *Ibid.*, para. 4.3.2.
154. *Ibid.*, para. 4.3.3.
155. *Ibid.*, paras 4.4.1–4.4.2.
156. *Ibid.*, para. 4.6.3.
157. *Ibid.*, para. 6.1.

patient could become aggressive or restless as he does not understand what is happening.[158] Some people refer to this as 'coffee' or 'apple sauce' euthanasia.

### *E. Request for Euthanasia by a Minor Patient*

*379.* If the patient is a minor aged between 16 and 18 years and is deemed to be capable of making a reasonable appraisal of his/her own interests, the attending physician may comply with a request made by such patient to terminate his/her life or provide physician-assisted suicide, after the parent or parents who has/have responsibility for him/her, or else the guardian has been consulted (Article 2.3).

*380.* If the patient is a minor aged between 12 and 16 and is deemed to be capable of making a reasonable appraisal of his own interests, the attending physician may comply with a request made by such patient to terminate his/her life or provide physician-assisted suicide, if the parent or parents who has/have responsibility for him/her, or else the guardian, agree(s). Article 2.2 shall apply *mutatis mutandis* (Article 2.4).

### *F. Notification to the Municipal Forensic Pathologist*

*381.* After euthanasia or physician-assisted suicide has been carried out, the attending physician must notify it to the municipal forensic pathologist. This is not provided for in the Euthanasia Act but in Article 7.2 of the Burial and Cremation Act.[159] The notification has to include a report, arguing that the due care criteria have been observed. A model report is available. The pathologist forwards the report to the competent regional euthanasia review committee regulated in Articles 3–19 of the Euthanasia Act.

### *G. The Regional Euthanasia Review Committees*

#### 1. Establishment and Composition

*382.* There are five regional euthanasia review committees. Each committee consists of a lawyer (chairperson), a physician and an expert on ethical and philosophical issues (Articles 3–7).

158. www.skipr.nl.
159. J. Legemaate and I. Bolt, 'The Dutch Euthanasia Act: Recent Developments', *European Journal Health Law,* 20 (2013) 453.

## 2. Duties and Responsibilities

*383.* The regional euthanasia review committee has to assess, on the basis of the report sent to the municipal forensic pathologist, whether the attending physician, in carrying out euthanasia or physician-assisted suicide, has acted in accordance with the due care criteria set out in Article 2 (Article 8.1). The committee may request the attending physician to supplement this report either orally or in writing if this is necessary for a proper assessment of the attending physician's conduct (Article 8.2). The committee may also obtain information from the municipal forensic pathologist, the independent physician(s) consulted by the attending physician or other involved healthcare providers if this is necessary for a proper assessment of the attending physician's conduct (Article 8.3).

*384.* The committee notifies the attending physician within six weeks after receiving the report sent to the municipal forensic pathologist of its motivated findings (Article 9.1). This timeline may be extended once for a maximum of six weeks. The committee has to notify the attending physician accordingly (Article 9.3). The committee is empowered to explain its finding to the attending physician orally. This oral explanation may be provided at the request of the committee or the attending physician (Article 9.4). If the committee concludes that the physician has complied with the due care criteria of Article 2.1., the procedure is completed.

*385.* The committee notifies the Assembly of Prosecutors General and the regional healthcare inspector of its finding that the attending physician did not act in accordance with the due care criteria (Article 9.2). These two bodies then determine whether any further steps are necessary and if so, what these will be. The committee is obliged to provide the public prosecutor with all the information that he/she may require for the purpose of assessing the attending physician's conduct or for the purpose of a criminal investigation. The committee notifies the attending physician that it has supplied information to the public prosecutor (Article 10). Between 2007 and 2011, the regional euthanasia review committees assessed almost 14,000 reports of euthanasia or physician-assisted suicide. In thirty-six cases, it was found that the physician had acted without due care.[160]

*386.* The findings of the regional euthanasia review committees on the reported cases are an important contribution to the clarification and operationalisation of the due care criteria for euthanasia and physician-assisted suicide.

## 3. Psychiatric Patients

*387.* The Supreme Court requires that in carrying out euthanasia or physician-assisted suicide on a psychiatric patient, the physician must act 'very cautiously'.[161]

160. *Ibid.*, 454.
161. Supreme Court 21 Jun. 1994, *NJ* (1994), 656.

According to the regional euthanasia review committees, this means that 'extra attention' must be paid specifically to the voluntary character of the request and the mental capacity.[162]

## 4. 'Tired of Life'

*388.* The Euthanasia Act does not apply to people who are 'tired of life' which means people whose suffering does not arise from a medically classifiable somatic or psychiatric illness or condition.[163]

*389.* In 1998 – before the Euthanasia Act – a GP assisted in the suicide of an 86-year-old man, *Brongersma*, on the grounds that he was suffering existentially as a consequence of a number of the side-effects of old age which had rendered him feeling increasingly undignified and socially isolated.

*390.* Following his death, the GP reported what had happened, and the authorities decided to prosecute. At first instance, the District Court in Haarlem accepted the defence that *Brongersma*'s suffering could not have been alleviated by other means and acquitted the GP (defence of necessity, Article 40 Criminal Code, *see* paragraph 355).[164] After considering whether it should be part of a physician's professional duty to relieve non-medical existential suffering, the Court of Appeal of Amsterdam concluded that although physicians should be concerned about such suffering, and should seek to relieve it, this should not extend to providing physician-assisted suicide. Thus, the GP was found guilty, although no punishment was imposed. This decision was upheld by the Supreme Court and played a prominent role in the Parliamentary discussions leading to the Euthanasia Act.[165]

*391.* The regional euthanasia review committees base their policy on situations concerning a patient who is 'tired of life' on this Supreme Court's ruling.[166]

*392.* For some time now, there has been public debate on the issue of whether people who consider their life as completed should be given help in ending their life in a dignified manner and at a time of their own choosing. In 2016, the then Minister of Health, Welfare and Sport and the Minister of Security and Justice made known to the House of Representatives the government's position on 'completed life'.[167]

---

162. J. Legemaate and I. Bolt, 'The Dutch Euthanasia Act: Recent Developments', *European Journal Health Law,* 20 (2013) 458.
163. Supreme Court 24 Dec. 2002, *NJ* (2003), 167.
164. District Court Haarlem 30 Oct. 2001, *Tijdschrift voor Gezondheidsrecht* (2001) 21.
165. S. Ost and A. Mullock, 'Pushing the Boundaries of Lawful Assisted Dying in the Netherlands? Existential Suffering and Lay Assistance', *European Journal Health Law,* 18 (2011) 166–167.
166. J. Legemaate and I. Bolt, 'The Dutch Euthanasia Act: Recent Developments', *European Journal Health Law,* 20 (2013) 459.
167. Letter of 12 Oct. 2016 from the Minister of Health, Welfare and Sport and the Minister of Security and Justice to the House of Representatives on the government position on 'completed life',

*H. The End-of-Life Clinic*

*393.* In 2011, the Dutch Right to Die Association proposed the establishment of a so-called end-of-life clinic. The purpose of such a clinic is to offer a solution for patients who make a request for euthanasia within the exiting legal framework but are confronted with the situation that their treating physician is not prepared to carry out euthanasia. The end-of-life clinic started its activities on 1 March 2012. As the Euthanasia Act does not contain any rules regarding the place where euthanasia has to be carried out, the end-of-life clinic seems to fit within the legal rules on euthanasia.[168] The end-of-life clinic has changed its name in the Dutch Centre for Euthanasia Expertise.[169]

## II. Withholding or Withdrawing (Cessation) of Treatment

*394.* If treatment has become futile, it has to be withdrawn. There is no medical indication anymore and neither a concrete treatment purpose. A patient or his/her legal representative cannot require the continuation of medically futile treatment.

*395.* Withdrawing life support from a patient in a persistent vegetative state was at stake in the case of Ine *Stinissen*. When she was for more than ten years in a persistent vegetative state, her husband – who had been appointed as her guardian – asked the nursing home where she was taken care of, to remove the feeding tube. The nursing home and her physician refused to do so. Mr *Stinissen* started legal proceedings, requesting a court order that artificial nutrition and hydration be stopped. The Court of First Instance refused the order referring to the ultimate responsibility of the treating physician in taking the decision to withdraw treatment.[170] It agreed, however, with Mr *Stinissen* that artificial nutrition and hydration is predominantly a medical intervention, although it involves elements of basic care. The case was then considered by the Court of Appeal of Arnhem. It agreed with the lower court that artificial nutrition and hydration is mainly a medical procedure because of the artificial situation the patient is in and because it takes place under strict medical control.[171] As to the basic issue whether continuation of artificial nutrition and hydration would be medically futile, the Court of Appeal considered that in the absence of a general, accepted policy and taking into account the disagreement, also in the wider society, the nursing home and the treating physician had the discretionary power to act according to their own ethical views. According to the court, there was no reason to presume that artificial nutrition and hydration was against the will

www.government.nl/documents; B.W. Florijn, 'Extending Euthanasia to Those "Tired of Living" in the Netherlands Could Jeopardize a Well-Functioning Practice of Physicians' Assessment of a Patient's Request for Death', *Heath Policy*, 122 (2018) 315–319.

168. J. Legemaate and I. Bolt, 'The Dutch Euthanasia Act: Recent Developments', *European Journal Health Law,* 20 (2013) 465–466.

169. E.C.A. Asscher and S. van de Vathorst, 'First Prosecution of a Dutch Doctor Since the Euthanasia Act of 2002: What Does the Verdict Mean', *Journal of Medical Ethics*, 46 (2020), 74.

170. Court of Almelo 1 Jul. 1987, *Tijdschrift voor Gezondheidsrecht* (1987) 50.

171. Court of Appeal Arnhem 31 Oct. 1989, *NJ* (1989) 909.

of Ms *Stinissen*. Finally, Mr *Stinissen* could have his wife transferred to another institution where the physicians might have different views.[172]

*396.* When the patient is incompetent and there is no unambiguous advance directive, and the decision to be made has serious consequences for the life and health of the patient, Dutch law leaves much discretion to the treating physician. This is also reflected in the Medical Treatment Agreement Act that provides that a physician need not comply with the wish of the patient's representative if his role as 'prudent physician' requires so (*see* paragraph 207). This means that if the interests at stake are high, the representative of the patient cannot refuse every intervention that the patient himself or herself could have refused. In case of a conflict, not the opinion of the representative but that of the physician will prevail.[173]

## III. Termination of Treatment at the Request of the Patient

*397.* Starting from the principle that patients have a right to refuse treatment, patients may refuse life-sustaining interventions (a right that, in a certain sense, becomes a 'right to die'). A patient's request to terminate treatment will have to be respected even if this eventually results in the patient's death. This is a direct consequence of the individual's right to integrity. A physician will, however, have to satisfy him/herself that the patient is fully aware of the consequences of his/her request and, moreover has made the request completely voluntarily. The removal of a feeding tube on the written request of a patient (a 'negative' advance directive) is considered a form of treatment refusal.[174]

*398.* Also, a minor of 12 years old (*see* paragraph 332) can autonomously take the decision to refuse a life-saving treatment (chemotherapy).[175]

## IV. Pain Relief with Life-Shortening Effects

*399.* Sometimes pain relief may have the inadvertent effect of hastening the patient's death. If pain relief is the intended objective, objective and remedy should be balanced. Moreover, a patient will, in principle, have to consent to pain relief. It should be noted, however, that a doctor is allowed to relieve pain on the grounds of presumed consent when a patient is not (or is no longer) able to consent.

172. S. Gevers, 'Withdrawing Life Support from Patients in a Persistent Vegetative State: the Law in the Netherlands', *European Journal Health Law,* 11 (2005) 348–349; I. de Beaufort, 'Patients in a Persistent Vegetative State: A Dutch Perspective', *The New England Journal of Medicine,* 352 (2005) 2373–2375.
173. S. Gevers, 'Withdrawing Life Support from Patients in a Persistent Vegetative State: I Law in the Netherlands', *European Journal Health Law,* 11 (2005) 350.
174. *Ibid.,* 354.
175. Court of Appeal Amsterdam 11 Jul. 2017, ECLI:NL:GHAMS:2017:2668.

## V. Palliative (Terminal) Sedation

*400.* Over the past years, a lot of discussion has taken place about 'terminal' or palliative sedation. This discussion dealt with the criteria and the conditions for palliative sedation and how it relates to euthanasia.[176] In September 2004, at the request of the Ministry of Health, Welfare and Sports, the DMA established a committee that was given the task to draw up a national guideline with respect to terminal sedation. In December 2005, this guideline was presented to the Secretary of State for Health, Welfare and Sports.

*401.* Already in 2004, Gevers had emphasised that 'what is needed is not so much specific legislation, but authoritative clinical guidelines providing a workable protocol on how physicians should proceed. That would show that terminal sedation can be part of accepted palliative care and that it can be practiced in a way consistent with the law'.[177]

*402.* The guideline aims to clarify questions and misunderstandings regarding palliative sedation, both at a conceptual level and in actual practice. The committee that drafted the guideline has taken the view that palliative sedation is a normal medical procedure that must be clearly distinguished from euthanasia because there is no evidence that palliative sedation – if administered carefully – hastens death.[178]

*403.* The general rules laid down in the Medical Treatment Agreement Act (*see* paragraph 159) also apply to palliative sedation. The main principle is of informed consent by the patient or his/her representative. In both cases, it is crucial that the information preceding consent (or refusal) is provided in a comprehensible way.[179]

*404.* In acute situations, there may not be time to ask for consent if the patient is experiencing unbearable suffering and is likely to die in the very near future (in a few minutes or hours). In those circumstances, responsibility for the decision lies with the attending physician(s). The patient's representative must, however, be informed as soon as possible of the decision and its consequences. In cases where the patient is incompetent, and no representative is available, the attending physician also has the discretion to decide to carry out palliative sedation on the basis of the principles listed in the guideline and any other relevant information (views expressed by the patient in the past, signs of suffering and so on).[180]

---

176. J. Legemaate et seq., 'Palliative Sedation in the Netherlands: Starting-Points and Contents of a National Guideline', *European Journal Health Law,* 14 (2007) 61.
177. S. Gevers, 'Terminal Sedation: A Legal Approach', *European Journal Health Law,* 10 (2003) 306.
178. J. Legemaate et seq., 'Palliative Sedation in the Netherlands: Starting-Points and Contents of a National Guideline', *European Journal Health Law,* 14 (2007) 64.
179. *Ibid.,* 68.
180. *Ibid.,* 70.

## VI. (Not-Physician) Assisted Suicide

*405.* Maria *Heringa* was a 99-year-old woman living in a nursing home who was tired of old age and concerned about her increasing loss of control over her life. She was assisted in her suicide by her stepson, Albert *Heringa,* who provided her with the necessary medication. A consultation with a physician had taken place to ascertain whether she could receive lawful assistance under the Euthanasia Act. The physician considered that she did not meet the due care criteria and that she did not express her wishes with clarity. Albert *Heringa* was questioned by the police, and the public prosecutor was contacted.[181]

*406.* The district court of Gelderland declared him guilty of assisting in suicide but did not impose him a penalty.[182] In the appeal, he was acquitted on the basis of 'force majeure'.[183] The Supreme Court annulled this judgment and sent the case to the Court of Appeal in Den Bosch.[184] This Court declared him guilty and imposed provisional detention of six months.[185]

*407.* In 2016, the then Minister of Health, Welfare and Sport and the Minister of Security and Justice made known to the Second Chamber the government's position on 'completed life'.[186] For some time, there has been public debate on the issue of whether people who consider their life as completed should be given help in ending their life in a dignified manner and at a time of their own choice. If a person does not have a serious medical condition, however, there is no medical dimension to his/her unbearable suffering without prospect of improvement. This means that he/she is not eligible for euthanasia or physician-assisted suicide as referred to in the Euthanasia Act.

*408.* During the debate on the 2014 budget for the Ministry of Health, Welfare and Sport, the right-wing liberal People's Party for Freedom and Democracy asked the Health Minister to commission a study to establish the legal scope for assisted suicide for people who regard their life as completed.

*409.* The government set up such a committee, chaired by Professor Paul Schnabel. In this committee's opinion, the current legal framework on euthanasia and physician-assisted suicide provides sufficient scope for the majority of people whose suffering relates to a feeling that their life is 'completed' because it often has a medical dimension. These people fall within the scope of the current legislation and would therefore be eligible for euthanasia or physician-assisted suicide. As regards

181. S. Ost and A. Mullock, 'Pushing the Boundaries of Lawful Assisted Dying in the Netherlands? Existential Suffering and Lay Assistance', *European Journal Health Law,* 18 (2011) 167–168.
182. District Court Gelderland 22 Oct. 2013 ECLI:NL:RBGEL:2013:3976.
183. Court of Appeal Arnhem-Leeuwarden 13 May 2015 ECLI:NL:GHARL:2015:3444.
184. Supreme Court 14 Mar. 2017 ECLI:NL:HR:2017:418.
185. Court of Appeal Den Bosch, 31 Jan. 2018, ECLI:NL:GHSHE:2018:345.
186. Letter of 12 Oct. 2016 from the Minister of Health, Welfare and Sport and the Minister of Security and Justice to the House of Representatives on the government position on 'completed life', www.government.nl/documents.

people who are not eligible, the committee noted that it did not have the impression that requests for assisted suicide are commonly made in these situations.

*410.* However, according to both ministers, the current system offers no options for people who regard their life as completed and whose desire to die cannot be met within the scope of the Euthanasia Act. To provide a solution for this group of people, the question has to be answered of how one can respond to the growing wish among people to have more autonomy in end-of-life decisions.

*411.* The guiding principle in the government's search for a solution is the question to what degree society can respond to the desire for greater autonomy among people who wish to die. Autonomy is a fundamental value and an important element in ethics and law. It is a basic principle that expresses the idea of shaping one's own life and the right to do so. In the thematic evaluation of the legislation, entitled 'Self-determination in care' autonomy is referred to as a moral and legal foundation of much of the legislation. It is also one of the guiding principles of the then government's coalition agreement.

*412.* The government believed that in cases where a person has a consistent, well-considered and active wish to end their life because they are suffering unbearably from life, without the prospect of improvement, but their suffering does not have a medical dimension, the scope should be created for autonomy by removing the obstacles in the current legislation for those cases.

*413.* Specifically, this means creating an extra immunity from criminal liability for anyone assisting another person's suicide on the basis of the right to autonomy and not, as in the current Euthanasia Act, as an act of compassion by a physician. This requires a separate legal framework, with different basic principles from the current Euthanasia Act, and aimed at a different group of people in society, thus safeguarding the achievements of the current Euthanasia Act. Like the Act, this new legal framework will have to ensure a maximum degree of due care, assessment and reviewability, and transparency, so that all members of society can feel safe. Stringent requirements will have to be set.

*414.* Assistance to aiding suicide would not be limited to physicians.[187] A specially trained end-of-life counsellor is the most logical option, according to this proposal. This new profession could draw from disciplines with experience in existential and psychosocial problems and in counselling people at the end-of-life, such as nurses, psychologists or physicians. New training will have to be developed that end-of-life counsellors must complete (a top-up course in addition to their medical training), in order to be allowed to practise. Family members may be present when the person dies. The details of this will need to be worked out. It is important that their role remain limited to prevent them from becoming criminally liable for assisting with suicide.

---

187. J. Doomen, 'The Struggle Unto Death', 5 *Biolaw* (2018) 225–230.

*415.* The above-described intentions have not been implemented until now. The District Court of Limburg condemned a man who had assisted his father's suicide.[188]

188. District Court Limburg, 26 Feb. 2019, ECLI:NL:RBLIM:2019:1740.

# Chapter 3. Specific Activities

## §1. Termination of Pregnancy (Abortion)

### I. Short Overview of the Existing Legal Rules on Termination of Pregnancy

*416.* The Act of 1 May 1981 contains rules on the termination of pregnancy (the Pregnancy Termination Act)[189] as well as the Pregnancy Termination Order. The Act came into force on 1 November 1981. Until November 1984, all actions aimed at the termination of pregnancy other than on medical grounds fell under the scope of the Criminal Code, particularly under 'offences against life', 'offences against common decency', as well as under 'violation of common decency'. The Pregnancy Termination Act was evaluated in 2020. This evaluation has not led to amendments in this Act.[190]

*417.* Article 296 of the Criminal Code states that any person who provides a woman with treatment and knows or may reasonably assume that pregnancy may be terminated as a result shall be liable to not more than four years and six months' imprisonment. Such an act shall not be punishable if the treatment is provided by a physician in a hospital or abortion clinic in which such treatment may be provided under the Pregnancy Termination Act.[191]

*418.* According to the district court in The Hague, the provision of a so-called abortion pill is covered by Article 296 Criminal Code.[192]

### II. Termination of Pregnancy by a Physician

*419.* For the purposes of the Act, the words 'termination of pregnancy' shall not mean the application of a method to prevent the nidation of a fertilised ovum in the uterus (Article 1.2 Termination of Pregnancy Act).

*420.* Treatment intended to terminate a pregnancy may only be carried out by a physician in a hospital or abortion clinic licensed to provide such treatment (Article 2). Articles 4 and 5-11 deal with these licences. For pregnancies that have lasted longer than thirteen weeks, the licensing conditions are more stringent (Article 6.2 Termination of Pregnancy Act).

*421.* Pregnancy shall be terminated not earlier than the sixth day after the woman has consulted the physician and on that occasion has discussed her intention

189. *OJ* 1987, 257.
190. M.C. Ploem et.al., *Tweede Evaluatie Wet Afbreking Zwangerschap*, The Hague, ZonMW, 2020.
191. S. Gevers, 'Abortion Legislation and the Future of the Counseling Model', *European Journal Health Law,* 13 (2006) 31–34.
192. District Court The Hague 6 Sep. 2017 ECLI:NL:2017:10060 (Woman on waves) confirmed by the Court The Hague, 12 Feb. 2019, ECLI:NL:GHDHA:2019:211.

with him/her (Article 3.1 and 3.2 Termination of Pregnancy Act). A physician who provides treatment intended to terminate a pregnancy at an earlier time shall be liable for a fine (Article 16.1 Termination of Pregnancy Act). Such an act shall not be punishable where the physician has provided treatment intended to terminate a pregnancy at an earlier time in order to avert an imminent danger to the woman's health (Article 16.3 Termination of Pregnancy Act).

*422.* The physician shall inform the woman as soon as possible whether he/she will provide the cooperation/assistance requested of him/her. This information must be provided not later than five days after the pregnant woman has first consulted but when there was already a therapeutic relation with the physician not later than three days (Article 3.3 Termination of Pregnancy Act).

*423.* By a general order, requirements (*see* paragraph 414) are set forth with regard to assistance and making of decisions in order to ensure that every decision to terminate a pregnancy is taken carefully and only carried out if the situation of distress in which the woman finds herself left with no other choice (Article 5.1 Termination of Pregnancy Act).

*424.* Which circumstances count as a situation of distress is not provided for by the legislator. However, Article 82a of the Criminal Code – a provision introduced by the Termination of Pregnancy Act – makes it clear that the woman's free will to experience a situation of distress is limited by the unborn child's viability. Article 82a provides that 'taking someone's life' includes 'the taking of the life of a foetus that reasonably can be expected to have the ability to keep alive outside its mothers' body'. Under normal conditions, viability is considered to be present when the child is twenty-four weeks old or more.[193] This term constitutes an absolute limit for permissible termination of pregnancy. Aborting a viable unborn child, in principle, equals a criminal offence, that is to say, of a homicide (infanticide or murder).[194] (*See* paragraph 416).

*425.* The requirements referred to in Article 5.1. aim to ensure in particular that:

(a) the woman who has the intention to terminate her pregnancy and has contacted a physician with a request in that regard is given assistance in particular through the provision of sound information regarding alternative solutions for her situation of distress than the termination of pregnancy;
(b) if the woman is of the opinion that her situation of distress cannot be ended by other means, the physician reassures that her request to terminate a pregnancy

193. Supreme Court 29 May 1990, *NJ* (1991), 217 cited by T.A.M. Te Braake, 'Late Termination of Pregnancy Because of Severe Foetal Abnormalities: Legal Acceptability, Notification and Review in the Netherlands', *European Journal Health Law*, 7 (2000) 391.

194. J.H.H.M. Dorscheidt, 'Developments in Legal and Medical Practice Regarding the Unborn Child and the Need to Expand Prenatal Legal Protection', *European Journal Health Law,* 17 (2010) 437–438.

is made and maintained voluntary, after careful consideration and in full awareness of her responsibilities towards the unborn child and of the consequences to herself and those nearest to her (this is the father and when she is a minor, her parents);

(c) that, without prejudice to Article 20 Termination of Pregnancy Act (conscientious objection, *see* paragraph 415), the physician terminates the pregnancy only if it can be considered justified on the basis of his/her findings; and

(d) that following the termination of pregnancy, the women and those nearest to her have access to adequate aftercare, including information regarding methods to prevent unwanted pregnancy (Article 5.2).

*426.* No person shall be obliged to provide a woman with treatment intended to terminate the pregnancy or to cooperate in carrying out such treatment (Article 20.1 Termination of Pregnancy Act). This provision does not detract a physician from his/her duty to provide other physicians with information concerning the woman's condition if requested to do so and provided the woman has given her consent (Article 20.3 Termination of Pregnancy Act). Where a physician has a conscientious objection to providing such treatment or arranging such a treatment, he/she shall inform the woman of this without delay after she has consulted him/her (Article 20.2 Termination of Pregnancy Act).

## III. Late Termination of Pregnancy

*427.* Until now, there is no specific legislation on the so-called late termination of pregnancy. Under the present legislation, termination of pregnancy in the third trimester is a crime and the physician carrying it out can only defend him or herself by invoking a state of emergency/necessity.[195] Cases of late termination of pregnancy can be divided into two categories according to the indication: foetal indications or maternal indications. With regard to foetal indications, the Dutch medical profession makes a distinction between category 1 and 2. Category 1 includes some 80% of all cases of all late terminations and involves babies diagnosed with severe and untreatable medical conditions incompatible with life. Category 2 refers to conditions resulting in serious and incurable functional abnormalities that hold a chance of survival, be it a rather limited one.[196]

*428.* To provide some room for late termination of pregnancy in case of a foetal indication, in 2007, the Minister of Health issued a decree establishing a national

195. S. Gevers, 'Late Abortion in Case of Severe Foetal Abnormality', *European Journal Health Law,* 20 (2013) 448.

196. J.H.H.M. Dorscheidt, 'Developments in Legal and Medical Practice Regarding the Unborn Child and the Need to Expand Prenatal Legal Protection', *European Journal Health Law,* 17 (2010) 438; T.A.M. Te Braake, 'Late Termination of Pregnancy Because of Severe Foetal Abnormalities: Legal Acceptability, Notification and Review in the Netherlands', *European Journal Health Law,* 7 (2000) 387–403.

multidisciplinary expert committee.[197] As of 15 March 2007, late terminations of category 2 have to be reported to this committee. The committee serves as an advisory board to the public prosecutor with regard to whether or not the physician who terminated the pregnancy has acted in accordance with special requirements of due care. Cases of late termination of pregnancy of category 1 must be reported directly to the judicial authorities. These cases are then discussed in a special committee of the Dutch obstetrical and gynaecology association.[198]

*429.* In 2013, an evaluation of this reporting procedure had been carried out. It turned out that much fewer cases than which had been expected were reported to the expert committee. According to Gevers, this can to a large extent be attributed to the lack of trust on the side of gynaecologists and paediatricians who are afraid that the expert committee is not independent enough of the criminal justice system. Another striking conclusion of this evaluation was that physicians performed a termination of pregnancy before the twenty-fourth week, given the relative liberal requirements for terminations of pregnancy in Dutch law. The evaluation report concluded that legalising late abortion for foetal abnormality under strict substantive and procedural conditions is a better alternative.[199]

*430.* In 2016, the regulation of 2006 had been replaced by more detailed rules: the so-called rules governing the evaluation committee on late abortion and termination of the life of newborns that came into force on 1 February 2016.[200] The Netherlands is the first (and only) country in the world that has legal rules on deliberately ending the life of severely ill neonates.[201]

*431.* According to the new rules, a physician terminates a late pregnancy with due care if this physician has come to the conclusion that the unborn is suffering from an illness or a combination of illnesses resulting in the withdrawal of treatment after birth; he/she is convinced that the unborn is suffering without prospect; the parents are completely informed of the diagnosis and prognosis; the mother has explicitly requested to terminate the pregnancy; at least one independent physician has been consulted, and the termination has been carried out in a medically careful way (Article 7).

*432.* The same rules apply *mutatis mutandis* in the case of the termination of the life of a newborn (Article 8). In this case, both parents have to give consent.

---

197. Directions on the non-prosecution of cases of termination of life not on request and late abortions, State Gazette (2007), 46.
198. J.H.H.M. Dorscheidt, 'Developments in Legal and Medical Practice Regarding the Unborn Child and the Need to Expand Prenatal Legal Protection', *European Journal Health Law,* 17 (2010) 439.
199. S. Gevers, 'Late Abortion in Case of Severe Foetal Abnormality', *European Journal Health Law,* 20 (2013) 448–449.
200. State Gazette (2016), 31345.
201. K. ten Cate, *Dutch Doctors & Dying: Do Doctors' Personal Views Influence Their Professional Care at the End of Life and Should They?* Amsterdam, PhD Thesis, 2019, 8.

## IV. Registration of Termination of Pregnancy by Physicians

*433.* Any physician who provides treatment intended to terminate pregnancy shall communicate the following data to the chief physician of the establishment at least once a month:

(a) the number of instances of treatment intended to terminate a pregnancy that he/she has provided over the period concerned, and any unusual occurrences that have arisen in connection with them;
(b) in respect of each woman treated, the duration of the pregnancy, the number of previous pregnancies and pregnancy terminations, her age, her province or, in the case of women living outside the Netherlands, her country of residence, her marital status and the number of her children; and
(c) the date on which he/she discussed the woman's intention with her, and, if the woman has been referred by a physician as referred to in Article 3.2., the time referred to in that Article and the medical qualification in which he/she offered the woman assistance; the question of whether other experts have been consulted, and if so in which cases, as well as the nature of the expert qualifications of the person consulted; the date of the termination procedure, provided that, in the case referred to Article 16.2, the special reasons are indicated; and the aftercare made available to the woman after the pregnancy termination (Article 11.1 Termination of Pregnancy Act).

*434.* The chief physician of the establishment shall ensure that all physicians employed in the establishment submit the data referred to in Article 11.1 to him/her in full and in good time, in such a manner that the data cannot be traced back to individual patients. He/she shall ensure that the data are retained for at least five years (Article 11.2 Termination of Pregnancy Act). Every three months, the chief physician shall submit to the Health inspector details of the totals derived from the data referred to above (Article 11.3 Termination of Pregnancy Act). The anonymity of the woman treated must be ensured whenever such data are provided (Article 11.4 Termination of Pregnancy Act). The data obtained may be used only: for statistical purposes and in connection with the supervision of compliance with this Act or the provisions made pursuant to it (Article 11.5 Termination of Pregnancy Act). The physician referred to in Article 11.1 shall likewise ensure that before the termination of pregnancy or as soon as possible after it, the findings which led to the termination are recorded. He shall be required to retain such records for at least five years and to keep the data contained in them at the disposal of the Health inspector, provided that they are not traceable to individual patients (Article 11.6 Termination of Pregnancy Act).

*435.* The chief physician of the establishment shall ensure that the Health inspector obtains access upon request to the data referred to in Article 11.2 and that such information as he may request and which he reasonably requires in order to fulfil his duties under this Act is made available to him, provided that such information is not traceable to individual patients (Article 12 Termination of Pregnancy Act).

### V. Wrongful Life

*436.* On 18 March 2005, the Supreme Court delivered for the first time a decision in a so-called wrongful life, the *Kelly (Molenaar*) case.[202] The case was a combination of a wrongful birth claim, by the parents of Kelly and a wrongful life claim by the 11-year-old Kelly represented by her parents. According to the parents, a prenatal genetic test had not been carried out, thus depriving them of their right to decide to terminate the pregnancy. The Supreme Court decided that the district court in first instance and the Court of Appeal had correctly held the midwife and the hospital liable and ordered both to pay lifelong medical and living expenses to Kelly ('s parents), including additional costs related to Kelly's impairments, monetary compensation to the parents for emotional damage as a result of a breach of the right to individual self-determination, monetary compensation to Kelly for the emotional damage she suffered herself and the costs of the psychiatric treatment of Kelly's mother.

## §2. Sterilisation

### I. Surgical Sterilisation

*437.* Sterilisation can be performed on both men and women. Because of the far-reaching consequences of such an operation, it is important for the patient to be informed clearly and adequately by the attending physician, prior to the treatment. In many cases, sterilisation does not serve a therapeutic purpose, which is why this form of treatment could be regarded as maltreatment (Articles 300–302 Criminal Code). This is one of the reasons why it is of the utmost importance that the sterilisation is carried out with the patient's consent. There are few cases imaginable in which the requirement of consent can be ignored as the sterilisation requires no immediate action and the non-performance of sterilisation entails no grave risks to the patient.

*438.* Consent can only be validly granted on the basis of complete information. This information includes the fact that there is a slight risk of permanent or recurring fertility as well as the limited chance of success of a reversal operation at a renewed wish for fertility. It is the physician's duty to supply this information correctly and intelligibly to the patient. If the physician fails to do so and cannot furnish adequate proof of his/her having supplied adequate information, he/she will,

202. Supreme Court 18 Mar. 2005, ECLI: NL: HR: 2005: AR5213, *NJ* (2006), 606; A. Hendriks, 'Wrongful Suits? Suing in the Name of Terri Schiavo and Kelly Molenaar', *European Journal Health Law,* 12 (2005) 99–102; I. Giesen, 'The Use and Influence of Comparative Law in Wrongful Life Cases', *Utrecht Law Review,* 8 (2012) 35–54; E. Hondius, 'The Kelly Case-Compensation for Undue Damage for Wrongful Treatment', in J.K.M. Gevers et seq. (eds), *Health Law, Human Rights and the Biomedicine Convention. Essays in Honour of Henriette Roscam Abbing* (Leiden, Martinus Nijhoff Publishers, 2005) 105–106; J.-P. Loof, 'Human Dignity in the Netherlands', in P. Becchi and K. Mathis (eds), *Handbook of Human Dignity in Europe* (Cham, Springer Nature Switzerland, 2019) 660.

for that reason, be held liable for default. In principle, the partner's consent is not required for sterilisation. It is, however, a routine procedure in the Netherlands to involve the partner, if any, in the decision-making process.

*439.* Most legal proceedings on sterilisation concern surgeon's or gynaecologist's liability for failed sterilisations. The damages granted for a proven physician's error do not exceed the cost of education of the child till its eighteenth year. Otherwise, there is no consensus, as yet, on the aspects qualifying for damages. Never has a court honoured the proposition that a woman should be obliged to have an abortion in order to limit the damage after a failed sterilisation. Courts have, however, ruled that a woman could claim damages for immaterial damage suffered from pregnancy after a failed sterilisation, which she had terminated.

*440.* As are most medical treatment contracts, sterilisation is regarded as a contract of effort. However, when inadequate information has been supplied on the (slight) risk of failure, jurisprudence assumes a contract of result to be in existence. This has consequences for procedural law: with a contract of result, the patient only needs to prove the absence of result, and subsequently, the physician has to prove circumstances beyond his control. When assuming the existence of a contract of effort, it is up to the patient to prove that the physician did not make the expected effort for the operation concerned. This way, the onus of proof is much harder for the patient.

## II. Sterilisation of Mentally Handicapped

*441.* The requirement of consent for sterilisation remains valid for the mentally handicapped as well. The decision to undergo or not undergo the operation then actually rests with the (legal) representative or the institution the patient is staying in. Under the Adult Mentor Act, the mentor decides on the sterilisation as part of the treatment. In general terms, a mentor can be assigned to an adult who is, temporarily or permanently, insufficiently capable of acting adequately in his own interests other than those concerning property, as a result of his mental or physical condition (*see* paragraph 202).

*442.* There are no legal regulations for the sterilisation of mentally handicapped people.

§3. Medically Assisted Procreation

## I. General Legal Framework

*443.* The general rules on patient's rights provided for in the Medical Treatment Agreement Act (*see* paragraph 159) also apply to the use of gametes and embryos for a regular in vitro fertilisation procedure.[203] No specific legal rules exist in this regard.

## II. Donation of Gametes for Procreation

*444.* The Act of 20 June 2002 containing rules relating to the use of embryos and gametes (Embryo Act)[204] provides rules regarding the donation of gametes for procreation. It came into force on 1 September 2002. Gametes are human spermatozoa and oocytes (Article 1b). This Act is the result of balancing human dignity and the respect for human life in general, on the one hand, and the future child's well-being and the well-being of infertile couples, on the other.[205]

*445.* Adults who are capable of making a reasonable assessment of their interests in this regard may make their gametes available in order to induce pregnancy in another person, without prejudice to cases in which the gametes are intended for the said adults' own medical use (Article 5.1 Embryo Act). Gametes may be made available only by means of a donation confirmed in writing and on a not-for-profit basis and only after the donor has been informed by the person storing the gametes regarding nature and the purpose thereof. The donor may revoke his/her decision at any time before the gametes are used, without giving reasons (Article 5.2 Embryo Act). If an invasive procedure is required in order to obtain gametes, the donor also has to be informed by the person who carries out the procedure of the possible risks and complications (Article 5.3 Embryo Act).

*446.* The information mentioned in Article 5 has to be supplied in such a way that it is reasonably certain that the donor has understood it and in the case referred to in Article 5.3 has to be supplied in writing. The donor shall be given sufficient time for reflection to allow him/her to make a carefully considered decision on the basis of the information provided, about making his/her gametes available (Article 6.1 Embryo Act). When gametes are made available in this way, the purposes for which the gametes may be used and the period for which they will be kept have to be laid down in writing. The person storing the gametes and the donor may jointly change the purposes and extend the storage period (Article 6.2 Embryo Act). If gametes are made available in order to induce pregnancy in another person, the

203. T.A.M. Te Braake, 'The Dutch 2002 Embryo Act and the Convention on Human Rights and Biomedicine: Some Issues', *European Journal Health Law,* 11 (2004) 141.

204. *State Journal* (2002), 338.

205. T.A.M. Te Braake, 'The Dutch 2002 Embryo Act and the Convention on Human Rights and Biomedicine: Some Issues', *European Journal Health Law,* 11 (2004) 139.

donor has to be given the opportunity to stipulate that his/her consent is required for the use of embryos created by using his/her gametes for any other purposes (Article 6.4 Embryo Act).

*447.* Unless they were made available for other purposes, the donated gametes shall, in any event, be destroyed upon expiry of the period for which they were made available and also if the decision to make them available is revoked. Furthermore, the gametes shall be destroyed if it has come to the attention of the person storing them that the donor has died unless the latter has expressly consented in writing to their being used after his/her death (Article 7 Embryo Act). Preceding to the destruction referred to in Article 7, gametes and embryos that will no longer be used for own medical use or other purposes may be used for purposes of quality assurance directly related with diagnostic processes or treatment processes in fertility care (Article 9a Embryo Act). Article 9a has been added into the Embryo Act by Article I.B of the Act of 1 July 2020 to modify the Embryo Act regarding the modification of the prohibition of gender selection and the use of gametes and embryos for quality assurance.[206] It entered into force on 1 October 2020.

*448.* Under Dutch law, gamete procurement from a dead or dying person is not explicitly regulated. In 2016, the State Commission on Parenthood Review highlighted the importance of prior consent to safeguard the 'right to self-determination of the deceased, because that right also extends to the use of his or her gametes on embryos after death'. In August 2018, the Dutch Association for Obstetrology and Gynaecology and the Association for Clinical Embryology published professional (not binding) guidelines on posthumous reproduction.[207]

*449.* It is prohibited to charge a fee for providing gametes made available pursuant to Article 5 to third parties if this fee exceeds the costs directly incurred as a result of procedures carried out using these gametes (Article 27 Embryo Act).

## III. Donation of Embryos for Procreation

*450.* The Embryo Act also provides rules regarding the donation of embryos for procreation. An embryo is a cell or a complex of cells with the capacity to develop into a human being (Article 1c Embryo Act).

*451.* Adults who are capable of making a reasonable assessment of their interests in this regard may make available embryos which have been created outside the body for their own pregnancy, but which will no longer be used for this purpose, *inter alia* to induce pregnancy in another person (Article 8.1a Embryo Act). Embryos may be made available only by means of a donation confirmed in writing and not on a profit basis and only after the persons concerned, including the gamete

206. *State Journal* (2020), 229.

207. N. Hyder-Rahman, 'Regulating Posthumous Reproduction in the Netherlands and the UK', *Family and Law,* April 2020, DOI: 10.5553/FenR/000046.

donor whose consent is required pursuant to Article 6.4 (*see* paragraph 437), have been informed by the person storing the embryos regarding nature and the purpose thereof. Where a difference of opinion arises between the parties concerned, the embryos shall not be made available. Any of the persons concerned may revoke his/her decision at any time before the embryos have been used, without giving reasons (Article 8.2 Embryo Act). Article 6 (information) and Article 7 Embryo Act (destruction) shall apply *mutatis mutandis* (Article 8.3 Embryo Act).

*452.* It is prohibited to charge a fee for providing embryos made available pursuant to Article 8 to third parties if this fee exceeds the costs directly incurred as a result of procedures carried out using these embryos (Article 27 Embryo Act).

## IV. Right to Know the Identity of the Donor of Gametes

*453.* On 1 June 2004, the Act of 25 April 2002 regulating the storage and provision of data of donors in case of artificial donor conception entered into force (Donor Data Act).[208] This Act has been accepted almost unanimously in Parliament. Artificial donor conception means the carrying out as a profession of procedures aimed at conceiving a pregnancy otherwise than in a natural way by making use of either sperm cells of another than the husband or registered partner or egg cells of another woman (Article 1c Donor Data Act).

*454.* In the case of a successful birth resulting from artificial donor conception, the person who carried out the artificial donor conception is obliged to register the following data of the gametes' donor and make them available for the Foundation on artificial donor conception: (a) medical data that may be of importance for the healthy development of the child; (b) physical characteristics, education and profession, social background and personal characteristics; and (c) name and data relating to his/her identity (Article 2.1 Donor Data Act). The data mentioned under (b) may not make it possible to identify the donor (Article 2.3 Donor Data Act). The person who carried out the artificial donor conception also has to register and make available to the Foundation, the data relating to the identity of the woman who has given birth and the day the conception took place. These data will be kept for eighty years (Article 2.2 Donor Data Act).

*455.* The Foundation makes the medical data of the donor available to the GP of the person who has been artificially conceived, at his/her request (Article 3a Donor Data Act); the Foundation makes the data mentioned in Article 2.1b available to the person who knows or who suspects having been artificially conceived and who has reached the age of 12, at his/her request and also to the parents of such a person who has not yet reached the age of 12, at their request (Article 3.1a, 3.1b and 3.1c Donor Data Act).

208. *State Journal* (2002), 240.

*456.* The identifying data of the donor are made available to anyone who knows or presumes having artificially been conceived and who has reached the age of 16, at his/her request and after written consent of the donor. If the donor refuses consent, the data are nevertheless made available to the person who requested this unless strong interests in favour of the donor plead against making the data available. The Act does not specify the nature of those strong interests (Article 3.2 Donor Data Act). Their acceptance should remain exceptional.[209] If the donor is dead or cannot be reached, his/her consent is presumed to have been refused unless his/her partner or a close relative gives written consent (Article 3.3 Donor Data Act).

*457.* The Foundation informs the donor without delay, in writing and motivated, that his/her identifying data are going to be made available. Within thirty days, the donor can object. After having taken a final decision, the Foundation makes the data to be available or not (Article 3.4 Donor Data Act). Donors are not obliged to have contact with their offspring. Nor do they have legal or financial obligations towards them.[210]

*458.* The Foundation takes care of the donor's data in a careful way for at least eighty years from the day it has received these data (Article 8).

*459.* The first children to be born under the Donor Data Act will have the opportunity to know their donor from 2021. Only then it will become apparent how many of them actually want to do so, and what impact this will have, according to the Health Council.[211]

## V. Surrogacy

*460.* Commercial arrangements regarding surrogacy are prohibited by the Criminal Code. Surrogacy as such is not prohibited.

*461.* Any person who, in the practice of a profession or in the conduct of a business, intentionally brings about or facilitates, either direct or indirect negotiations between a surrogate mother or a woman who wishes to be a surrogate mother and another person or arranges an appointment in order to carry out the intention of bearing a child for another person, shall be liable to a term of imprisonment not exceeding one year or a fine of the fourth category (Article 151b.1 Criminal Code). Any person who: (a) publicly offers services to bring about or facilitate such negotiations or such an appointment, or (b) makes public that a woman would like to become a surrogate mother or is available as such, or that a woman is being sought

209. D. Boddaert, 'Wet Donorgegevens Wordt niet Goed Uitgevoerd', *Nederlands Juristenblad* (2018) 640.

210. P.M.W. Janssens et al., 'A New Dutch Law Regulating Provision of Identifying Information of Donors to Offspring: Background, Contents and Impact', *Human Reproduction*, 4 (2006) 853.

211. Health Council of the Netherlands, *The Maximum Number of Children per Sperm Donor: An Evaluation of the Current Guideline* (The Hague, 2013), Publication No. 2013/18, 17–18.

who would like to become a surrogate mother or is available as such shall be liable to the same punishment (Article 151b.2 Criminal Code).

*462.* A surrogate mother shall be deemed to be a woman who has become pregnant with the intention of bearing a child for another person who wishes to acquire parental authority over the child or otherwise wishes to assume on a permanent basis responsibility for the permanent care and raising of the child (Article 151b.3 Criminal Code).

*463.* Any person who, in the practice of a profession or in the conduct of a business, intentionally brings about or facilitates, either direct or indirect negotiations between a woman and another person or arranges an appointment in respect of her wish to have another person assume on a permanent basis responsibility for the care and raising of her child, shall be liable to a term of imprisonment not exceeding six months or a fine of the third category (Article 151c.1 Criminal Code).

*464.* Without prejudice to the provisions of Article 151b.1 (*see* previous paragraph), Article 151c.1 shall not apply: (a) if the bringing about or facilitation is done by the Child Protection Board or a legal person appointed by the Child Protection Board; (b) if the bringing about or facilitation involves a referral to an organisation as referred to in (a) (Article 151c.2 Donor Data Act).

## §4. Human Genetics

### I. Genetic Testing and Insurances

*465.* *See* paragraph 246, Medical Examinations Act.

### II. Clinical Genetics

*466.* Article 1h of the Order of 3 July 2014 designating special medical procedures that require a licence by the Minister of Health refers to clinical genetic diagnosis and counselling, including pre-implantation genetic diagnostics. The legal basis of this Order is the Special Medical Procedures Act of 1999.[212]

## §5. Removal and Transplantation of Organs

### I. The Scope of the Organ Donation Act

*467.* The Act of 24 May 1996 regulating the procurement of organs (Organ Donation Act) regulates the removal, the preservation and the allocation of organs,

212. *State Journal* (3 Mar. 1999).

both from living and deceased donors. It entered into force on 1 September 1998.[213] It has been amended by the Act of 27 March 2018 with regard to the establishment of an active donor registration system that entered into force on 1 July 2020.[214] The Organ Donation Act has also been amended by the Act of 30 October 2019 in order to provide a legal basis for the protocols to determine death on the basis of circulatory criteria and some other modifications that also entered into force on 1 July 2020.[215] Donors who died after circulatory death make up more than half of post-mortem donors. Organ transplantation has not been regulated as this is a medical procedure covered by the Medical Treatment Agreement Act.

*468.* The Organ Donation Act does not only aim at regulating the removal of organs for transplantation purposes but also removal from deceased donors for other purposes (Article 12 Organ Donation Act). For instance, the use of organs or tissue for transplantation-related research and (industrial) preparation.

## II. Removal of Organs from Living Donors

### *A. General Conditions*

*469.* Consent to the removal of an organ in order to receive a remuneration that exceeds the costs, inclusive of the lost income incurred by the removal is void (Article 2 Organ Donation Act). Only the expenses of the donor and/or of those whose consent to the removal of an organ is required may be compensated (Article 7). Removal of an organ while alive is only allowed when consent to it has been given in accordance with Articles 3, 4 or 5 Organ Donation Act (Article 8).

### *B. Adult Living Donors*

*470.* An adult who is capable to reasonably assess his/her interests in this regard can give consent to remove an organ with a view to transplanting it in a well-determined person (Article 3.1 Organ Donation Act). The person responsible for the removal takes care that the donor has been informed clearly, both orally and in writing and if wished by audio-visual means regarding the nature and the aim of the removal and the to-be-expected consequences and risks for his/her health and other living conditions. This person must also be reassured that consent is given in a free and informed way, also regarding the legal rules concerning the compensation of the costs to remove the organ (Article 3.2 Organ Donation Act). When the removal can reasonably be expected to cause permanent damage to the health of the donor, it will only be carried out if the envisaged recipient is in mortal danger which cannot be averted in any other way just as well (Article 3.3 Organ Donation Act).

213. *State Journal* (1996), 370.
214. *State Journal* (2018), 95; Decree of 15 May 2020 determining the date of entering into force, *State Journal* (2020), 153.
215. *State Journal* (2019), 405.

*471.* Removal of an organ from an adult who is not capable to reasonably assess his/her interests in this regard is only allowed if it concerns a regenerative organ and the removal has no permanent consequences for the health of the donor. The recipient has to be a close relative who is in mortal danger which cannot be averted in any other way just as well. The donor also has to have a serious interest in averting this danger (Article 4.1 Organ Donation Act). The consent of the legal representative is required or when there is no legal representative, of the partner of the donor, his/her parent or his/her adult child. Also, the court has to give consent (Article 4.2 Organ Donation Act). Article 3.2 is applicable *mutatis mutandis* (Article 3.3 Organ Donation Act).

*472.* The information referred to in Articles 3.2, 4.3 and Article 5.3 contains, in any case, a reference to the information referred to in the Annex to Directive 2004/23/EU of 31 March 2004 on setting standards of quality and safety for the donation, procurement, testing, processing, preservation, storage and distribution of human tissues and cells (Article 5a.1).

*473.* Consent has to be always given in a handwritten, dated and signed statement. It can be revoked at any time before the removal (Article 6 Organ Donation Act).

### *C. Minor Living Donors*

*474.* Removal of an organ from a minor of 12 years or older is only allowed if it concerns a regenerative organ and the removal has no permanent consequences for the health of the donor. The recipient has to be a relative up to and including the second degree who is in mortal danger which cannot be averted in any other way just as well. The consent of the minor as well as of his/her parents or his/her guardian and the juvenile court is required (Article 5.1 Organ Donation Act).

*475.* Removal of an organ from a minor of less than 12 years old or from a minor older than 12 years who is not capable to reasonably assess his/her interests in this regard is only allowed if it concerns a regenerative organ and the removal has no permanent consequences for the health of the donor. The recipient has to be a relative up to and including the second degree who is in mortal danger which cannot be averted in any other way just as well. The donor also has to have a serious interest in averting this danger. The consent of the parents of the minor or his/her guardian and the juvenile court is required (Article 5.2 Organ Donation Act). Article 3.2. is applicable *mutatis mutandis* (Article 5.3 Organ Donation Act).

*476.* Consent has to be always given in a handwritten, dated and signed statement. It can be revoked at any time before the removal (Article 6 Organ Donation Act).

## III. Removal of Organs after Death

### *A. Persons Competent to Give Consent or to Object*

*477.* Adults and minors of 12 years or older who are capable to reasonably assess their interests in this regard, may consent to the removal of their organs after death or of certain organs specified by them or may object to removal. The legal representative of a minor who is not capable to reasonably assess his interest regarding organ donation may give consent in his name to the removal of his organs after death or certain organs specified by him or object to this (Article 9.1).

*478.* If a minor person dies before the age of 16 and he has given consent to the removal of his organs according to Article 9.1, no removal may take place if one of his parents or his guardian objects to it. In case both parents or the guardian are absent or cannot be reached, no removal of organs can take place (Article 12).

If a person has left the decision concerning the removal of organs to his relatives once death has been determined, consent to the removal of his organs may be given by his spouse, registered partner or other life companion or when these are absent or cannot be reached, by the adult kinsmen up to the second degree included who can be immediately reached or when they are absent or cannot be reached by the relatives up to the second degree including who can be immediately reached (Article 11.1). If a person has left the decision concerning the removal of organs to a specific person once death has been determined, consent to the removal of his organs may be given by that person. If this person is absent or cannot be reached, consent can be given by the kinsmen referred to in Article 11.1 (Article 11.3). If a minor of 12 years or older has left the decision concerning the removal of organs to a specific person, this person may give consent to the removal once death has been determined. If this person is absent or cannot be reached, consent can be given by the parents or the guardian (Article 11.5). For minors less than 12 years old, the decision to remove organs can be taken by the parents or the guardian once death has been determined (Article 11.7). In case of disagreement between kinsmen or relatives or parents as referred to in Article 11.1–11.7, no consent can be given to the removal of organs (Article 11.8).

### *B. Declaration of Will and Registration of Donor Form*

*479.* In order to consent or to object, a donor form as referred to in Article 10 has to be filled in and registered. If a person referred to in Article 9.1 wants to leave the decision to remove his organs to his relatives or to a specific person, he may indicate this in the donor form (Article 9.2). A declaration of will regarding the removal of organs can at all times be withdrawn by filling in and registering another donor form (Article 9.3). A declaration of will regarding the removal of organs can also be expressed in a handwritten, dated and signed statement (Article 9.4). A withdrawal in general terms of a disposition of will does not imply the withdrawal of such a declaration of will (Article 9.5).

*480.* The Minister of Health takes care that to each resident, a donor form is sent when he has attained the age of 18 years. Such donor form is also made available on request and for free (Article 10.1). A donor registry is established in which in order to make knowable the declaration of will of the concerned, the following is registered: the consent or objection expressed in such donor form regarding the removal of organs after death or the wish to leave the decision to relatives or to a specific person according to Article 11 (Article 10.2). The donor registry can be consulted day and night by or on behalf of a physician when this is necessary in view of an intended removal of an organ (Article 10.3). A royal decree provides more detailed rules concerning the form, the contents and the way of sending the donor form and the way the donor registry is kept and can be accessed (Article 10.4). Article 2.1c of the royal decree of 21 April 2020 containing rules to implement the Organ Donation Act stipulates that consenting to or not objecting to removal regards to the extent that the person concerned has not provided otherwise, the following organs: pancreas, blood vessels, bone tissue, cartilage, tendons, intestines, heart, heart valves, skin, liver, lungs, kidneys, eye tissue and nerve tissue.[216]

*481.* When the donor form is sent, explicit mention is made that an adult of whom no declaration of will is available six weeks after a reminder has been sent, will be registered in the donor registry as a person who does not object to the removal of his organs (Article 10.4). Six weeks after thc donor form has been sent, a reminder will be sent to the person concerned together with a new donor form (Article 10a.1). If after six weeks, no reply is received, the person concerned will be registered as having no objection to the removal of his organs after death (Article 10a.2). Within six weeks after having been registered as not objecting, the person concerned or if applicable his legal representative receives a confirmation of this together with a message that he may at any time ask to modify this registration by filling in and registering a donor form (Article 10a.3 and 10a.5). As soon it has become apparent or plausible that a person who has not responded within six weeks after a reminder is not capable to reasonably assess his interests, the registered consent is replaced by a registration that leaves the decision to a specific person, being his legal representative. The person concerned receives a confirmation of this change within six weeks (Article 10a.4).

*482.* The major takes care that an adult who is a resident receives written information about donor registration and the way he may consult his registration and modify it when he requests a national passport, a Dutch identity card or a driving license (Article 10b.1).

*483.* Unless the person who has given consent or has not objected to the removal of organs has provided explicitly otherwise, this consent or no objection is applicable to implantation, including implantation for scientific research if the organ after removal appears to be not suitable (Article 13).

216. *State Journal* (2020), 128.

*C. Diagnosis of Death*

*484.* Before the removal of an organ, death has to be diagnosed by a physician who is not involved in the removal or implantation. If there is intention to remove an organ, death has to be diagnosed in accordance with the most recent scientifically accepted methods and criteria to diagnose brain death or circulatory death by a physician who is qualified in the matter. The way the brain death has been diagnosed has to be recorded in a statement following the model provided in the protocol referred to in Article 15.1 (Article 14.1). Brain death is defined as the complete and irreparable loss of functions of the brain, including the brain stem and elongated marrow. Diagnosis of brain death only occurs after a deadly brain injury with a known cause that cannot be treated. It only occurs when it becomes plausible that other causes of unconsciousness and reactionlessness are not present (Article 14.2). Circulatory death is defined as an irreversible absence of circulation and breathing (Article 14.3). Having regard to Article 14.2 and 14.3, the Health Council determines the most recent scientifically accepted methods and criteria to diagnose with certainty brain death or circulatory death. Based on these, the Health Council determines protocols prescribing procedures and investigations to diagnose brain death or circulatory death in a hospital when it is intended to remove an organ. These protocols are confirmed by a royal decree (15.1). In 2015, the Health Council had recommended amending the Organ Donation Act in this way. According to the Council, procedural requirements for determining circulatory death had to be included in the Act, and the asymmetry with respect of brain death had to be stopped.[217]

*485.* In case of the removal of an organ from a corpse, the autopsy may not be performed by a physician involved in the removal or implantation of the organ (Article 16). In case of a not natural death or suspicion of such a death, no organ may be removed before its authorisation by the public prosecutor (Article 17).

*D. Notification and Allocation of Available Organs*

*486.* The responsible person referred to in Article 23 immediately notifies to an organ centre that presumably organs for implantation will become available (Article 18.1). This organ centre determines who may qualify as a recipient of an organ (Article 18.2). In determining this, no other elements may be taken into account than the blood and tissue correspondence between the donor and the recipient of the organ, the medical urgency of the recipient and other with the state of the organ related circumstances or, if these elements do not lead to a definite decision, the waiting time of the recipient. A royal decree may specify rules in this regard (Article 18.3).

217. Health Council of the Netherlands, *Determining Death in Postmortal Organ Donation: Protocols and Criteria, Including an Updated Brain Death Protocol* (The Hague, 2015), Publication No. 2015/13.

*E. Preparatory Actions and Removal of Organs*

*487.* When there is a reasonable chance that a person will die within a foreseeable time and, in any case, as soon as possible after his death has been diagnosed, the responsible person referred to in Article 23 checks what has been registered concerning that person in the donor registry unless it is already apparent that from a medical point of view he does not qualify as a donor of organs (Article 20.1). The responsible person informs the relatives who can immediately be reached of the registered data in the donor registry. In the case this person is an adult who is apparently or plausibly not capable of assessing his interests, the responsible also informs the legal representative if he is present and can be reached (Article 20.2). If the registration does not correspond with another available declaration of will as referred to in Article 9.4 (*see* paragraph 479), the most recent of both takes precedence (Article 20.3). If the person concerned has been registered in the donor registry as having given consent or objected to the removal of organs and a declaration of will as referred to in Article 9.4 that determines otherwise is available, the latter takes precedence (Article 20.4). If the person concerned has been registered in the donor registry as having given consent or objected to the removal and there is no other declaration of will while the relatives as referred to in Article 11.1 (*see* paragraph 478) make it plausible that the registration does not correspond to the wish of the deceased, this information takes precedence (Article 20.5). If no registration concerning a person is available or if this person has made use of the possibility referred to in Article 9.2 (*see* paragraph 479), the responsible person gives adequate information with regard to the possibility of organ donation once it is reasonably certain that the person concerned will die in a foreseeable time, to the person(s) who is/are competent to give consent to the removal of organs. Once death has been diagnosed, he requests this person/them to give consent to the removal unless his/their objection has already turned out otherwise. Only when it may be expected that a circulatory death will be diagnosed the responsible may already request consent after having provided adequate information (Article 20.6). The responsible person informs the relevant relatives who can be reached immediately about the way an effect has been given to a consent or a refusal (Article 20.7). If the person concerned has himself given consent, the person responsible referred to in the protocol in Article 23 (*see* paragraph 490) informs the relevant relatives who can be reached immediately about the way an effect has been given to this consent (Article 20.8). The application of Article 20 takes place with respect for the rules determined in the protocol referred to in Article 23. The responsible person records this application in a report by filling out a paper or digital form provided by the organ centre (Article 20.9). The responsible persons referred to in Article 20 may access the medical file of the patient to the extent that this is necessary to accomplish their tasks (Article 20.10).

*488.* The removal of an organ after death is only allowed if: (a) it has been established according to Article 20 that the deceased has consented in or not objected to removal of organs; (b) the responsible person referred to in Article 23 has reassured that the deceased was competent at the moment consent has been given or registered as referred in Article 10a; (c) Articles 14, 16 and 17 have been respected; and (d) the organ for implantation has been notified to a transplant centre according to Article 18 (Article 21).

*489.* If a person has been registered in the donor registry as a person who has consented to or has not objected to removal of an organ after his death and if it is reasonably certain that this person will die in a foreseeable time, already before the diagnosis of his death preparatory measures may be taken to the extent that they are not conflicting with the medical treatment of this person and postponement until death has been diagnosed is not possible. Such preparatory measures may consist of investigations necessary to prepare an implantation; starting with or maintaining artificial respiration; maintaining artificial circulation of blood and other measures to keep organs suitable for implantation (Article 22.1). If regarding a person no registration is available in the donor registry or if use has been made of the possibility provided for in Article 9.2, these preparatory measures may already be taken before death has been diagnosed to the extent that: (a) it is reasonably certain that this person will die in a foreseeable time; (b) they are not conflicting with the medical treatment of this person; (c) postponement until death has been diagnosed is not possible and the procedure to give information as referred to in Article 20.6 has not yet led to objection to the preparatory measures by the person or persons who according to Article 11 are competent to give consent to the removal (Article 22.2). If regarding a person no registration is available in the donor registry or if use has been made of the possibility provided for in Article 9.2, the preparatory measures may be taken after death has been diagnosed, as long as the procedure to obtain the legally required consents to removal has not yet led to their refusal (Article 22.3).

### *F. The Protocol*

*490.* The management of a hospital takes care of the determination of a protocol to make organs available for implantation and supervises its application (Article 23.1). In this protocol, the persons are appointed who within the hospital are tasked to implement Articles 18.1 and 20. The protocol also contains rules concerning: (a) the way to check whether a deceased qualifies as a donor; (b) the way to consult the donor registry according to Article 20.1, to inform the persons referred to in Article 20.2, to inform the relatives referred to in Article 20.5 is dealt with, the persons referred to in Article 20.6 have been asked to give consent, the persons referred to in Article 20.7 have been informed; (c) the procedure to notify an organ to an organ centre; (d) the way aftercare is given to persons referred to in Article 20.6 and 20.7; and (e) the information in the hospital with regard to the rules contained in the protocol (Article 23.2). If it is possible in a hospital to diagnose brain death, the protocol has to contain the applicable methods and criteria and the procedures and investigations to be followed as provided in Article 15.1 (Article 23.4).

*G. Organ Centres*

*491.* Mediating to obtain, typify and transport organs of donors as well as to allocate these organs to a suitable recipient may only be performed by an organ centre licensed by the minister (Article 24.1). Such license may only be granted to a not-for-profit legal person that is not a tissue organisation (Article 25.1).

## §6. RESEARCH

### I. Research with Human Persons

*A. Research with Human Persons That Is Not a Clinical Trial on Medicinal Products for Human Use*

*492.* Medical research with human persons is regulated by the Act of 26 February 1998 on Medical Research with Humans (Medical Research Act) last amended by the Act of 22 March 2017 modifying the Medical Research Act and the Medicines Act regarding the implementation of Regulation (EU) 536/2014 of 16 April 2014 on clinical trials on medicinal products.[218] The Act of 22 March 2017 has not yet entered into force. In what follows the modifications that result from this Act are not yet integrated.

1. General Dispositions (Paragraph 1 Medical Research Act)

a. Definitions

*493.* Article 1 provides definitions of frequently used notions in the Medical Research Act. Scientific research is defined as medical-scientific research, including subjecting persons to procedures or imposing upon them a certain way of behaviour (Article 1.1b Medical Research Act). Such persons are (research) subjects (Article 1.1c Medical Research Act). Subjecting persons to procedures or imposing upon them a certain way of behaviour merely as a means to provide care to them is no scientific research (Article 1.2 Medical Research Act).

b. Positive Opinion of a Research Ethics Committee on the Research Protocol

*494.* Scientific research is carried out in accordance with a research protocol. A research protocol requires a positive opinion of a research ethics committee. In general, this is a medical research ethics committee that has been accredited by the central committee on research involving human subjects according to Article 16 Medical Research Act (Article 2.2a). Scientific research, including research on different sites, is evaluated by one competent research ethics committee indicated by the person who performs out the research (Article 2a). According to Article 1f, this

218. *State Journal* (2017), 147.

is the person, undertaking, institution or organisation that takes the responsibility to start, manage or finance scientific research. According to Article 1g, the person who carries out the research is a physician or a person with expertise in carrying out scientific research who is responsible for carrying it out.

*495.* In the following cases, this positive opinion has to be given by the central committee on research involving human subjects itself, which is established by Article 14 Medical Research Act: after an appeal against an opinion of a medical research ethics committee, in case of non-therapeutic research with a minor and cases of research specified in a general administrative order (Article 2.2b) Medical Research Act).

## 2. Rules Governing Scientific Research with Subjects (Paragraph 2 Medical Research Act)

### a. General Rules

*496.* A competent medical research ethics committee can only issue a positive opinion on the research protocol if: the scientific research contributes to new insights in the field of medical science (Article 3.1a Medical Research Act); such new insights can only be obtained through research with subjects and not with less intrusive research (Article 3.1b Medical Research Act); the importance of the research to the subjects and other current or future patients is in proportion to the objections (burden) and the risk for the subject, taking into account the circumstances of persons belonging to the group of the subjects (Article 3.1c Medical Research Act); the study involves only a minimal risk and a minimal burden compared to the standard treatment of the subject's condition in the case of non-therapeutic research with subjects under the age of 16 years or with incapacitated adult subjects (Article 3.1d Medical Research Act); the research meets the requirements of a proper methodology of scientific research (Article 3.1e Medical Research Act); the research is carried out in appropriate institutes and by or under the supervision of professionals (Article 3.1f Medical Research Act); any compensation paid to the subject did not have influenced giving consent to participating in the study if the subject is under 18 years of age (minor) (Article 3.1g Medical Research Act); any compensation paid to the subject did not disproportionately have influenced giving consent to participating in the study if the subject is 18 years of age or above (adult) (Article 3.1h Medical Research Act); the person who carries out the research and the institution where the research is carried out receive a compensation not exceeding an amount that is reasonable in relation to the nature, extent and aim of the research (Article 3.1i Medical Research Act); the protocol clearly states how burdensome the research is for the subject and the extent to which the subject can benefit from the research (Article 3.1j); the protocol indicates which scientifically appropriate criteria subjects must meet in order to participate in the research (Article 3.1k Medical Research Act); the results of the research will be made publicly available by the central committee on research involving human subjects through its register unless the person who carries out the research objects to this (Article 3.1l

Medical Research Act) and the research complies with any other reasonable requirements (Article 3.1m Medical Research Act).

*497.* If in the case of non-therapeutic research with subjects under the age of 16 years or with incapacitated adult subjects, there is no standard treatment; the competent committee may issue a positive opinion if the research involves only minimal risk and a minimal burden considering the nature and severity of the subject's condition (Article 3.2 Medical Research Act).

*498.* A medical research ethics committee or the central committee on research involving human subjects may postpone the application of its positive opinion or withdraw it when there are justified reasons to assume that the continuation of scientific research will provoke unacceptable risks to the subject (Article 3a.1 Medical Research Act).

### b. Research with Minor and Incapacitated Subjects

*499.* It is prohibited to carry out scientific research with persons who have not reached the age of 16 or who are not capable of reasonably assessing their interests in this regard.[219] This prohibition does not apply to research which is also of direct benefit to the research subject (therapeutic) and to non-therapeutic research which can only be conducted with that group of persons (Article 4 Medical Research Act).

*500.* If a subject objects to the procedures he/she is subjected to or to the behaviour imposed upon him/her, the research cannot be carried out with this subject (Article 10a.1 Medical Research Act).

### c. Research with Vulnerable Subjects

*501.* It is prohibited to carry out scientific research with persons who cannot reasonably consent freely to participate given their legal or factual state of dependency in respect of the researcher. This prohibition does not apply to research which is also of direct benefit to the research subject (therapeutic) and regarding non-therapeutic research which can only be conducted with that group of persons (Article 5 Medical Research Act).

*502.* If a subject objects to the procedures he/she is subjected to or to the behaviour imposed upon him/her; the research cannot be carried out with this subject (Article 10a.1 Medical Research Act).

---

219. The original, restricted provisions have been amended by the Act of 26 Oct. 2016, *State Journal* (2016), 424. *See* for the original rules, M.J.H. Kenter, 'Legislation and Review of Medical Research with Minors in the Netherlands', *European Journal Health Law,* 15 (2008) 145–151.

d. Informed Consent

*503.* It is prohibited to carry out scientific research with a subject who has reached the age of 16 without his or her written consent (Article 6.1a Medical Research Act). If the subject cannot write, consent may be given in the presence of at least one witness (Article 6.2 Medical Research Act).

*504.* If the subject has reached the age of 12 but not yet of 16 and is capable of reasonably assessing his/her interests in that regards, the written consent of the subject and of his/her parents or guardian is required (Article 6.1b Medical Research Act).

*505.* If the subject has reached the age of 12 and is not capable of reasonably assessing his/her interests in that regard, the written consent of one of the following is required: the parents or the guardian if the subject has not reached the age of 16; otherwise of the legal representative, or, if such a representative lacks, the husband/partner or the parents or an adult child or an adult brother or sister (Article 6.1c Medical Research Act). The substituted consent has to reflect the will of the subject (Article 6.3 Medical Research Act).

*506.* If the subject has not reached the age of 12, the written consent of the parents or the guardian is required (Article 6.1d Medical Research Act). The substituted consent has to reflect the will of the subject (Article 6.3 Medical Research Act).

*507.* The subject or the person who is competent to give substituted consent may at any time and without giving reasons withdraw the consent. No compensation is due (Article 6.9 Medical Research Act).

e. Research in an Emergency Case

*508.* If the scientific research can only be carried out in a state of emergency, and the required consent cannot be obtained while the research is in the benefit of the subject, all procedures to carry out the research are allowed without this consent as long as the emergency impedes obtaining it (Article 6.4 Medical Research Act).

f. Information Prior to Consent

*509.* Before asking for consent, the person whose consent is required has to be informed in writing and if he/she wishes so, in an interview on the following: the aim, nature and duration of the research; the risks that the research may entail for the health of the subjects; the risks that the withdrawal from the research may entail for the health of the subjects and the burden that the research may pose for the subjects (Article 6.5 Medical Research Act).

3. Liability and Insurance (Paragraph 3 Medical Research Act)

*510.* The scientific research may only be carried out if, at the moment of its start, an insurance has been concluded that covers damage by death or physical damage to the subject caused by the research (Article 7.1 Medical Research Act).

*B. Clinical Trials on Medicinal Products for Human Usage*

*511.* Clinical trials are regulated in Regulation (EU) No. 536/2014 of the European Parliament and of the Council of 16 April 2014 on clinical trials on medicinal products from human use, and repealing Directive 2001/20/EC on the approximation of the laws, regulations and administrative provisions of the Member States relating to good clinical practice in the conduct on medicinal products for human use (The Clinical trials Regulation).[220] The Regulation entered into force on 16 June 2014. It will probably become applicable in December 2021. Nevertheless, in this section, the rules laid down in the Regulation and in the Act of 22 March 2017 amending the Medical Research Act that will implement this Regulation are described.

*512.* Directive 2001/20/EC (the Clinical Trials Directive) aimed to simplify and harmonise the administrative provisions governing clinical trials in the Union. However, experience had shown that a harmonised approach to the regulation of clinical trials had only partially achieved. This made it particularly difficult to perform a given clinical trial in several Member States (Recital 4 in the Preamble to Regulation No. 536/2014 (the Clinical Trials Regulation)). Experience had also indicated that the legal form of a Regulation would present advantages for sponsors and investigators, for example, in the context of clinical trials taking place in more than one Member State, they will be able to rely on its provisions directly. Divergences of approach among different Member States will, therefore, be kept to a minimum (Recital 5 in the Preamble to the Clinical Trials Regulation).[221]

1. Field of Application of the Clinical Trials Regulation

*513.* The Clinical Trials Regulation applies to all clinical trials conducted in the Union (Article 1). Although there appears to be some uncertainty as to the application of the Clinical Trials Regulation in relation to clinical trials conducted only within one Member State,[222] it follows from different Articles of the Clinical Trials

220. *OJ* 2014, L 158/1-76.

221. M.L. Flear, 'The EU Clinical Trials Regulation: Key Priorities, Purposes and Aims and the Implications for Public Health', *Journal of Medical Ethics,* 42 (2016) 193–194.

222. J.V. McHale, 'Reforming the EU Clinical Trials Directive: Streamlining Processes of a Radical "New" Agenda?', *European Journal Health Law,* 20 (2013) 368; T.K. Hervey and J.V. McHale, *European Union Health Law: Themes and Implications* (Cambridge: Cambridge University Press, 2015) 307.

Regulation that it also applies to clinical trials conducted only within one Member State. For instance, Article 5.1(4) provides that if ( … ) the clinical trial involves only one Member State, that Member State shall be the reporting Member State. *See also* Article 30 in this regard (*see* below, paragraph 516).

*514.* A 'clinical trial' means a clinical study which fulfils any of the following conditions: (a) the assignment of the subject to a particular therapeutic strategy is decided in advance and does not fall within the normal clinical practice of the Member State concerned; (b) the decision to prescribe the investigational medicinal products is taken together with the decision to include the subject in the clinical study; or (c) diagnostic or monitoring procedures in addition to normal clinical practice are applied to the subjects (Article 2. 2(2) Regulation). A 'clinical study' means any investigation in relation to humans intended: (a) to discover or verify the clinical, pharmacological or other pharmacodynamics effects of one or more medicinal products; (b) to identify any adverse reactions to one or more medicinal products; or (c) to study the absorption, distribution, metabolism and excretion of one or more medicinal products; with the objective of ascertaining the safety and/or efficacy of those medicinal products (Article 2.2(1) Regulation). 'Normal clinical practice' means the treatment regime typically followed to treat, prevent, or diagnose a disease or a disorder (Article 2.2(6)).

*515.* Article 1j Medical Research Act defines scientific research with medicinal products as a clinical trial to which the Regulation is applicable.

*516.* Low-intervention clinical trials fall within the field of application of the Clinical Trials Regulation but are subjected to less stringent rules because they pose only a minimal additional risk to the subject's safety compared to normal clinical practice (Recital 11 in the Preamble). 'Low-intervention clinical trial' means a clinical trial which fulfils all of the following conditions: (a) the investigational medicinal products, excluding placebos, are authorised; (b) according to the protocol of the clinical trial, (i) the investigational medicinal products are used in accordance with the terms of the marketing authorisation; or (ii) the use of the investigational medicinal products is evidence-based and supported by published scientific evidence on the safety and efficacy of those investigational medicinal products in any of the Member States concerned; and (c) the additional diagnostic or monitoring procedures do not pose more than minimal additional risk or burden to the safety of the subjects compared to normal clinical practice in any Member State concerned (Article 2.2(3)).

*517.* The Clinical Trials Regulation does not apply to non-interventional studies (Article 1). A 'non-interventional study' means a clinical study other than a clinical trial (Article 2.2(4)). The precise scope of the Clinical Trials Regulation in this respect is not very clear.[223]

223. J. Herringa and J. Dute, 'The Proposed EU-Regulation on Clinical Trials on Medicinal Products', *European Journal of Health Law,* 20 (2013) 349.

## 2. The Protection of Subjects in Clinical Trials

*518.* A 'subject' means an individual who participates in a clinical trial, either as a recipient of an investigational medicinal product or as a control (Article 2.2.17).

*519.* Human cells and human tissues in clinical trials are applied to the human body should comply with the quality and safety standard laid down in Directive 2004/23/EC of the European Parliament and of the Council of 31 March 2004 on setting standards of quality and safety for the donation, procurement, testing, processing, preservation, storage and distribution of human tissues and cells (Recital 11 in the Preamble of Directive 2004/23/EC).

### a. Prior Authorisation

*520.* According to Article 4, the first sentence a clinical trial has to be subjected to scientific and ethical review and authorised in accordance with the Clinical Trials Regulation. In order to obtain an authorisation, the sponsor has to submit an application dossier to the intended Member States concerned through the portal referred to in Article 80 (the 'EU portal') (Article 5.1). 'Sponsor' means an individual, company, institution or organisation which takes responsibility for the initiation, for the management and for setting up the financing of the clinical trial (Article 2.2(14)). The sponsor proposes one of the Member States concerned as reporting Member State (Article 5.1). Within ten days from the submission of the application dossier, the reporting Member State validates the application taking into account considerations expressed by the other Member States concerned (Article 5.3). The date on which the sponsor is notified that the application is validated by the reporting state is the validation date of the application (Article 5.6).

*521.* The ethical review and the authorisation referred to in Article 4 are both the responsibility of the reporting Member State and the Member State concerned. This shared responsibility is clarified in Recital 6 in the Preamble as follows: 'The Member States concerned should cooperate in assessing a request for authorisation of a clinical trial. This cooperation should not include aspects of an intrinsically national nature, such as informed consent.'

*522.* Unlike in the Clinical Trials Directive, an ethical review by an ethics committee is not an obligation. In the proposed Clinical Trials Regulation, the concept of an ethics committee was not mentioned at all.[224] The Clinical Trials Regulation leaves it to the Member States to determine which body is competent for the ethical review and the authorisation. Recital 18 in the Preamble states the following in this

224. H. Nys, 'New European Rules Regarding the Approval of Clinical Trials: The Role of Ethics Committees and the Protection of Subjects', *Archives Immunology Experimental Therapy,* 30 (2012) 409; J. Herringa and J. Dute, 'The Proposed EU-Regulation on Clinical Trials on Medicinal Products', *European Journal of Health Law,* 20 (2013) 347–362; C. Pertini, 'What Is the Role of Ethics Committees after Regulation (EU) 536/2014?', *Journal of Medical Ethics,* 42 (2016) 186–188.

respect: 'It should be left to the Member State concerned to determine the appropriate body or bodies to be involved in the assessment of the application to conduct a clinical trial and to organise the involvement of ethics committees within the timelines for the authorisation of that clinical trial as set out in this Regulation. Such decisions are a matter of internal organisation for each Member State.' At first sight, this is in contradiction with Article 4, second sentence that begins as follows: 'The ethical review shall be performed by an ethics committee in accordance with the law of the Member State concerned.' That seems to imply the obligation for the Member States to delegate the ethical review to an ethics committee. However, the second sentence of Article 4 goes as follows: 'The review by the ethics committee may encompass aspects addressed in Part I of the assessment report for the authorisation of a clinical trial as referred to in Article 6 and in Part II of that assessment report as referred to in Article 7 as appropriate for each Member State concerned'. Those aspects form the core of the ethical review, which may be evaluated by an ethics committee without this being an obligation. According to Hervey and McHale, the need for research ethics committee approval for publication in journals is probably enough to secure the continued use of research ethics committees across the EU.[225]

*523.* The Clinical Trials Regulation defines 'ethics committee' and contains provisions concerning the composition and the management of such a committee or the body that is responsible for the ethical review and the authorisation. According to Article 2(11), an 'ethics committee' means an independent body established in a Member State in accordance with the law of that Member State and empowered to give opinions for the purposes of this Regulation, taking into account the views of laypersons, in particular patients or patients' organisations. Article 9 contains more detailed provisions concerning the persons that validate and assess the application without mentioning ethics committees. Member States have to ensure that these persons do not have conflicts of interest, are independent of the sponsor, of the clinical trial site and the investigators involved and of persons financing the clinical trial, as well as free of any other undue influence.[226] In order to guarantee independence and transparency, the Member States ensure that persons admitting and assessing the application as regards the aspects addressed in Parts I and II of the assessment report have no financial or personal interests which could affect their impartiality. These persons have to make an annual declaration of their financial interests (Article 9.1). The Central Committee on research involving human subjects that is responsible for the ethical review has to determine its procedure in a regulation. This regulation has to provide that the review has to take place in accordance with Article 9.1 of the Regulation (Article 14.7 Medical Research Act). The Member States ensure that the assessment is done jointly by a reasonable number of persons who collectively have

225. T.K. Hervey and J.V. McHale, *European Union Health Law: Themes and Implications* (Cambridge, Cambridge University Press, 2015) 315.

226. This condition may pose problems in small countries because it may be difficult to find independent researchers in the case of large multisite trials, *see* Nordic Trial Alliance Working Group on Ethics, *Report on the Ethical Review Process for Clinical Trials in the Nordic Countries-The Challenges and Opportunities of the New Clinical Trials Regulation*, 2016, 30 http://nta.nordforsk.org/files/NordForsk_NTAREPORT_Ethics.pdf.

the necessary qualifications and experience (Article 9.2). At least one layperson has to participate in the assessment (Article 9.3).

*524.* The reporting Member State has to assess among other aspects the compliance with Chapter V of the Clinical Trials Regulation with respect to the anticipated therapeutic and public health benefits and the risks and conveniences for the subject (Article 6.1a (i) and (ii)). Both but especially the second one are very important in view of the protection of the subject. This is also highlighted by the title of Chapter V: 'Protection of subjects and informed consent'. After the assessment of these and other aspects, the reporting Member State draws up an assessment report. The assessment of these aspects constitutes Part I of the assessment report (Article 6.2). Given the themes treated in Part I, it is obviously not correct to state that Part I is merely scientifically.[227] The reporting Member State submits, through the EU portal, the final Part I of the assessment report, including its conclusion (acceptable; acceptable subject to compliance with specific conditions; not acceptable, *see* Article 6.3) to the sponsor and to the other Member States concerned within forty-five days from the validation date (Article 6.4).

*525.* For clinical trials involving more than one Member State, the assessment process includes three phases: (a) an initial assessment phase performed by the reporting Member State within twenty-six days from the validation date. During this phase, the reporting Member State develops a draft Part I of the assessment report and circulates it to all other Member States concerned; (b) a coordinated review phase performed within twelve days from the end of the initial assessment phase involving all Member States concerned. During this phase, all Member States concerned jointly review the application based on the draft Part I of the assessment report and share any considerations relevant to the application; (c) a consolidation phase performed by the reporting Member State within seven days from the end of the coordinated review phase. During this phase, the reporting Member State takes due account of the considerations of the other Member States concerned when finalising Part I of the assessment report and records how all such considerations have been dealt with. The reporting Member State submits the final Part I of the assessment report to the sponsor and all other Member States concerned within forty-five days from the validation date (Article 6.5). The date on which the final Part of the assessment is submitted is the reporting date (Article 6.6). Between the validation date and the reporting date, only the reporting Member State may request additional information from the sponsor. For the purpose of obtaining and reviewing this additional information from the sponsor, the reporting Member State may extend the period referred to in paragraph 4 by a maximum of thirty-one days (Article 6.8).

---

227. I. Vranken, 'Krachtlijnen van de Europese Verordening klinische proeven', *Tijdschrift Gezondheidsrecht/Revue droit de la santé,* 20 (2014–2015) 264; Shaw and Townend also state that 'ethics committees can also consider part 1 issues in their deliberation', D. Shaw and D. Townend, 'Division and Discord in the Clinical Trials Regulation', *Journal of Medical Ethics,* 42 (2016) 729. *See also* at p. 731: 'While the Clinical Trials Regulation does allow ethics committees to consider part 1 issue, they should really be listed as a specific responsibility of the ethics committee.'

*526.* Each Member State concerned assesses, for its own territory, the application with respect to the following aspects: (a) compliance with the requirements for informed consent as set out in Chapter V; (b) compliance of the arrangements for rewarding or compensating subjects with the requirements set out in Chapter V and investigators; (c) compliance of the arrangements for the recruitment of subjects with the requirements set out in Chapter V; (d) compliance with Directive 95/46/EC (protection of personal data); (e) compliance with Article 49 (suitability of individuals involved in conducting the clinical trials); (f) compliance with Article 50 (suitability of clinical trials sites); (g) compliance with Article 76 (damage compensation); (h) compliance with the applicable rules for the collection, storage and future use of biological samples of the subject. The assessment of the aspects referred constitutes Part II of the assessment report (Article 7.1). Each Member State concerned completes its assessment within forty-five days from the validation date and submit, through the EU portal, Part II of the assessment report, including its conclusion, to the sponsor. Each Member State concerned may request, with justified reasons, additional information from the sponsor regarding the aspects referred to in Article 7.1 only within the period of forty-five days (Article 7.2). For the purpose of obtaining and reviewing this additional information, the Member State concerned may extend the period of forty-five days by a maximum of thirty-one days (Article 7.3). Regarding the period within which the ethical review has to be finished, one also has to take account of Article 4 that provides that the Member States ensure that the timelines and procedures for the review by the ethics committees are compatible with the timelines and procedures set out in this Regulation for the assessment of the application for authorisation of a clinical trial.

*527.* Each Member State concerned notifies the sponsor through the EU portal as to whether the clinical trial is authorised, whether it is authorised subject to conditions, or whether an authorisation is refused. Notification has to be done by way of one single decision within five days from the reporting date (Article 8.1). Where the Member State concerned has not notified the sponsor of its decision within this period, the conclusion on Part I of the assessment report is deemed to be the decision of the Member State concerned on the application for authorisation of the clinical trial (Article 8.6).

*528.* Where the conclusion of the reporting Member State as regards Part I of the assessment report is that the conduct of the clinical trial is acceptable or acceptable subject to compliance with specific conditions, that conclusion is deemed to be the conclusion of the Member State concerned. Notwithstanding this, a Member State concerned may disagree with the conclusion of the reporting Member State as regards Part I of the assessment report only on the following grounds: (a) when it considers that participation in the clinical trial would lead to a subject receiving an inferior treatment than in normal clinical practice in the Member State concerned; (b) infringement of its national law as referred to in Article 90 (specific requirements for special groups of medicinal products); (c) considerations as regards subject safety and data reliability and robustness (Article 8.2).

*529.* A Member State concerned refuses to authorise a clinical trial if it disagrees with the conclusion of the reporting Member State as regards Part I of the assessment report on any of the grounds referred to in the previous paragraph, or if it finds, on duly justified grounds, that the aspects addressed in Part II of the assessment report are not complied with, or where an ethics committee has issued a negative opinion which in accordance with the law of the Member State concerned is valid for that entire Member State. That Member State has to provide for an appeal procedure in respect of such refusal (Article 8.4).

*530.* Where the conclusion of the reporting Member State as regards Part I of the assessment report is that the clinical trial is not acceptable, that conclusion is deemed to be the conclusion of all Member States concerned (Article 8.5).

*531.* If no subject has been included in the clinical trial in a Member State concerned within two years from the notification date of the authorisation, the authorisation expires in that Member State concerned unless an extension, on request of the sponsor, has been approved following the procedure set out in Chapter III (Article 8.9).

*532.* The central committee is responsible for: (a) the communication that Netherland is prepared to act as the reporting Member State, as referred in Article 5.1 Regulation; (b) the validation of the application dossiers and substantial modifications referred in Articles 5.3, 17.2 and 20.1 Regulation; (c) the allocation of application dossiers as referred to in Article 5.1 Regulation to review committees with the exception of those that have to be reviewed by the central committee itself according to Article 2.2b Medical Research Act; (d) the access to the EU portal referred to in Article 80 Regulation; and (e) administratively supporting the review committees that have to review the application dossiers with regard to scientific research that is not exclusively carried out in the Netherlands (Article 17a.1 Medical Research Act). When allocating an application file to a review committee according to Article 17a.1c, the central committee may consider the experience, the composition and the procedure of the review committee concerned (Article 17a.2 Medical Research Act). The review committee reviews the application dossier that has been allocated to it and respects the provisions of the Regulation (Article 17a.3 Medical Research Act). If the Central Committee itself reviews an application dossier, it respects the provisions of the Regulation (Article 17a.4 Medical Research Act).

*533.* The Central Committee may issue guidelines concerning the language in which an application dossier is drafted. It may provide information concerning scientific research in accordance with the Regulation to the competent authorities of other Member States to the extent that they need this information to perform their tasks (Article 24a.1 and 24a.2 Medical Research Act).

*534.* An interested party may appeal to the central committee against a decision taken by a committee on the basis of the Regulation (Article 23b Medical Research Act).

b. General Provisions for the Protection of Subjects

*i. General Principle*

*535.* A clinical trial may be conducted only if the rights, safety, dignity and well-being of subjects are protected and prevail over all other interests and if it is designed to generate reliable and robust data (Article 3). Recital 27 in the Preamble explicitly refers to the Charter of Fundamental Rights of the EU: 'Human dignity and the right to the integrity of the person are recognised in the Charter of Fundamental Rights of the European Union (the "Charter"). In particular, the Charter requires that any intervention in the field of biology and medicine cannot be performed without free and informed consent of the person concerned.' Moreover, 'Directive 2001/20/EC contains an extensive set of rules for the protection of subjects. These rules should be upheld.'

*ii. Proportionality Requirement (Balance Benefits-Risks)*

*536.* A clinical trial may be conducted only where the anticipated benefits to the subjects or to public health justify the foreseeable risks and inconveniences and compliance with this condition is constantly monitored (Article 28.1a).

*iii. Informed Consent*

*537.* The Clinical Trials Regulation contains the following definition of informed consent: 'a subject's free and voluntary expression of his or her willingness to participate in a particular clinical trial, after having been informed of all aspects of the clinical trial that are relevant to the subject's decision to participate or, in case of minors and of incapacitated subjects, an authorisation or agreement from their legally designated representative to include them in the clinical trial' (Article 2.2.26; Article 1v Medical Research Act). In order to certify that informed consent is given freely, the investigator should take into account all relevant circumstances which might influence the decision of a potential subject to participate in a clinical trial, in particular, whether the potential subject belongs to an economically or socially disadvantaged group or is in a situation of institutional or hierarchical dependency that could inappropriately influence her or his decision to participate (Recital 31 in the Preamble).

**Express Informed Consent As a Rule**

The subjects have to be informed in accordance with Article 29.2–29.6 (Article 28.1b).

Information given to the subject has to enable the subject to understand: (i) nature, objectives, benefits, implications, risks and inconveniences of the clinical trial; (ii) the subject's rights and guarantees regarding his or her protection, in particular, his or her right to refuse to participate and the right to withdraw from the clinical trial at any time without any resulting detriment and without having to provide any justification; (iii) the conditions under which the clinical trial is to be conducted, including the expected duration of the subject's participation in the clinical trial; and (iv) the possible treatment alternatives, including the follow-up measures if the participation of the subject in the clinical trial is discontinued (Article 29.2a).

The information has to include information about the applicable damage compensation system referred to in Article 76.1 and has to include the EU trial number and information about the availability of the clinical trial results (Article 29.2d and 29.2e).

The subject has to be informed that the summary of the results of the clinical trial and a summary presented in terms understandable to a layperson will be made available in the EU database, referred to in Article 81 (the 'EU database'), pursuant to Article 37.4, irrespective of the outcome of the clinical trial, and, to the extent possible, when the summaries become available (Article 29.6).

The subject has to be provided with the contact details of an entity where further information can be received in case of need (Article 28.1g).

The information has to be kept comprehensive, concise, clear, relevant, and understandable to a layperson (Article 29.2b).

The information has to be provided in a prior interview with a member of the investigating team who is appropriately qualified according to the law of the Member State concerned (Article 29.2c). In this interview, special attention has to be paid to the information needs of specific patient populations and of individual subjects, as well as to the methods used to give the information. In this interview, it has to be verified that the subject has understood the information (Article 29.4 and 29.5).

The information has to be prepared in writing and be available to the subject (Article 29.3).

Informed consent has to be written, dated and signed by the person performing the interview referred to in paragraph 379 and by the subject after having been duly informed in accordance with Article 29.2. Where the subject is unable to write, consent may be given and recorded through appropriate alternative means in the presence of at least one impartial witness. In that case, the witness signs and dates the informed consent document (Article 29.1). According to Recital 30 in the Preamble, appropriate alternative means are, for instance, audio or video recorders.

The subject has to be provided with a copy of the document (or the record) by which informed consent has been given. Informed consent has to be documented. Adequate time has to be given for the subject to consider his or her decision to participate in the clinical trial (Article 29.1).

### Implicit Informed Consent for Cluster Trials

Article 30.3 Clinical Trials Regulation determines the conditions following which informed consent can be obtained for so-called cluster trials that are conducted exclusively in one Member State. The Clinical Trials Regulation does not define cluster trials, but from Recital 33 of the Preamble, it can be deduced that these are clinical trials where the methodology of the trial requires that groups of subjects rather than individual subjects are allocated to receive different investigational medicinal products. In those clinical trials, the investigational medicinal products are used in accordance with the marketing authorisations, and the individual subject receives a standard treatment regardless of whether he/she accepts or refuses to participate in the clinical trial, or withdraws from it so that the only consequence of non-participation is that data relating to him/her are not used for the clinical trial. Such clinical trials serve to compare established treatments. It is appropriate to allow that informed consent be obtained by simplified means for such clinical trials.

The simplified means to obtain informed consent for such clinical trials means that informed consent is deemed to have been obtained if the information required by Article 29.2 has been given, and this information makes clear, in particular, that the subject can refuse to participate in, or withdraw at any time from, the clinical trial without any resulting detriment and the potential subject, after being informed, does not object to participating in the clinical trial (Article 30.2). This is called implicit, tacit or non-verbal consent. It is not a presumed consent because the will of the subject is known.

Informed consent may be obtained by this simplified means if all the following conditions are fulfilled: (a) it does not contradict national law in the Member State concerned; the amended Medical Research Act does not prohibit obtaining informed consent by this simplified means; (b) the methodology of the clinical trial requires that groups of subjects rather than individual subjects are allocated to receive different investigational medicinal products in a clinical trial; (c) the clinical trial is a low-intervention clinical trial (*See* above, paragraph 354) and the investigational medicinal products are used in accordance with the terms of the marketing authorisation; (d) there are no interventions other than the standard treatment of the subjects concerned; (e) the protocol justifies the reasons for obtaining informed consent with simplified means and describes the scope of information provided to the subjects, as well as the ways of providing information (Article 30.3).

The investigator has to document all refusals and withdrawals and has to ensure that no data for the clinical trial are collected from subjects that refuse to participate in or have withdrawn from the clinical trial (Article 30.4).

### Withdrawal of Informed Consent

Any subject may, without any resulting detriment and without having to provide any justification, withdraw from the clinical trial at any time by revoking his or her informed consent. Without prejudice to Directive 95/46/EC, the withdrawal of the informed consent will not affect the activities already carried out and the use of data obtained based on informed consent before its withdrawal (Article 28.3).

The fact that withdrawal is not retrospective has to be included in the consent process so that subjects are aware of it.[228]

228. J.V. McHale, 'Reforming the EU Clinical Trials Directive: Streamlining Processes of a Radical "New" Agenda?', *European Journal Health Law,* 20 (2013) 375.

*iv. Respect for the Rights to Physical and Mental Integrity, to Privacy and to Data Protection*

*538.* The rights of the subjects to physical and mental integrity, to privacy and to the protection of the data concerning them in accordance with Directive 95/46/EC are safeguarded (Article 28.1d).

*v. As Little Pain, Discomfort, Fear and any Other Foreseeable Risk*

*539.* The clinical trial has to be designed to involve as little pain, discomfort, fear and any other foreseeable risk as possible for the subjects and both the risk threshold and the degree of distress have to be specifically defined in the protocol and constantly monitored (Article 28.1e).

*vi. Medical Care under the Responsibility of an Appropriately Qualified Medical Doctor/Dental Practitioner*

*540.* The medical care provided to the subjects is the responsibility of an appropriately qualified medical doctor or, where appropriate, a qualified dental practitioner (Article 28.1f; Article 13d, c Medical Research Act).

*vii. No Undue Influence*

*541.* No undue influence, including that of a financial nature, is exerted on subjects to participate in the clinical trial (Article 28.1h).

*viii. Protection of Subjects During the Clinical Trial*

*542.*

- Conduct in Accordance with the Protocol and Good Clinical Practice Principles: The sponsor of a clinical trial and the investigator ensure that the clinical trial is conducted in accordance with the protocol and with the principles of good clinical practice (Article 47; Article 13b Medical Research Act).
- Adequate Monitoring of the Conduct of the Clinical Trial: In order to verify that the rights, safety and well-being of subjects are protected, that the reported data are reliable and robust, and that the conduct of the clinical trial is in compliance with the requirements of the Clinical Trials Regulation, the sponsor adequately monitors the conduct of a clinical trial. The extent and nature of the monitoring are determined by the sponsor on the basis of an assessment that takes into consideration all characteristics of the clinical trial, including the following characteristics: (a) whether the clinical trial is a low-intervention clinical trial; (b) the

objective and methodology of the clinical trial; and (c) the degree of deviation of the intervention from normal clinical practice (Article 48).

- Qualified Investigator: The investigator has to be a medical doctor as defined in national law, or a person following a profession which is recognised in the Member State concerned as qualifying for an investigator because of the necessary scientific knowledge and experience in patient care. Other individuals involved in conducting a clinical trial have to be suitably qualified by education, training and experience to perform their tasks (Article 49).
- Suitable Facilities: The facilities where the clinical trial is conducted have to be suitable for the conduct of the clinical trial in compliance with the requirements of the Clinical Trials Regulation (Article 50).
- Notification of Serious Breaches of Safety and Rights of a Subject: The sponsor has to notify the Member States concerned about a serious breach of the Clinical Trials Regulation or of the version of the protocol applicable at the time of the breach through the EU portal without undue delay but not later than seven days of becoming aware of that breach. For the purposes of this Article, a 'serious breach' means a breach likely to affect to a significant degree the safety and rights of a subject or the reliability and robustness of the data generated in the clinical trial (Article 51).
- No Costs to be Borne by the Subject: Without prejudice to the Member States' competence for the definition of their health policy and for the organisation and delivery of health services and medical care, the costs for investigational medicinal products, auxiliary medicinal products, medical devices used for their administration and procedures specifically required by the protocol are not to be borne by the subject, unless the law of the Member State concerned provides otherwise (Article 92; Article 13d, b Medical Research Act).
- Damage Compensation: the Member States ensure that systems for compensation for any damage suffered by a subject resulting from participation in a clinical trial conducted on their territory are in place in the form of insurance, a guarantee, or a similar arrangement that is equivalent as regards its purpose and which is appropriate to the nature and the extent of the risk. The sponsor and the investigator make use of that system in the form appropriate for the Member State concerned where the clinical trial is conducted. Member States may not require any additional use of that system for low-intervention clinical trials if any possible damage that could be suffered by a subject resulting from the use of the investigational medicinal product in accordance with the protocol of that specific clinical trial on the territory of that Member State is covered by the applicable compensation system already in place (Article 76).
- Summary of the Results of the Clinical Trial Within One Year: Irrespective of the outcome of a clinical trial, within one year from the end of a clinical trial in all Member States concerned, the sponsor has to submit to the EU database a summary of the results of the clinical trial (*see* for the content of that summary Annex IV to the Clinical Trials Regulation). It has to be accompanied by a summary written in a manner that is understandable to laypersons (*see* for the content of that summary Annex V to the Clinical Trials Regulation). However, where, for scientific reasons detailed in the protocol, it is not possible to submit a summary of the results within one year, the summary of results has to be submitted as soon

as it is available. In this case, the protocol has to specify when the results are going to be submitted, together with a justification (Article 37.4).

c. Clinical Trials on Incapacitated Subjects

*i. Incapacitated Subject*

*543.* An incapacitated subject is a subject who is, for reasons other than the age of legal competence to give informed consent, incapable of giving informed consent according to the law of the Member State concerned (Article 2.2.19). For the purposes of the Clinical Trials Regulation, a subject which falls under the definition of both 'minor' and 'incapacitated subject' is deemed to be an incapacitated subject (Article 2.3). This explains why the Clinical Trials Regulation does not refer to adult incapacitated subjects.

*544.* In the case of incapacitated subjects who have not given, or have not refused to give, informed consent before the onset of their incapacity, a clinical trial may be conducted only where, in addition to the conditions set out in Article 28, all of the conditions provided for in Article 31 are met (Article 31.1.).

*545.* It follows from the wording of Article 31.1. that it is not applicable when an incapacitated person has given or refused informed consent before the onset of his or her incapacity. In that situation, the consent or refusal will remain valid.[229]

*ii. Informed Consent of the Legally Designated Representative*

*546.* The informed consent of the legally designated representative of the incapacitated person has to be obtained (Article 31.1a).

*547.* The rules concerning the determination of the legally designated representatives of incapacitated persons diverge in the Member States. It is therefore left to the Member States to determine the legally designated representatives of incapacitated persons (*see* Recital 27 in the Preamble).

*548.* The subject may as far as possible take part in the informed consent procedure (Article 31.3). The Clinical Trials Regulation is without prejudice to national law requiring that both the signature of the incapacitated person and the signature of his or her legally designated representative may be required on the informed consent form (Article 29.7).

*549.* The incapacitated subjects must have received the information referred to in Article 29.2 in a way that is adequate in view of their capacity to understand it

229. *Ibid.*

(Article 31.1b). It is evident that also the representative of this incapacitated person has to receive all the information referred to in Article 29.2.

*iii. Respect for the Explicit Wish to Refuse or Withdraw Consent*

*550.* The explicit wish of an incapacitated subject who is capable of forming an opinion and assessing the information referred to in Article 29.2 to refuse participation in, or to withdraw from, the clinical trial at any time, has to be respected by the investigator (Article 31.1c). It is evident that this explicit will also has to be respected by the legally designated representative.

*iv. No incentives or Financial Inducements*

*551.* No incentives or financial inducements may be given to the subjects or their legally designated representatives, except for compensation for expenses and loss of earnings directly related to the participation in the clinical trial (Article 31.1d).

*v. The Clinical Trial is Essential and No Alternative*

*552.* The clinical trial has to be essential with respect to incapacitated subjects and data of comparable validity cannot be obtained in clinical trials on persons able to give informed consent, or by other research methods (Article 31.1e; Article 13f, a Medical Research Act).

*vi. Directly Related to the Medical Condition of the Subject*

*553.* The clinical trial has to relate directly to a medical condition from which the subject suffers (Article 31.1f; Article 13f,a Medical Research Act). As a consequence, it is not possible to include in a clinical trial an incapacitated person who does not suffer from any medical condition or when the clinical trial does not directly relate to a medical condition the subject is suffering from.

*vii. A Direct Benefit for the Subject … or …*

*554.* There have to be scientific grounds for expecting that participation in the clinical trial will produce a direct benefit to the incapacitated subject outweighing the risks and burdens involved (Article 31.1g(i)). As a consequence, an incapacitated subject cannot participate in a non-therapeutic clinical trial.

### *viii. ... Some Benefit for the Population Represented by the Subject and Directly Related to the Life-Threatening or Debilitating Medical Condition from Which the Subject Suffers*

*555.* If no direct benefit to the subject is to be expected, there have to be scientific grounds for expecting his or her participation in the clinical trial will produce some benefit for the population represented by the incapacitated subject concerned. In that case, the clinical trial has to relate directly to the life-threatening or debilitating medical condition from which the subject suffers and the trial may pose only minimal risk to and may impose only minimal burden on, the incapacitated subject concerned in comparison with the standard treatment of the incapacitated subject's condition (Article 31.1g(ii)). The possibility of including an incapacitated person in a clinical trial with no direct benefit to the subject has not been provided for in Article 13f Medical Research Act. This is in conformity with Article 31.2 of the Clinical Trials Regulation.

*556.* Unlike the Clinical Trials Directive that did not allow for non-therapeutic clinical trials on incapacitated persons,[230] the Clinical Trials Regulation does allow for such trials under strict conditions. This is remarkable, the more so as the draft Clinical Trials Regulation did not differ from the Clinical Trials Directive in this respect.[231] Only one Recital in the Preamble is devoted to this fundamental change and in a rather superficial way: 'In order to improve treatments available for vulnerable groups such as frail or older people, people suffering from multiple chronic conditions, and people affected by mental health disorders, medicinal products which are likely to be of significant clinical value should be fully and appropriately studied for their effects in these specific groups, including as regards requirements related to their specific characteristics and the protection of the health and well-being of subjects belonging to these groups.'(Recital 15 in the Preamble).

*557.* The criterion of minimal risk and minimal burden appears in many guidelines and regulations and is generally accepted. However, the Clinical Trials Regulation adds to this 'in comparison with the standard treatment of the subject's condition'. Westra argues correctly that this condition can be interpreted in a way that may lead to exploitation of vulnerable research subjects. The added wording sets a relative standard for the concepts of minimal risk and minimal burden: the meaning of 'minimal' depends on the severity of the standard treatment: if, for

230. And for this was severely criticised, *see* H. Visser, 'Non-therapeutic Research in the EU in Adults Incapable of Giving Consent', *The Lancet* (2001) 818–819; *see also* A.E. Westra, 'Ambiguous Articles in the New EU Regulation May Lead to Exploitation of Vulnerable Research Subjects', *Journal of Medical Ethics,* 42 (2016) 189: 'A total ban on so called non-therapeutic with incompetent subjects would make it impossible to improve healthcare for these groups.'

231. J.V. McHale, 'Reforming the EU Clinical Trials Directive: Streamlining Processes of a Radical "New" Agenda?', *European Journal of Health Law,* 20 (2013) 376; H. Nys, 'New European Rules Regarding the Approval of Clinical Trials: The Role of Ethics Committees and the Protection of Subjects', *Archives Immunology Experimental Therapy,* 30 (2012) 411.

example, the standard treatment for the subjects' condition includes muscle biopsies, the risk and burdens of such biopsies for these subjects may be regarded as minimal.[232]

*558.* The ethical and legal delicateness of this condition is highlighted in Article 31.2, that leaves without prejudice more stringent national rules prohibiting the conduct of those clinical trials on incapacitated subjects, where there are no scientific grounds to expect that participation in the clinical trial will produce a direct benefit to the subject outweighing the risks and burdens involved.

##### *ix. Ethical Assessment on the Basis of Expertise in the Relevant Disease*

*559.* Specific consideration has to be given to the assessment of the application for authorisation of a clinical trial on the basis of expertise in the relevant disease and the patient population concerned or after taking advice on clinical, ethical and psychosocial questions in the field of the relevant disease and the patient population concerned (Article 10.2; Article 13f, b Medical Research Act).

#### d. Clinical Trials on Minors

*560.* A minor is a subject who is, according to the law of the Member State concerned, under the age of legal competence to give informed consent (Article 2.2(18)).

##### *i. Basic Rule*

*561.* In the case of minors, a clinical trial may be conducted only where, in addition to the conditions set out in Article 28, all of the conditions provided for in Article 32 are met (Article 32.1.).[233]

##### *ii. Informed Consent*

*562.*

- Informed Consent of the Legally Designated Representative: The informed consent of the legally designated representative has to be obtained (Article 32.1a).

232. A.E. Westra, 'Ambiguous Articles in the New EU Regulation May Lead to Exploitation of Vulnerable Research Subjects', *Journal of Medical Ethics,* 42 (2016) 189–190.
233. Paragraph 5 of the European Parliament resolution of 15 Dec. 2016 on the regulation on paediatric medicines (2016/2902(RSP)) stresses the importance of cross-border trials for research into many paediatric and rare illnesses and therefore welcomes Regulation 536/2014; Paragraph 26 of the European Parliament resolution of 14 Feb. 2017 on promoting gender equality in mental health and clinical research (2016/2096(INI)) 'suggests that clinical trials should also take account of specific vulnerable population groups such as paediatric and geriatric patients and persons from ethnic minorities'.

As the rules concerning the determination of the legally designated representatives of minors diverge in the Member States, it is left to the Member States to determine the legally designated representatives of minors (*see* Recital 27 in the Preamble).

- Participation of the Minor: The minor has to take part in the informed consent procedure in a way adapted to his or her age and mental maturity (Article 32.2).
- Assent of the Minor: The Clinical Trials Regulation is without prejudice to national law requiring that, in addition to the informed consent given by the legally designated representative, a minor who is capable of forming an opinion and assessing the information given to him or her, also has to assent in order to participate in a clinical trial (Article 29.8).
- Informed Consent of the Minor When he Reaches the Age of Legal Competence: If during a clinical trial the minor reaches the age of legal competence to give informed consent as defined in the law of the Member State concerned, his or her express informed consent has to be obtained before that subject can continue to participate in the clinical trial (Article 32.3).

#### *iii. Information to Be Provided to the Minor*

*563.* The minors have to receive the information referred to in Article 29.2 in a way adapted to their age and mental maturity and from investigators or members of the investigating team who are trained or experienced in working with children (Article 32.1b).

#### *iv. Explicit Wish to Refuse Is Respected*

*564.* The explicit wish of a minor who is capable of forming an opinion and assessing the information referred to in Article 29.2 to refuse participation in, or to withdraw from, the clinical trial at any time, has to be respected by the investigator (Article 32.1c).

#### *v. No Incentives or Financial Inducements*

*565.* No incentives or financial inducements should be given to the subject or his or her legally designated representative except for compensation for expenses and loss of earnings directly related to the participation in the clinical trial (Article 32.1d).

#### *vi. A Medical Condition That Only Occurs in Minors … or …*

*566.* The clinical trial has to be intended to investigate treatments for a medical condition that only occurs in minors (Article 32.1e). In this respect, the question arises how this provision relates to Article 31.3 of the Clinical Trials Regulation.

Probably the answer is that the clinical trial has to be halted once the minor has reached the age of legal competence to give informed consent.

*vii. ... Essential to Validate Alternatives*

*567.* If the clinical trial has no intention to investigate treatments for a medical condition that occurs only in minors, the clinical trial has to be essential with respect to minors to validate data obtained in clinical trials on persons able to give informed consent or by other research methods (Article 32.1e; Article 13e, a Medical Research Act).

*viii. Directly Related to the Medical Condition of the Minor or No Alternative but Minors*

*568.* The clinical trial either has to relate directly to a medical condition from which the minor concerned suffers or has to be of such a nature that it can only be carried out on minors (Article 32.1f).

*ix. A Direct Benefit for the Minor ... or ...*

*569.* There have to be scientific grounds for expecting that participation in the clinical trial will produce a direct benefit to the minor concerned outweighing the risks and burdens involved (Article 32.1g (i)). This means that a minor cannot participate in a non-therapeutic clinical trial.

*x. ... Some Benefit for the Population Represented by the Minor*

*570.* If there are no scientific grounds for expecting that participation will produce a direct benefit to the minor, there have to be scientific grounds for expecting that participation in the clinical trial will produce some benefit for the population represented by the minor concerned (Article 13e, a Medical Research Act). Moreover, the clinical trial should pose only minimal risk to and should impose a minimal burden on, the minor concerned in comparison with the standard treatment of the minor's condition (Article 32.1g(ii)).[234]

*571.* Compared with the conditions for such a clinical trial with adult incapacitated persons, it is remarkable that the condition regarding the life-threatening or debilitating medical condition from which the subject suffers is not provided for here. The Clinical Trials Directive was already more flexible for non-therapeutic

234. K. Wade, 'Defining the Threshold of Permissible Risk for Non-therapeutic Clinical Trials with Children in Europe', *European Journal of Health Law,* 24 (2017) 414–431.

clinical trials on minors than on incapacitated persons. This possibly explains why for clinical trials on minors, a provision analogous to Article 31.1g(ii) is lacking.

### *xi. Ethical Assessment on the Basis of Paediatric Expertise*

*572.* Specific consideration has to be given to the assessment of the application for authorisation of a clinical trial on the basis of paediatric expertise or after taking advice on clinical, ethical and psychosocial problems in the field of paediatrics (Article 10.1).

### e. Clinical Trials on Pregnant or Breastfeeding Women

*573.* A clinical trial on pregnant or breastfeeding women may be conducted only where, in addition to the conditions set out in Article 28 (*see* above, paragraphs 515 et seq.) the following conditions are met: (a) the clinical trial has the potential to produce a direct benefit for the pregnant or breastfeeding woman concerned, or her embryo, foetus or child after birth, outweighing the risks and burdens involved; or (b) if such clinical trial has no direct benefit for the pregnant or breastfeeding woman concerned, or her embryo, foetus or child after birth, it can be conducted only if: (i) a clinical trial of comparable effectiveness cannot be carried out on women who are not pregnant or breastfeeding; (ii) the clinical trial contributes to the attainment of results capable of benefitting pregnant or breastfeeding women or other women in relation to reproduction or other embryos, foetuses or children; and (iii) the clinical trial poses a minimal risk to, and imposes a minimal burden on, the pregnant or breastfeeding woman concerned, her embryo, foetus or child after birth; (c) where research is undertaken on breastfeeding women, particular care is taken to avoid any adverse impact on the health of the child; and (d) no incentives or financial inducements are given to the subject except for compensation for expenses and loss of earnings directly related to the participation in the clinical trial (Article 33).

*574.* Specific consideration has to be given to the assessment of the application for authorisation of a clinical trial on the basis of expertise in the relevant condition and the population represented by the subject concerned (Article 10.3).

### f. Clinical Trials on Other Vulnerable Subjects

*575.* Member States may maintain additional measures regarding persons performing mandatory military service, persons deprived of liberty, persons who, due to a judicial decision, cannot take part in clinical trials, or persons in residential care institutions (Article 34). Residential care institutions are accommodations providing uninterrupted assistance for persons who necessitate such assistance.

*576.* These four categories of persons have in common that they are in a situation of subordination or factual dependency and therefore may require specific protective measures (*see* Recital 35 in the Preamble).

*577.* It is not clear which additional measures can be provided for persons who, due to a judicial decision, cannot take part in clinical trials because, by definition, they cannot take part in a clinical trial.

*578.* Article 34 does not mention economically or socially disadvantaged groups and does not provide any specific protection for them.[235]

*579.* If according to the protocol a clinical trial provides for the participation of specific groups or subgroups of subjects, where appropriate, specific consideration has to be given to the assessment of the application for authorisation of that clinical trial on the basis of expertise in the population represented by the subjects concerned (Article 10.4).

### g. Clinical Trials in Emergency Situations

*580.* By way of derogation from Article 28.1b (information to the subject or his legal representative) and Article 28.1c (informed consent), Article 31.1a and 31.1b (obligation to inform and obtain informed consent for a clinical trial on an incapacitated person) and Article 32.1a and 32.1b (obligation to inform and obtain informed consent for a clinical trial on a minor), informed consent to participate in a clinical trial may be obtained, and information on the clinical trial may be given, after the decision to include the subject in the clinical trial, provided that this decision is taken at the time of the first intervention on the subject, in accordance with the protocol for that clinical trial and that all of the following conditions are fulfilled:

(a) due to the urgency of the situation, caused by a sudden life-threatening or other sudden serious medical condition, the subject is unable to provide prior informed consent and to receive prior information on the clinical trial;
(b) there are scientific grounds to expect that participation of the subject in the clinical trial will have the potential to produce a direct clinically relevant benefit for the subject resulting in a measurable health-related improvement alleviating the suffering and/or improving the health of the subject, or in the diagnosis of its condition;
(c) it is not possible within the therapeutic window to supply all prior information to and obtain prior informed consent from his or her legally designated representative;
(d) the investigator certifies that he/ or she is not aware of any objections to participate in the clinical trial previously expressed by the subject;
(e) the clinical trial relates directly to the subject's medical condition because of which it is not possible within the therapeutic window to obtain prior informed consent from the subject or from his or her legally designated representative and to supply prior information, and the clinical trial is of such a nature that it may be conducted exclusively in emergency situations;

235. E. Gennet, R. Andorno and B. Elger, 'Does the New EU Regulation on Clinical Trials Adequately Protect Vulnerable Research Participants,' *Health Policy,* 119 (2015) 928.

(f) the clinical trial poses minimal risk to and imposes a minimal burden on, the subject in comparison with the standard treatment of the subject's condition (Article 35.1).

*581.* Following an intervention pursuant to Article 35.1, informed consent in accordance with Article 29 has to be sought to continue the participation of the subject in the clinical trial, and information on the clinical trial has to be given, in accordance with the following requirements:

(a) regarding incapacitated subjects and minors, the informed consent has to be sought by the investigator from his or her legally designated representative without undue delay and the information referred to in Article 29.2 has to be given as soon as possible to the subject and to his or her legally designated representative;
(b) regarding other subjects, the informed consent has to be sought by the investigator without undue delay from the subject or his or her legally designated representative, whichever is earlier and the information referred to in Article 29.2 has to be given as soon as possible to the subject or his or her legally designated representative, whichever is earlier. Where informed consent has been obtained from the legally designated representative, informed consent to continue the participation in the clinical trial has to be obtained from the subject as soon as he/ or she is capable of giving informed consent (Article 35.2).

*582.* If the subject or, where applicable, his or her legally designated representative does not give consent, he/she has to be informed of the right to object to the use of data obtained from the clinical trial (Article 35.3).

*583.* In any application for authorisation of a clinical trial in an emergency situation, specific consideration has to be given to the circumstances of the conduct of the clinical trial (Article 10.5).

## II. Research with Gametes, Embryos in Vitro and Foetuses

*584.* Research with gametes, embryos in vitro and foetuses is governed by the Act of 20 June 2002 containing rules relating to the use of gametes and embryos (Embryo Act).

### *A. Research with Gametes*

*585.* Adults who are capable of making a reasonable assessment of their interests in this regard may make their gametes available for research purposes (Article 5.1 Embryo Act). Gametes may be made available only by means of a donation confirmed in writing and on a not-for-profit basis and only after the donor has been informed by the person storing the gametes regarding nature and the purpose thereof. The donor may revoke his/her decision at any time before the gametes are used, without giving reasons (Article 5.2 Embryo Act). If an invasive procedure is required in order to obtain gametes, the donor is to be informed by the person who carries out the procedure of the possible risks and complications (Article 5.3 Embryo Act).

*586.* When making his/her gametes available, the donor may stipulate that research may be performed using the gametes in question only after he/she has been informed about the purposes of the research and has given his/her express consent for such research (Article 6.3 Embryo Act).

*587.* Research involving gametes leading to the creation of embryos is considered to research with embryos (Article 3.1 Embryo Act).

### B. *Research with Embryos*

#### 1. Common Provisions

##### a. Positive Opinion on the Research Protocol

*588.* Research involving embryos has to be carried out in accordance with a specifically drafted research protocol which contains a complete description of the intended research (Article 3.1 Embryo Act). Such research is only allowed if a positive opinion regarding the research protocol has been given by the central committee on research with human subjects established by Article 14 of the Medical Research Act (*see* paragraph 476) (Article 3.2 Embryo Act).

##### b. Donation of Embryos for Research

*589.* Adults who are capable of making a reasonable assessment of their interests in this regard may make available embryos which have been created outside the body for their own pregnancy, but which will no longer be used for this purpose, to carry out research that is permissible under this Act using those embryos (Article 8.1c Embryo Act).

*590.* Embryos may be made available for research only by means of a donation confirmed in writing and on a not-for-profit basis and only if the donors have been informed by the person storing the embryos regarding nature and the purpose thereof. Where a difference of opinion arises between the donors, the embryos shall not be made available. Any of donors may revoke his/her decision at any time before the embryos have been used, without giving reasons (Article 8.2 Embryo Act). Articles 6 and 7 shall apply *mutatis mutandis*.

## 2. Research with Embryos Outside the Human Body Which Does Not Induce Pregnancy

*591.* Paragraph 3 of the Embryo Act contains rules governing research with embryos outside the human body while this research does not induce pregnancy.

*592.* The central committee on research with human subjects deliver a positive opinion on a research protocol concerning research with embryos which does not induce pregnancy only if: (a) it can reasonably be assumed that the research will lead to new insights in the field of medical science; (b) it can reasonably be assumed that the insights referred to under (a), cannot be achieved through any forms or methods of research other than research with the embryos in question or through a less invasive form of research; (c) the research in question meets the standards of proper research methodology; (d) the research is carried out by or under the direction of persons who are expert in the relevant research area; and (e) the research also satisfies requirements which might reasonably be imposed on it in other respects (Article 10 Embryo Act).

*593.* Carrying out research with embryos created specifically for this purpose is prohibited. This prohibition does not apply to research which is reasonably likely to lead to new insights in the fields of infertility, artificial reproduction techniques, hereditary or congenital diseases or transplant medicine, and which can only be performed by making use of such embryos (Article 11 Embryo Act). This disposition has not yet entered into force.

*594.* Carrying out research is prohibited unless these embryos or the gametes from which they were created, were made available for that purpose (Article 12.1 Embryo Act).

*595.* The person who commissions the research is responsible for compliance with Article 3 (Article 13 Embryo Act). The person carrying out the research is responsible for ensuring that the privacy of the individuals from whom the gametes originate and those who have made an embryo available is protected as far as possible (Article 14 Embryo Act). The person carrying out the research is responsible for ensuring that, before the research commences, those individuals whose professional cooperation is required in the performance of the research are informed about its nature and purpose (Article 15 Embryo Act).

## 3. Research with Embryos Outside the Human Body Which is Intended to Induce Pregnancy

*596.* Paragraph 4 of the Embryo Act contains rules governing research with embryos outside the human body, which is intended to induce pregnancy.

*597.* The central committee on research with human subjects shall deliver a positive opinion on a research protocol concerning research with embryos outside the human body which is intended to induce pregnancy only if: (a) it can reasonably be assumed that the research will lead to new insights with regard to research or therapeutic methods that are aimed at inducing pregnancy and the birth of a healthy child; (b) it can reasonably be assumed that the new insights referred to under (a), cannot be achieved through any forms or methods of research other than research with embryos with which pregnancy is intended to be induced or through a less invasive form of research; (c) it can reasonably be assumed that the interests to be served by the research are proportional to the burdens and risks for the potential child and the woman in question; and (d) the requirements laid down in Article 10 c, d and e Embryo Act (*see* paragraph 569) have been satisfied (Article 16 Embryo Act).

*598.* Carrying out such research without the written consent of the woman and her husband, registered partner or other life companion is prohibited. Consent may only be given by adults who are capable of making a reasonable assessment of their interests in this regard. Before consent is requested, the person carrying out the research shall ensure that the persons from whom consent is required are informed in writing about the purpose and nature of the research, their time to reflect, their right to withdraw and the protection of their privacy. The information shall be supplied in such a way that it is reasonably certain that the persons from whom consent is required have understood it. If required, the information supplied shall be supplemented. The persons from whom consent is required shall be given sufficient time for reflection to enable them to make a carefully considered decision regarding consent. A person who has given consent may withdraw it at any time, without giving reasons. He/she shall not be obliged to pay any compensation in respect of the withdrawal (Article 18 Embryo Act).

*599.* The person who commissions the research is responsible for compliance with Article 3. The person carrying out the research is responsible for ensuring that the privacy of the individuals from whom the gametes originate and those who have made an embryo available is protected as far as possible. The person carrying out the research is responsible for ensuring that, before the research commences, those individuals whose professional cooperation is required in the performance of the research are informed about its nature and purpose (Article 18 Embryo Act).

### *C. Research with Foetuses*

*600.* A foetus is defined as 'an embryo in the human body' (Article 1e Embryo Act).

*601.* Paragraph 5 of the Embryo Act contains rules governing scientific research with foetuses. According to Article 3 research with foetuses is allowed if: (a) it concerns scientific research where the foetus is not subjected to invasive procedures or the condition of the foetus is not deliberately altered, and the research protocol has received a positive opinion of a medical research ethics committee referred to in

Article 16 of the Medical Research Act (*see* paragraph 475); or (b) it concerns scientific research where the foetus is subjected to invasive procedures or the condition of the foetus is deliberately altered, and the research protocol has received a positive opinion of the central committee on research with human subjects (Article 3.3 Embryo Act). However, this central committee can determine that also research mentioned under (a) has to be evaluated by itself (Article 3.4).

*602*. The central committee on research with human subjects or a medical research ethics committee referred to in Article 16 Medical Research Act (*see* paragraph 475) shall deliver a positive opinion on a research protocol concerning research with foetuses only if: (a) it can reasonably be assumed that the research will lead to new medical insights in relation to unborn and newborn children or regarding the continuation of pregnancies to term; (b) it can reasonably be assumed that the objective referred to under (a), cannot be achieved through any forms or methods of research other than research with foetuses or via a less invasive form of research; (c) it can reasonably be assumed that the interests to be served by the research are proportional to the burdens and risks for the foetus and the woman in question; and (d) the requirements laid down in 10 c, d and e Embryo Act (*see* paragraph 569) have been satisfied (Article 19 Embryo Act).

*603*. Research using a foetus is permitted only if it might contribute to the diagnosis, prevention or treatment of serious diseases in the foetus concerned and if it cannot be postponed until after the birth or if it can contribute to this in other foetuses and the risks for this foetus and the pregnant woman are minimal (Article 20 Embryo Act).

*604*. Carrying out research using a foetus without the written consent of the pregnant woman is prohibited. If she is a minor and under 16 years of age, written consent is also required from her parents or guardian. If the pregnant woman in question is not capable of making a reasonable assessment of her interests in this regard, consent may be given by her parents or guardian or, if she is adult by her legal representative or, in the absence of the latter, by her husband, registered partner or other life companion (Article 21.1 and 21.2 Embryo Act).

*605*. Before consent is requested, the person carrying out the research shall ensure that the persons from whom consent is required are informed in writing regarding: (a) the purpose, nature and duration of the research; (b) the risks which the research may entail for the health of the pregnant woman and the foetus; (c) the risks which premature termination of the research may entail for the health of the pregnant woman and the foetus; and (d) the burden which the research may entail for the pregnant woman and the foetus (Article 21.3 Embryo Act).

*606*. The pregnant woman, or, if she is not competent to give consent, the person who is competent on her behalf, may withdraw consent at any time, without giving reasons. She shall not be obliged to pay any compensation (Article 21.5 Embryo Act).

*607.* If the research should take a course which is significantly less favourable for the pregnant woman or the foetus than is foreseen in the research protocol, the person carrying out the research shall notify the person who has given consent and the competent research committee that has given the opinion referred to in Article 3 and request a further opinion from that committee. The research shall be suspended until this further opinion is given unless the health of the pregnant woman or of the foetus does not permit immediate suspension (Article 22.1 Embryo Act). If further opinion is negative, the research shall be terminated unless the health of the pregnant woman or the foetus does not permit immediate termination (Article 22.2 Embryo Act). The person carrying out the research shall issue a reasoned notification of the termination to the competent research committee that has given the latest opinion (Article 22.3 Embryo Act).

*608.* Articles 13, 14 and 16 Embryo Act (*see* paragraph 572) are *mutatis mutandis* applicable (Article 23 Embryo Act).

### D. *Prohibited Uses of Gametes and Embryos*

*609.* Division 6 of the Embryo Act provides rules prohibiting certain uses of gametes and embryos.

#### 1. Creation of Embryos for Research

*610.* Article 24a Embryo Act prohibits creating an embryo specifically for research purposes or for purposes other than the induction of pregnancy and using such an embryo in research or for purposes other than the induction of pregnancy. According to Article 33.2 Embryo Act, Article 24a shall lapse on a date to be determined by decree. Initially, a three to five years moratorium on the creation of embryos for research had been provided for in the Embryo Act. In the original version of Article 33.2, it was provided that the moratorium had to be lifted at the latest before September 2007.[236] On 6 November 2008, an amendment of Article 33.2 has been accepted in order to continue the moratorium while at the same, the opportunity to lapse Article 24a remained open. The government actually in power (until 2021) has decided not to lift the moratorium.

#### 2. Other Prohibited Uses of Gametes and Embryos

*611.* Creating an embryo specifically and using such an embryo for purposes other than the induction of a pregnancy or the purposes for which it may be made available pursuant to Article 9.1 (Article 24b Embryo Act; this provision has not yet entered into force); using gametes and embryos other than those referred to under

236. N. Zeegers, 'Convergence in European Nations' Legal Rules Concerning the Use of Human Embryos in Research?', *European Journal Health Law,* 21 (2014) 461.

(b), for purposes other than those for which they may be made available pursuant to this Act (Article 24c Embryo Act); using gametes and embryos for purposes permissible under the terms of this Act if they have not been made available for such purposes (Article 24d Embryo Act); allowing an embryo to develop outside the human body for longer than fourteen days (Article 24e Embryo Act); performing procedures with gametes or embryos with a view to the birth of genetically identical human individuals (reproductive cloning) (Article 24f Embryo Act); intentionally modifying the genetic material of the nucleus of human germ-line cells with which a pregnancy is to be induced (Article 24g Embryo Act); using cells cultured from an embryo for purposes other than those for which it is permissible to make them available under the terms of Article 8.1b and Article 9.1a, respectively (Article 24h Embryo Act).

#### 3. Prohibition to Create a Chimera or a Hybrid

*612.* The following procedures are prohibited: (a) combining a human and an animal gamete with a view to creating a multicellular hybrid; (b) allowing a chimaera created from human and animal (or exclusively human) embryonic cells to develop for longer than fourteen days or implanting this chimaera into a human being or an animal; (c) implanting an embryo into an animal; and (d) implanting an animal embryo into a human being (Article 25 Embryo Act).

#### 4. Prohibition of Procedures Aimed at Gender Selection, Unless

*613.* Performing procedures with gametes or embryos with a view to select the gender of a potential child is prohibited (Article 26.1 Embryo Act). This prohibition does not apply if, according to scientifically sound medical opinion, there is a risk of a serious gender-linked hereditary disease in the child and the procedures are intended to prevent that disease. The prohibition also does not apply if, according to scientifically sound medical opinion, there is a risk to serious hereditary disease with an unequal sex incidence to the child and with the aim to diminish that risk (Article 26.2 Embryo Act as amended by Article I.C of the Act of 1 July 2020, *see* paragraph 436). Offering services consisting of procedures prohibited by this Article is prohibited (Article 26.3 Embryo Act).

### III. Research with Personal Data

*614.* Without prejudice to the provisions of Article 7:457-1 Civil Code (medical secrecy; *see* paragraph 197), information about the patient or access to the documents referred to in Article 7:454 (medical file; *see* paragraph 194) may, if requested, be supplied to another person for the purpose of statistics or scientific research in the field of public health without the patient's consent, if: (a) consent cannot reasonably be requested and guarantees are provided that the patient's privacy will not be inordinately infringed by the conduct of the research; or (b) consent cannot reasonably be requested given the nature and purpose of the research, and the care provider has ensured that the data are supplied in such a form as to ensure that they cannot be traced back to individual natural persons (Article 7:458-1 Civil Code).

*615.* Information may be provided in accordance with paragraph 1 only if: (a) the research is in the public interest; (b) the research cannot be conducted without the information in question; and (c) the patient in question has not explicitly objected against the possibility that information will be provided for this purpose (Article 7:458.2 Civil Code).

*616.* The fact that information has been provided under paragraph 1 shall be noted in the patient's records (Article 7:458-3 Civil Code).

## IV. Research with Human Bodily Material

### *A. Research with Anonymous Human Bodily Material*

*617.* Anonymous substances or parts secreted from the body may be used for medico-statistical, or other medico-scientific research insofar the patient from whom the bodily material originates has not objected against this, and the research is carried out with due care. Research using anonymous substances or parts is defined as research which guarantees that the bodily material used for research purposes and the data obtained therefrom cannot be traced back to the person from whom they originated (Article 7:467 Civil Code).

### *B. Research with Organs*

*618.* Unless the person who has given consent or has not objected to removal of organs has provided explicitly otherwise, this consent or no objection is applicable to implantation, including implantation for scientific research if the organ after removal appears to be not suitable (Article 13 Organ Donation Act).

### *C. Research with Foetal Tissues*

*619.* The Act of 8 November 2001 containing rules regarding the availability and use of foetal tissue[237] provides that the preservation and use of foetal tissues are only allowed, among others, for scientific research (Article 2.1). The consent of the

237. *State Journal* (2001), 573.

woman or her legal representative in case she is legally or factually incapacitated is required. This consent has to be handwritten, dated and signed (Article 3).

## V. Population Screening

### *A. Definition of Population Screening*

*620.* The definition of population screening, as laid down in the Population Screening Act of 29 October 1992 is: 'medical research in persons carried out on an entire population or a category thereof aimed at the detection of certain types of disease or certain risk indicators for the benefit of the participating subjects' (Article 1c). The Act entered into force on 1 July 1996.

*621.* This definition contains a number of elements:[238]

- It must concern a medical research within the population screening. The research must be carried out in the entire population, or a category thereof. The investigator must be presented to the population or the population group through, for example, individual consultations, advertisements or other general communication, such as in the waiting room of the practice of the investigator.
- The screening should partly take place for the benefit of the participants so that the individual results of the research can be offered to every participant as a healthcare benefit. With 'partly' is meant that the research can possibly also be a 'trial population research' and may have a medical/scientific character.
- The term 'disease' is defined in the wider sense to include disorders, pain, injuries, deficiencies, or other physical or psychological conditions.
- Risk indicators are seen to be 'information on an individual containing details concerning the level of risk to that individual defined within a set time period and clinical manifestation. These increase the chance of contracting certain diseases'.

### *B. Licensing Requirements*

*622.* There are three categories of population research for which a licence is required: population screening whereby ionising radiation is used; population cancer screening and population screening of serious diseases or defects for which there is no treatment and prevention possible (Article 2.1). A licence must be obtained from the Ministry of Health, Welfare and Sport for population research (Article 3.1). In the case of screening for which a licence is required, the Health Council is asked to give advice prior to the minister reviewing the screening and issuing a licence (Article 6).

*623.* There is uncertainty about the interpretation of some notions in the Act. This concerns, among others, the criterion 'serious diseases or defects for which no

238. www.ccmo.nl/en/population-research.

treatment or prevention exists' which is decisive for the question as to whether a licence is required. In an advisory report, the committee on population screening of the Health Council examined how these terms have been interpreted to date and the limitations of that interpretation. From a legal point of view, the licensing criterion, 'serious diseases or defects for which no treatment or prevention exists', is an all or nothing criterion. Given the purpose of the Act of protecting people, the committee advises against too easily assuming that a condition can be treated. When in doubt, the qualification 'treatable or untreatable' should be based on the scientific knowledge of the anticipated favourable effect on the clinical result of the treatments available for a particular condition. When assessing the licensing criterion 'serious diseases or defects for which no treatment or prevention exists', the seriousness of the condition and the severity of the consequences of the condition play an important role as well. After all, according to the Act, a licence is only required when a condition that is both untreatable and unpreventable is also serious.[239]

### *C. Protection of Research Subjects*

*624.* Research subjects who participate in population screening for which a licence is required are also protected. The Population Screening Act has its own protection regime that has been mainly implemented in the Population Screening Decree of 1 August 1995 that entered into force on 1 July 1996. Article 2 requires the written consent of the participant or his/her legal representative. It can always be revoked. The information to be provided before consent is given is regulated in Article 3 of the decree.

*625.* According to van Hellemondt a.o., besides the practical problems and shortcomings, the Act is not in accordance with EU law. The definition of population screening and the licence requirements are ambiguous. The permit system of the Act does not meet the rules of the Internal Market because of the absence of objective advance announce criteria. A permit system without foreseeable and accessible licence criteria could be an invitation to arbitrariness.[240]

---

239. *Population Screening Act: Essential Terms Explained,* 7 Mar. 2017, www.gezondheidsraad.nl.
240. R.E. van Hellemondt et seq., 'Regulating the Use of Genetic Tests: Is Dutch Law an /Example for Other Countries with Regard to DTC Genetic Screening?', *Amsterdam Law Forum,* 3 (2011) 23.

# Part III. The Physician and the Healthcare System

## Chapter 1. Relations with Other Healthcare Providers

### §1. PHARMACISTS

### I. The Practice of Pharmacy

*626.* The profession of a pharmacist is one of the so-called Article 3 IHCP Act professions. As a consequence, the disciplinary jurisprudence rules apply to pharmacists (Article 47 IHCP Act).

*627.* The domain of expertise of the pharmacist is the preparation, conservation in circumstances that are suitable according to the actual state of science, handing over of medicinal products and advising patients to whom medicinal products are handed over about their use and surveillance of this use (Article 23 IHCP Act; Article 61.1a Medicine's Act). To the extent that a GP or a military doctor is authorised on the basis of the Medicine's Act to prepare or handover medicinal products, this preparation or handing over belongs to his domain of expertise (Article 19.2 IHCP Act; Article 61.1b Medicine's Act). The rules to obtain a licence to prepare and handover medicinal products as a GP are laid down in Article 61.10–61.15 Medicine's Act.

*628.* Article 7:459-1 Civil Code provides that actions in the context of a medical treatment agreement may not be observed by any other individual than the patient unless the patient has given permission for doing so. The Act of 15 March 2007 (*see* paragraph 167 has added to this that if the care provider is a pharmacist, this obligation is not applicable to the extent that it concerns visual observation by others than the patient.

### II. Professional Relations Between Physicians and Pharmacists

*629.* A pharmacist may not handover a so-called prescription-only medicinal product without a prescription. However, in emergency cases, he is authorised to handover such a medicinal product without a prescription if he has reassured sufficiently that there is no danger of abuse (Article 61.9 Medicine's Act). It is prohibited to remotely offer for sale, remotely sale or handover medicinal products otherwise than determined by ministerial decree to implement Directive 2001/83 on the Community Code relating to medicinal products for human use (Article 67a.1 Medicine's Act).

*630.* A pharmacist may with the explicit consent of the patient, request, consult and keep the laboratory results that are necessary to handover a medicinal product to this patient. He requests these results from the person who keeps these results (Article 66a Medicine's Act).

### §2. Dentists

*631.* The profession of a dentist is one of the so-called Article 3 IHCP Act professions. As a consequence, the disciplinary jurisprudence rules apply to dentists (Article 47 IHCP Act).

*632.* The domain of expertise of the dentist is the carrying out of activities in the domain of dentistry (Article 21 IHCP Act).

*633.* Dentists are authorised to carry out the following reserved procedures: the practice of surgical procedures which means activities in the field of medicine that disturb the cohesion of tissues of the body which does not immediately restore, limited to the extent that this belongs to their legal domain (Article 36.1 IHCP Act); the practice of injections (Article 36.5); the practice of anaesthetising patients under certain conditions (Article 36.7); the practice of activities in the field of individual healthcare by making use of radioactive products or ionising radiation under certain conditions (Article 36.8); the prescription of medicinal products (Article 36.14).

### §3. Healthcare Psychologists

*634.* The profession of a healthcare psychologist is one of the so-called Article 3 IHCP Act professions. As a consequence, the disciplinary jurisprudence rules apply to healthcare psychologists (Article 47 IHCP Act).[241]

*635.* The domain of expertise of the healthcare psychologist is carrying out of psychological examination and assessing its results and of psychological treatment methods (Article 25 IHCP Act). According to Article 11.1 of the Healthcare Psychologists Decree,[242] these treatment methods consist of: (a) establishing a relationship with the patient by the healthcare psychologist for the benefit of the treatment

241. F.A.G. Hout et al., 'Practice of the Statutory Disciplinary System for Healthcare Psychologists in the Netherlands', *European Journal Health Law,* 14 (2007) 75–91.
242. *State Journal* (1998), 156.

as well as maintaining that relationship; (b) bringing about behavioural changes that lead to a reduction in complaints; (c) bringing the patient into contact with his feelings and meaning; (d) influencing the position of the patient in the social environment in which the disorder or complaint originated or which plays a role in its maintenance; and (e) guiding his close relatives with a view to the patient's complaints. According to Article 11.2, the methods referred to in section 1 are based on the scientific field of psychology and ortho-pedagogic and are always practised on the basis of psycho-diagnostics and needs assessment.

*636.* There are two recognised specialisations within healthcare psychology: clinical psychologist and clinical neuropsychologist.

### §4. Psychotherapists

*637.* The profession of a psychotherapist is one of the so-called Article 3 IHCP Act professions. As a consequence, the disciplinary jurisprudence rules apply to psychotherapists (Article 47 IHCP Act).

*638.* The domain of expertise of the psychotherapist is carrying out examinations of and influencing moods, behaviours and attitudes of a person with a mental illness, disturbance or complaint in order to make it disappear or diminish (Article 27 IHCP Act). According to Article 11.1 of the Psychotherapeutic Decree of 17 March 1998,[243] the methods referred to in Article 27 IHCP mean: (a) establishing a relationship with the patient by the psychotherapist for the benefit of the treatment as well as maintaining that relationship; (b) bringing about behavioural changes that lead to a reduction in the patient's complaints; (c) bringing the patient into contact with his inner world of feelings and meaning; and (d) influencing the position of the patient in the social environment in which the disorder or complaint originated or which plays a role in its maintenance. The methods referred to in section 1 are based on one or more of the following theories: psychoanalytical theories; learning and cognitive theories; experiential theories and system theories.

### §5. Physiotherapists

*639.* The profession of a physiotherapist is one of the so-called Article 3 IHCP Act professions. As a consequence, the disciplinary jurisprudence rules apply to physiotherapists (Article 47 IHCP Act).

*640.* The domain of expertise of the physiotherapist is the carrying out of activities in the field of physiotherapy described in a royal decree insofar as they belong to medicine (Article 29.1 IHCP). Next to these activities, the physiotherapist also carries out activities that directly relate to a person and which aim to promote and

243. *State Journal* (1998), 155.

to monitor his health status and that correspond with the activities described in section 1 but that do not belong to medicine (Article 29.2 IHCP Act). Article 5 of the royal decree of 13 October 1997 prescribing training requirements and required expertise of physiotherapists[244] as amended by the royal decree of 6 July 2011 reformulating the training requirements and regulating the direct accessibility[245] implements Article 29.1. The professional domain of physiotherapists consists of: (a) recognising risk factors and symptoms in the patient that possibly indicate a condition for which the expertise of a physician is desired or necessary and refer to a physician if these are found; (b) examining a patient's abilities and habits with regard to the posture and movement as well as for the presence of disorders and limitations of his support and locomotor apparatus and the functionally involved organs and control systems and, on the basis of the data obtained, establishing the diagnosis and if necessary drawing up a treatment plan; (c) treating the patient by applying physiotherapeutic methods, aimed at eliminating, reducing or compensating for disorders or limitations of the support and locomotor apparatus and the organs and control systems involved, as well as normalising the posture and movement capacity; and (d) giving advice to the patient (Article 5.1). The physiotherapeutic methods referred to in section 1 comprise: (a) movement therapy, which is understood to mean the by the physiotherapist performed movements or by the patient performed movements; (b) massage therapy, which is understood to mean the methodical application of specific handles on the body of the patient; and (c) physical therapy in the narrow sense, which is understood to mean the administration of physical stimuli other than ionising rays to the patient (Article 5.2).

### §6. Midwives

*641.* The profession of a midwife is one of the so-called Article 3 IHCP Act professions. As a consequence, the disciplinary jurisprudence rules apply to midwives (Article 47 IHCP Act).

*642.* The domain of expertise of the midwife is the carrying out of activities in the field of the obstetrics determined by royal decree as well as the carrying out of other activities determined by royal decree, with respect for the limitations prescribed by this decree; also a royal decree may indicate the medical products and medical devices, the prescription, administration or application of which belongs to the professional domain of a midwife as well as apparatus the use of which belongs to this domain (Article 31). Article 5.1 of the royal decree of 3 July 2008 prescribing training requirements and required expertise of midwives[246] provides that the domain of expertise of a midwife consists in the pursuit of obstetrical activities and other activities aimed at an optimal outcome of pregnancy, the promotion and supervision of a natural course of pregnancy, the delivery and the childbirth and the prevention of abnormalities in the mother or the child by recognising the warning signs

244. *State Journal* (1997), 516.
245. *State Journal* (2011), 364.
246. *State Journal* (2008), 300.

during the pregnancy, the delivery and the childbirth and based on these signs to give advice and assistance and if necessary consult a physician or refer to a physician. The obstetrical activities referred to in section 1 encompass medical supervision of the pregnancy and the delivery, the birth, the first developments of the child and the recovery of the mother after childbirth; vaginal examinations without apparatus or with the use of apparatus designated by ministerial decree; elimination of positional deviations by means of external handles and pursuit of amniotomies during the delivery (Article 5.2). To the other activities referred to in section 1 belong psychological accompaniment of the woman during her pregnancy, delivery and childbirth; prescription and administration of medicinal products or medical devices as indicated in a ministerial decree to the woman or the child; pursuit of episiotomies or suture of lesion of perineum or labium with or without the application of local anaesthesia by making use of means designated by ministerial decree; taking of blood for examination of the woman by means of a puncture or not; removal of material of the cervix and vagina for a cytological apparatus or culture; for examination of the child removal of blood by a puncture of the heel; removal from the woman of urine by catheterisation; pursuing or letting pursue laboratory examinations; giving advice to the woman regarding her life style during the pregnancy; giving of nutritional advices to the women or for the benefit of the child, among which advice on breast feeding; informing and counselling the woman and if applicable her partner concerning the possibilities of prenatal and neonatal screening and prenatal diagnosis; indicating a prenatal diagnosis; advising the woman and if applicable her partner with regard to contraception and family planning; resuscitating the new born; intervening in case of an acute shock or excessive blood loss, including insertion of an IV and by way of an intravenous drip or intravenous injection administering medicinal products designated by ministerial decree (Article 5.3).

*643.* Midwives are authorised to carry out the following reserved procedures: the practice of surgical procedures which means activities in the field of medicine that disturb the cohesion of tissues of the body which does not immediately restore under certain conditions (Article 36.1); the practice of obstetrical procedures under certain conditions (Article 36.2); the practice of catheterisations under certain conditions (Article 36.4); the practice of injections under certain conditions (Article 36.5); the practice of punctures under certain conditions; (Article 36.6) and the prescription of medicinal products (Article 36.14).

## §7. Nursing Profession

### I. The Practice of Nursing

*644.* The nursing profession is one of the so-called Article 3 IHCP Act professions. As a consequence, the disciplinary jurisprudence rules apply to nurses (Article 47 IHCP Act).

## II. Professional Relations Between Physicians and Nurses

*645.* The domain of expertise of nurses consists of carrying out, on the one hand, activities in the field of observation, assistance, nursing and care (the 'traditional' nursing activities) and, on the other hand, activities delegated by a practitioner in the field of individual healthcare that are connected to his/her diagnostic and therapeutic activities (Article 33a and 33b IHCP Act).

*646.* Nurses can obtain a so-called dependent qualification on the basis of Article 35.2. IHCP Act. A person who is legally competent to carry out reserved procedures (in all cases a physician) can delegate this competence to a nurse who considers him or herself competent to carry out the delegated procedure and on the condition to respect the instructions, if any, given by the physician (Article 35.1).

*647.* Article 39 provides the so-called functional autonomy: if it is required by proper exercise of individual healthcare, a royal decree provides that the field of expertise of a given category of healthcare professionals includes the practice of a given category of reserved procedures without supervision or intervention of the physician who orders this procedure. Article 39 has been implemented by the royal decree of 24 October 1997 that provides specific rules for nurses and ambulance nurses with regard to the practice of reserved procedures (Decree Functional Autonomy).[247] According to Article 2 and notwithstanding Article 33 IHCP Act, the field of expertise of a nurse includes practising without the supervision or intervention of a physician: (a) giving a subcutaneous, intramuscular or intravenous injection; (b) catheterisation of the bladder in adults as well as insertion of a stomach tube or an intravenous drip; and (c) performing a venepuncture and a heel prick in neonates. Notwithstanding Article 2 of this Decree, the field of expertise of an ambulance nurse includes practising without the supervision or intervention of a physician: (a) applying elective cardioversion; (b) applying defibrillation; (c) in- or extubate the trachea with an oral or nasal tube; (d) using a drainage puncture for a tension pneumothorax; and (e) performing a coniotomy.

*648.* Article 36.14 IHCP Act provides that the prescription of medicinal products belongs to the legal authority of nurses under certain conditions. The ministerial decree of 19 November 2013 regulating the prescription of prescription-only medicinal products by certain categories of nurses has implemented Article 36.14.[248] According to Article 3, a nurse with expertise in the field of diabetes mellitus may prescribe blood glucose regulating drugs to the extent that a physician diagnosed a patient with diabetes mellitus and insofar as the nurse follows the relevant guidelines, standards and protocols derived therefrom. According to Article 5, a nurse with expertise in the field of oncology may prescribe antidiarrheal drugs, antiemetics, benzodiazepines, laxatives, pain relief agents and secretion inhibitors to the extent that a physician diagnosed a patient with cancer and insofar as the nurse follows the relevant guidelines, standards and protocols derived therefrom.

247. *State Journal* (1997), 524.
248. *State Journal* (2013), 33354.

According to Article 7, a nurse with expertise in the field of asthma and Chronic Obstructive Pulmonary Disease (COPD) may prescribe inhalation medication to the extent that a physician diagnosed a patient asthma or COPD and insofar as the nurse follows the relevant guidelines, standards and protocols derived therefrom.

*649.* The Regional Disciplinary Board of Groningen cancelled the entry in the registry (the heaviest disciplinary sanction) of a nurse who autonomously had decided not to reanimate a patient contrary to the relevant guidelines, standards and protocols derived therefrom.[249]

## §8. Physician Assistants

*650.* The profession of a physician assistant is one of the so-called Article 3 IHCP Act professions. As a consequence, the disciplinary jurisprudence rules apply to physician assistants (Article 47 IHCP Act).

*651.* The domain of expertise of physician assistants includes the performance of activities described by royal decree in that area of medicine in which the physician assistant was trained, all this with due observance of the restrictions imposed by royal decree. These acts include examining, treating and counselling of patients with common conditions within that area of medicine (Article 33b IHCP Act). Article 5 of the royal decree of 18 April 2018 determining training requirements and field of experience of physician assistants[250] describes these activities. They include examining, treating and counselling patients with common conditions within the area of medicine they have been trained (Article 5.1). The activities referred to in section 1 include: (a) examining and assessing a patient, making a diagnosis and drawing up a treatment plan on the basis of the data obtained; (b) implementing the treatment plan and performing usual medical procedures for this purpose; (c) performing actions for which the physician assistant is authorised pursuant to Article 36 IHCP Act; (d) setting indications and recognising complications of medical actions and procedures and anticipating them; (e) providing emergency care, monitoring vital bodily functions and where necessary, taking measures to restore them; (f) referring to, consulting and collaborating with physicians and other healthcare professionals; and (g) providing advice, information and preventive care (Article 5.2). The actions referred to in section 2, under c are only performed insofar as it concerns: (a) acts of limited complexity; (b) routine actions; (c) actions for which the risks are manageable; and (d) actions performed in accordance with nationally applicable guidelines, standards and protocols derived therefrom (Article 5.3). To sum up, the physician assistant supports the physician (medical specialist) by autonomously performing medical tasks. Given the field of expertise of the physician assistant, he works within a partnership of which at least one physician (medical specialist) is a member.[251]

249. 29 September 2017, ECLI:NL:TGZRGRO:2017:19.
250. *State Journal* (2018), 130.
251. Note of information to the decree of 14 Apr. 2018, *State Journal* (2018), 130.

*652.* Physician assistants are authorised to carry out the following reserved procedures: the practice of surgical procedures which means activities in the field of medicine that disturb the cohesion of tissues of the body which does not immediately restore, limited to the extent that this belongs to their legal domain (Article 36.1 IHCP Act); endoscopies (Article 36.3); catheterisations (Article 36.4); the practice of injections (Article 36.5); elective cardioversion (Article 36.9); defibrillation (Article 36.10); prescription of medicinal products to the extent that this belongs to their expertise (Article 36.14).

*653.* Also, with regard to the physician assistant, the general requirement applies that there is only legal authority for a reserved procedure if there is factual competence to perform this in view of the provision of Article 35a.1 IHCP Act.[252]

## §9. Clinical Technologists

*654.* The profession of a clinical technologist is one of the so-called Article 3 IHCP Act professions. As a consequence, the disciplinary jurisprudence rules apply to clinical technologists (Article 47 IHCP Act).

*655.* The field of expertise of a clinical technologist includes optimising existing medical procedures as well as designing and developing new diagnostic methods and therapies using technology and the performance of activities described by a royal decree within the technical-medical area of medicine in which the clinical technologist has been trained, with due observance of the restrictions of the royal decree (Article 33d.1 and 33d.2 IHCP Act). This Article has been implemented by the royal decree of 6 March 2020 on the educational requirements and field of expertise of the clinical technologist.[253]

*656.* The field of expertise of the clinical technologist includes the optimisation of existing technical-medical actions as well as the design and the development of new diagnostic methods and therapies with the aid of technology and the performance of complex technical-medical actions within the technical-medical sub-area of medicine in which the clinical technologist has been trained (Article 5.1 Decree Clinical Technologist). The complex technical-medical actions referred to in section 1 also include: (a) examining and assessing a patient as a diagnosis and drawing up a treatment plan based on the data obtained; (b) performing actions that the clinical technologist is authorised to do on the basis of Article 36 IHCP Act; (c) implementing the treatment plan, accompanying the patient and performing common and complex technical-medical procedures; (d) setting indications and recognising complications of common and complex technical-medical actions and procedures and anticipating them; and (e) referring to, consult and collaborating with physicians and other healthcare professionals (Article 5.2). The actions referred to in section 2, under b are only performed insofar as they fall within the

252. *Ibid.*
253. *State Journal* (2020), 96.

expertise of common and complex technical-medical actions as referred to in section 1 and 2, and in accordance with nationally applicable guidelines, standards and the protocols derived thereof (Article 5.3).

*657.* Clinical technologists are authorised to practise the following reserved procedures: the practice of surgical procedures which means activities in the field of medicine that disturb the cohesion of tissues of the body which does not immediately restore, limited to the activities that belong to their legal domain of expertise (Article 36.1 IHCP Act): the practice of catheterisations (Article 36.4); the practice of injections (Article 36.5); the practice of punctures (Article 36.6); the practice of electronic convulsion (Article 36.9) and the practice of applying defibrillation (Article 36.10).

### §10. Orthopedagogics-generalist

*658.* The profession of an orthopedagogic-generalist is one of the so-called Article 3 IHCP Act professions. As a consequence, the disciplinary jurisprudence rules apply to orthopedagogics-generalist (Article 47 IHCP Act).

*659.* The field of expertise of the orthopedagogic-generalist includes conducting examinations and diagnostics and treating and accompanying persons who are in a dependent personal relationship with learning, behavioural and development problems (Article 33f IHCP Act).

### §11. Bachelors Medical Care Providers

*660.* A royal decree of 13 September 2018 on the temporary autonomous competence of the bachelor medical care provider has created the legal basis for the temporary registration of bachelors medical providers. It entered into force on 1 January 2019.[254] This royal decree is based upon Article 36a IHCP Act that makes it possible to register on a temporary basis so-called experimental healthcare professions in order to stimulate the development of new healthcare professions. Article 36a has been inserted in the IHCP Act by the law of 7 November 2011 in order to enable task reallocation.[255] According to Article 36a.7, Article 47 IHCP Act (disciplinary jurisprudence rules) is also applicable to these professionals.

*661.* The field of expertise of the bachelor medical care provider includes the performance of activities in the field of acute care, intervention care and diagnostics within which the bachelor medical care provider was trained. These actions include emergency or life-saving actions that are included in a treatment plan or recorded in a protocol, as well as actions aimed at monitoring the patient's health status (Article 6.1 royal decree 18 September 2018). The activities referred to in section 1 include:

254. *State Journal* (2018), 323.
255. *State Journal* (2011), 568.

(a) examining and assessing a patient and making a diagnosis and drawing up a treatment plan on the basis of the data obtained; (b) implementing the treatment plan and performing usual medical procedures for this purpose; (c) the performance of reserved procedures as referred to in Article 7; (d) providing protocol emergency care, monitoring vital bodily functions and, where necessary, taking measures to restore them; and (e) referring to, consulting and collaborating with other healthcare professionals (Article 6.2).

*662.* The bachelor medical care provider is authorised to practise the following reserved procedures: (a) giving a subcutaneous, intramuscular or intravenous injection; (b) performing a bladder catheterisation in adults as well as inserting a stomach tube or an IV; (c) performing a venepuncture; (d) performing elective cardioversion; (e) performing the following actions in the context of acute care: (i) applying defibrillation; (ii) inserting or extubating the trachea with oral or nasal tubes; (iii) the use of a drainage puncture for a tension pneumothorax (Article 7.1). The authority referred to in section 1 applies only insofar it concerns (a) actions that fall within the field of expertise referred to in Article 6; (b) acts of limited complexity; (c) routine actions; (d) actions for which the risks are manageable; and (e) actions that are performed in accordance with applicable national guidelines, standards and protocols derived therefrom (Article 7.2).

## §12. Registered Dental Hygienists

*663.* The royal decree of 17 May 2019 on the temporal autonomous authority of the registered dental hygienist has implemented Article 36a.1 IHCP Act (*see* paragraph 660 for this category of healthcare professionals.[256]

*664.* The field of expertise of the registered dental hygienist includes: (a) examining and assessing the condition of the patient's teeth and of the tissues surrounding the teeth with respect to plaque-related conditions and based on the data obtained, establishing the diagnosis and developing a treatment plan; (b) screening for dental abnormalities and referring to a dentist or physician if necessary; (c) applying oral care treatments aimed at preventing or repairing disorders of the teeth and remedying or reducing disorders of the tissues surrounding the teeth and if necessary refer to a dentist or a physician; (d) providing dental health education to an individual for the purpose of encouraging behaviour that promotes oral health; (e) for eligible patients (1°) applying ionising radiation in the context of an examination referred to under (a) insofar as this is necessary for the exercising of the authorised actions of the registered dental hygienist; (2°) applying local anaesthesia by giving injections of agents for conduction or infiltration anaesthesia to support the examination referred to under (a) or the treatment referred to under (c); and under 3 and (3°) treatment of primary cavities by preparation for restauration with plastic fillers (Article 7 Decree 17 May 2019).

256. *State Journal* (2019), 192.

*665.* The registered dental hygienist is authorised to perform the following reserved procedures: (a) performing surgical procedures; (b) giving injections; and (c) carrying out activities involving the use of radioactive materials or devices that emit ionising radiation. This authority only applies insofar as it concerns actions that fall within the expertise referred to in Article 7 and are performed in accordance with nationally applicable guidelines, standards and protocols derived therefrom (Article 8 royal decree 17 May 2019).

### §13. Paramedical Professions

*666.* Article 34.1 IHCP Act contains the legal basis for the registration of the so-called Article 34 professions or paramedical professions. Registration gives the registered person the right to use the title of his/her professions (Article 34.3). Using such a title by others is prohibited (Article 34.4).

#### I. Dieticians

*667.* The field of expertise of the dietician includes: (a) recognising risk factors and symptoms in the patient that indicate the possible presence of a condition for which expertise from other disciplines is desired or necessary and, if these are identified, refer to that other disciplines; (b) examining the patient, aimed at determining his nutritional status and determining or locating certain nutrition-related syndromes, and drawing up a treatment plan on the basis of the data obtained; (c) treating the patient by applying dietary therapy or giving dietary advice, aimed at eliminating, reducing or compensating for nutrition-related or nutrition-influenceable diseases or complaints; and (d) providing nutrition and diet information to a person, with the aim of preventing nutrition-related or nutritionally influenceable diseases or complaints (Article 5 royal decree 24 October 1997 on dieticians).[257]

#### II. Occupational Therapists

*668.* The field of expertise of the occupational therapist includes: (a) recognising risk factors and symptoms in the patient that indicate the possible presence of a condition for which expertise from other disciplines is desired or necessary and, if these are identified, refer to that other disciplines; (b) examining the patient whether and to what extent the abilities or skills are present to perform actions derived from daily life or work, and drawing up a treatment plan on the basis of the data obtained; (c) treating the patient with the aim of eliminating, reducing or compensating psychological disorders, limitations or disabilities by obtaining or optimising the skills required for performing actions as referred to under (a) or by providing information, instruction or advice to the patient, and in appropriate cases, to his relatives,

257. *State Journal* (1997), 532 as revised.

aimed at ensuring that the patient functions as independently as possible in his living, housing or work situation; (d) in appropriate cases manufacturing aids for the patient or advising the patient about provisions to be made in or adjustments to his living, housing or work situation, within the framework of treatment referred to under (b); (e) giving advice, information and instructions to a person with the aim of preventing obstacles to independent functioning in living, housing or work situation (Article 9 royal decree 24 October 1997 on occupational therapists).[258]

## III. Speech Therapists

*669.* The field of expertise of the speech therapist includes: (a) recognising risk factors and symptoms in the patient that indicate the possible presence of a condition for which expertise from other disciplines is desired or necessary and, if these are identified, refer to that other disciplines; (b) the external examination of the patient whether and if so to what extent the abilities to speak, learn to speak and use language are present; whether the abilities to eat, drink and swallow safely and efficiently are present; whether the hearing, voice or speech organs function, including the influence of breathing on the voice; whether there are impairments in the use of language or speech related to the personality of the patient and his relationship to his environment and drawing up a treatment plan on the basis of the data obtained; (c) treating the patient aimed at restoring, improving or maintaining the functioning of his hearing, voice or speech organs or the regulation of his breathing necessary for the using of the voice; the removal of disturbances present in the patient in speaking or learning to speak or in the use of the language or in adequate eating, drinking and swallowing, whether or not in connection with the necessary influencing of movement or behaviour; guiding the patient in the context of the treatment in the use of aids that promote the functioning of the hearing, voice or speech organs or that replace these organs in whole or in part; and (d) examining a person or giving speech therapy advice to a person with the aim to preventing disorders in the functioning of the hearing, voice or speech organs, or in speaking or using the language (Article 13 royal decree 24 October 1997 on speech therapists).[259]

## IV. Dental Hygienists

*670.* The field of expertise of the dental hygienist includes: (a) examining and assessing the condition of the patient's teeth and of the tissues surrounding the teeth with respect to plaque-related conditions and based on the data obtained, establishing the diagnosis and developing a treatment plan; (b) screening for dental abnormalities and referring to a dentist or physician if necessary; (c) with the exception of the preparation of primary cavities as referred to in subsection e, applying oral care treatments aimed at preventing or repairing disorders of the teeth and remedying or reducing disorders of the tissues surrounding the teeth; (d) providing dental

258. *Ibid.*
259. *Ibid.*

health education to an individual for the purpose of encouraging behaviour that promotes oral health; (e) for eligible patients on prescription of a dentist (1°) applying ionising radiation in the context of an examination referred to under (a), (2°) applying local anaesthesia by giving injections of agents for conduction or infiltration anaesthesia to support the examination referred to under (a), or the treatment referred to under (c); and under 3 and (3) treatment of primary cavities by preparation for restauration with plastic fillers (Article 17 royal decree 24 October 1997 on dental hygienists).[260] Without prejudice of the Article 17, the expertise of the dental hygienist also includes the use of local anaesthesia by giving an injection and the treatment of primary cavities by means of preparation for restoration with plastic filling materials without supervision and intervention by the physician who delegated this task (Article 4 Decree Functional Autonomy).[261]

## V. Remedial Therapists

*671.* The field of expertise of the remedial therapist includes: (a) recognising risk factors and symptoms in the patient that indicate the possible presence of a condition for which expertise from a physician is desired or necessary and, if these are identified, refer to a physician; (b) examining the patient on his posture and movement abilities and habits and on the presence of disorders and limitations of his support and movement apparatus and the functionally involved organs and control systems according to the remedial therapy based on the movement theory Cesar or the method Mensendieck, and on the basis of the data obtained, establishing the diagnosis and, if necessary drawing up a treatment plan; (c) treating the patient, aiming to eliminate, reduce or compensate for disorders or limitations of the support and locomotor apparatus and the organs and control systems involved and the normalisation of the posture and movement capacity, by performing exercises, derived from and aimed at daily functional movements and elementary movement skills, according to the movement principles and standards of the movement theory Cesar, or to practice skills derived from daily actions by means of information and guidance according to the method Mensendieck; (d) examining a person or giving advice, information and instruction on the basis of the movement theory Cesar or the method Mensendieck, with the aim of promoting good posture and physical movement in living, housing, working and sports situations (Article 21 royal decree 24 October 1997 on remedial therapists).[262]

## VI. Orthoptists

*672.* The field of expertise of the orthoptist includes: (a) recognising risk factors and symptoms in the patient that indicate the possible presence of a condition for

260. *Ibid.*
261. *State Journal* (1997), 524.
262. *State Journal* (1997), 532 as revised.

which expertise from other disciplines is desired or necessary and, if these are identified, refer to that other disciplines; (b) examining the patient for the presence of monocular and binocular functions and of disturbances in the monocular and binocular vision with the aid of appropriate equipment or by administering eye drops appropriate for this examination, and preparing on the basis of the data obtained a treatment plan; (c) treating the patient's monocular or binocular vision disturbances by providing instruction and advice to the patient regarding monocular and binocular vision; remedial therapy with orthoptic aids and equipment; amblyopia treatment with occlusion material; accommodation decreasing eye drops or specially prescribed spectacle lenses; the fitting of spectacle lenses or special spectacle corrections; (d) advising the ophthalmologist on indications for surgical eye muscle corrections (Article 25 royal decree 24 October 1997 on orthoptists).[263]

## VII. Podiatrists

*673.* The field of expertise of the podiatrist includes: (a) recognising risk factors and symptoms in the patient that indicate the possible presence of a condition for which expertise from other disciplines is desired or necessary and, if these are identified, refer to that other disciplines; (b) examining the patient whether and to what extent there is a deviation from or an obstruction in the position or function of the foot and drawing up a treatment plan based on the data obtained; and (c) the treatment of the patient with the aim of eliminating, reducing or compensating for disorders in the functioning of the support and locomotor apparatus by means of orthoses or prostheses or other aids on the foot, the external treatment of skin disorders present on the foot, prevention or combating nail abnormalities or giving advice (Article 29 royal decree 24 October 1997 on podiatrists).[264]

## VIII. Pharmacy Assistants

*674.* The field of expertise of the pharmacy assistant includes the preparation, supply and management of medicinal products, the supply and management of medical devices as well as giving pharmaceutical advice under the supervision of a pharmacist or a dispensing GP (Article 3 royal decree training and expertise of the pharmacy assistant).[265]

## IX. Skin Therapists

*675.* The field of expertise of the skin therapist includes: (a) recognising risk factors and symptoms in the patient that indicate the possible presence of a condition

263. *Ibid.*
264. *Ibid.*
265. *State Journal* (1997), 501.

for which expertise from a physician is desired or necessary and, if these are identified, refer to a physician; (b) examining a patient with a disorder, limitation or disability of the skin, as a result of a pathological trauma or congenital abnormality and drawing up a treatment plan on the basis of the data obtained; (c) treating the patient with the aim of remedying, reducing or compensating for a disorder, limitation or disability of the skin, optimising skin functions as well as providing advice and instruction; (d) measuring and supplying medical devices as well as prostheses, as well as providing advice with regard to their use; and (e) providing advice and information to a patient (Article 5 royal decree 10 October 2002 training and expertise of the skin therapist).[266]

## X. Clinical Physicists

*676.* The field of expertise of the clinical physicist includes: (a) advising on and guiding the use of medical, physical methods, techniques and models as well as medical equipment and physical agents in the diagnosis or treatment of patients; (b) performing dosimetry and monitoring the correct and safe use of physical agents in the diagnosis or treatment of patients; and (c) guiding and monitoring the development, introduction, quality and safety of the medical equipment and aids used for diagnostics and treatment (Article 17 royal decree training and expertise of the clinical physicist).[267]

## XI. Optometrists

*677.* The field of expertise of the optometrist includes: (a) screening the client for eye disorders with the aid of appropriate equipment or by administering the necessary pharmaceuticals for the examination, designated by the minister and referring to a GP or ophthalmologist if an eye disorder is diagnosed; and (b) to carry out follow-up examinations with regard to eye disorders in eligible patients with chronic diseases on referral of a GP or an ophthalmologist using appropriate equipment or by administering the pharmaceuticals referred to under (a) (Article 5.1 royal decree training and expertise of the optometrist).[268] The referral under (b) is made in writing, dated and signed by the physician concerned and contains at least the diagnostic data he deems relevant for the examination of the patient by the optometrist (Article 5.2).

## XII. Radiodiagnostic and Radiotherapeutic Laboratory Technicians

*678.* The field of expertise of the radiodiagnostic laboratory technician includes carrying out a radio diagnostic examination on behalf of a physician or a dentist.

266. *State Journal* (2002), 528.
267. *State Journal* (2005), 265.
268. *State Journal* (2000), 297.

This includes: (a) preparing and planning the total examination process; (b) guiding the patient during the entire examination process, monitoring his physical and psychological condition and providing advice to the patient regarding the influences that the radiodiagnostic examination may entail; (c) displaying or recording the condition of a particular body part or organ of the patient using ionising rays; (d) conducting the examination in such a way that the radiation load is kept as low as possible; (e) determining the correct examination and registration technique that is tailored to the body part or organ of the patient to be recorded; (f) checking and interpreting all radiation parameters; and (g) assessing and interpreting the technical quality of the images produced (Article 26 royal decree 19 November 1997 education and expertise of the radiodiagnostic and radiotherapeutic laboratory technicians).[269]

*679.* The field of expertise of the radiotherapeutic laboratory technician includes the performance of radiation treatment on behalf of a physician. This implies: (a) the manufacture of individual aids or the formulation of an assignment for this so that good fixation, shielding and adjustment of dose distribution are guaranteed during the irradiation; (b) locating and stimulating, with appropriate equipment, the target areas to be irradiated; (c) draft and after approval from the physician implement individual radiation plans; (d) introducing into and removing closed radioactive sources if a container is provided in the patient for this purpose; (e) checking, interpreting and recording radiation parameters of the individual patient; (f) identifying and reporting changes in the physical and psychosocial condition of the patient during treatments; and (g) guiding the patient during the entire treatment process, monitoring his physical and psychological condition and providing advice to the patient regarding the influences the radiation treatment can bring about (Article 27 royal decree training and expertise of the radiodiagnostic and radiotherapeutic laboratory technicians).

## XIII. Dental Prosthetists

*680.* The field of expertise of the dental prosthetist includes: (a) examining the patient's mouth to obtain the data necessary for the application of a dental prosthesis; (b) measuring, manufacturing, fitting and adjusting a complete dental prosthesis for the upper and lower jaw in a patient whose jaw walls have recovered from dental extraction; (c) measuring, manufacturing, fitting and adjusting a dental prosthesis for the upper jaw or the lower jaw in a patient whose jaw wall in question has been recovered from the dental extraction and in whose oral cavity there are no teeth or other elements that serve to support a dental prosthesis; (d) providing a patient with advice and information regarding the dental prosthesis or its use (Article 4.1 royal decree training and expertise of the dental prosthetist).[270] The field of expertise of the dental prosthetist also includes measuring, manufacturing, fitting and adjusting a dental prosthesis on a patient's referral by the dentist concerned, in

269. *State Journal* (1997), 551.
270. *State Journal* (1997), 477.

whose oral cavity there are dental elements or other elements that serve to support the dental prosthesis (Article 4.2). The referral referred to in section 2, is made in writing, is dated and signed by the dentist concerned and contains at least the diagnostic information he considers relevant for the care to be provided by the dental prosthetist (Article 4.3).

## XIV. Carers in Individual Healthcare

*681.* The field of expertise of a carer in individual healthcare includes: (a) performing activities in the field of care, nursing, observation and guidance in care and non-complex treatment and nursing situations; and (b) the performance upon delegation by an individual healthcare provider of actions related to the latter's diagnostic and therapeutic activities (Article 2 royal decree 1 October 1999 on the carer in individual healthcare).[271]

271. *State Journal* (1999), 463.

## Chapter 2. Relations with Healthcare Provisions

### §1. Hospitals

*682.* Since 2006, hospital planning is based on the Act of 20 October 2005 on the admission of healthcare facilities.[272] This Act has introduced a shift from central planning towards a decentralised demand-driven system in which the governmental role is restricted to setting preconditions. These preconditions concern safeguarding public interests such as accessibility, quality and efficiency of intramural care. As such, the Act sets requirements for hospital admission, organisational structure and management, and 'healthcare governance'. The rationale is that consumer demand and competition in the healthcare providers market will determine the required hospital capacity. Therefore, withdrawal of governmental interference in capacity planning was replaced by promoting entrepreneurship, creating a level playing field between competing health insurers and contracting hospitals, liberalising healthcare prices, thus achieving equilibrium between demand and supply.

*683.* A basic tool is the so-called admission, i.e., a licence to provide healthcare covered by health insurance legislation. Admission should guarantee the quality of care provided, accessibility of specific (emergency) services, financial transparency and sound management. It is up to the Health Inspectorate to supervise whether healthcare institutions comply with the law. If not, the ultimate sanction imposed is the withdrawal of admission. Without such an admission, healthcare institutions are not entitled to deliver healthcare under the Health Insurance Act.

*684.* Admission is open to each institution providing 'medical specialist care', e.g., traditional hospitals but also to private clinics, irrespective their legal status. Traditionally, most healthcare institutions can be legally classified as civil law foundations. Under the Act, a for-profit basis category of outpatient healthcare entities was introduced, providing *inter alia*, audiology services, intensive care for thrombotic patients, dental, pharmaceutical and obstetrical care and transportation services. Funded by collective means, these entities can be established on a for-profit basis.

*685.* Next, there is the Special Medical Procedures Act of 1997 that has frequently been amended (*see* paragraph 466).

*686.* Nearly all hospitals have outpatient and inpatient facilities. Outpatient services are provided primarily by specialists who carry out pre-admission diagnostic examinations and outpatient treatment. Except in case of emergency, patients are not allowed to go directly to an outpatient department of an acute care hospital.

---

272. *State Journal* (2005), 571.

*687.* There are eight University Medical Centres (UMC's). In a UMC, the Faculty of Medicine, with its responsibility for the initial training of physicians and for scientific research, is merged with the Academic Hospital, with its responsibility for tertiary care and clinical research and innovation. All medical faculties and academic hospitals in the Netherlands are now a UMC. Each UMC is a private non-profit enterprise with strong links to the University and with an executive board, including a dean of medicine. The finances come from the Department of Education and Science, the Department of Health, as well as from the health insurance companies. The eight UMC's have a special position in the healthcare system because although they are legally private entities, they have a distinct public mission. This mission can be divided into three core responsibilities: teaching and training, basic and clinical research and (tertiary) patient care.

*688.* Within the category of general hospitals, there are considerable differences from hospital to hospital, with some smaller hospitals providing only basic specialist care. The other hospitals are speciality hospitals, which limit their care to selective illnesses or patient groups.

*689.* Hospitals have increased their capacity through mergers and expansion, which decreased the number of acute care beds by over a third since 1980.

*690.* Hospital management has been streamlined, with middle management gaining responsibility for departmental functions at the expense of central managers. Greater integration of medical specialists into the hospital administrative structure has also occurred. Also, administrators with broader roles have replaced directors of nursing.

*691.* Top management has gained overall power and professionalism (compared to physicians) as a result of the changes. Medical specialists continue to have great influence over hospital operations but are more dependent on executive leadership than they used to be. Hospital governors currently play a more supervising role in decisions, and major policy responsibility is delegated to administrators.

*692.* Gradually, it has led to an increased sense of interdependence between hospital management and medical professionals. The financing system provoked a real shift in the organisation of the hospitals. Traditionally, the organisational structure of hospitals was based on grouping activities by function. The traditional hospital organisation consisted of separate, strong, functional departments, which were linked together only at the top of the organisation. Under external pressure and increasing, mutual interdependence between specialists and hospital management, another type of hospital organisation was required.

## §2. Relations Between Hospitals and Physicians

*693.* Over the past decades, there have been attempts to integrate medical specialists in hospital governance.[273] They resulted in 2015 in a financial structure and incentives for collaboration between hospital boards and medical specialists. A so-called integral tariff has been introduced for medical care in hospitals, and two budgets which were formerly distinct and separated are now unified: the budget of the hospital and the fee for services budget for medical specialists.

*694.* Until 2015, most self-employed medical specialists were organised in so-called partnerships (maatschap): a group of specialists, who usually practised the same speciality for a particular patient group. After the 2015 reform, this partnership structure came under pressure. Apart from the salaried model where the self-employed physicians become employees of the hospital, there are two models among which medical specialists have to make a choice. The first model is the so-called cooperation model, where medical specialists organise themselves in a so-called specialist medical company that concludes a collective collaboration agreement with the hospital that replaces the individual agreements between the medical specialists and the hospital. The second model is the so-called participation model where medical doctors become co-owners of the hospital. So far, in most hospitals, medical specialists have chosen for the cooperation second model.[274]

## §3. Health Insurance

*695.* *See* above, paragraphs 60 et seq.

273. J.-L. Denis and N. van Gestel, 'Medical Doctors in Healthcare Leadership: Theoretical and Practical Challenges', *BMC Health Services Research,* 16 (2016) 51.
274. *Ibid.*, 52.

# Selected Bibliography


Asscher, E.C.A. & S. van de Vathorst, 'First Prosecution of a Dutch Doctor Since the Euthanasia Act of 2002: What Does the Verdict mean', *Journal of Medical Ethics,* 46 (2020): 71–75.

Blankenburg, B. et al., 'Access to Justice voor 12- tot 16 jarigen bij niet nakoming van de geneeskundige behandelingsovereenkomst?', *Tijdschrift voor Jeugdrecht,* 2 (2020): 94–100.

Bongers, L.M.H., 'Disclosure of Medical Data to Relatives after the Patient's Death: Recent Developments with Respect to Relatives' Entitlements in the Netherlands', *European Journal of Health Law,* 11 (2011): 255–275.

Bongers, L.M.H. & D.M.R. Townend, 'The Implementation of the Directive on the Application of Patients' Rights in Cross-Border Healthcare in the Netherlands', *European Journal of Health Law,* 21 (2014): 65–78.

Cuperus-Bosma, J.M., Van Der Wal, G. & P.J. Van Der Maas, 'Physician-Assisted Death: Policy-Making by the Assembly of Prosecutors General in the Netherlands', *European Journal of Health Law,* 4 (1997): 225–238.

de Beaufort, I., 'Patients in a Persistent Vegetative State: A Dutch Perspective', *New England Journal of Medicine,* 352 (2005): 2373–2375.

De Bijl, N. & I. Nederveen-Van De Kragt, 'Legal Safeguards Against Medical Practice by Not Suitably Qualified Persons: A Comparative Study in Seven EU-Countries', *European Journal of Health Law,* 4 (1997): 5–18.

de Boer, M et al., 'Pressure in Dealing with Requests for Euthanasia of Assisted Suicide: Experiences of General Practitioners', *Journal of Medical Ethics,* 45 (2019): 425–429.

Defloor, S; 'The Medically Examined Applicant for Private Insurance and His/Her Right to Informed Consent: A Comparative Analysis', *European Journal of Health Law,* 18 (2011): 319–330.

Dondorp, W., Legemaate, J. & H. van de Klippe, 'The Retention of Medical Records: Dutch Health Council Report in Favour of Future Change', *European Journal of Health Law,* 11 (2004): 273–282.

Doomen, J., 'The Struggle Unto Death', *Biolaw,* 5 (2018): 225–230.

Dorscheidt, J.H.H.M., 'Developments in Legal and Medical Practice Regarding the Unborn Child and the Need to Expand Prenatal Legal Protection', *European Journal of Health Law,* 17 (2010): 433–454.

Flear, M.L., 'The EU Clinical Trials Regulation: Key Priorities, Purposes and Aims and the Implications for Public Health', *Journal of Medical Ethics,* 42 (2016): 192–198.

Florijn, B.W., 'Extending Euthanasia to Those "Tired of Living" in the Netherlands Could Jeopardize a Well-Functioning Practice of Physicians' Assessment of a Patient's Request for Death', *Heath Policy*, 122 (2018): 315–319.

Frederiks, B, et al., 'Reporting of Use of Coercive Measures from a Dutch Perspective', *Advances in Mental Health and Intellectual Disabilities*, 11 (2017): 65–73.

Gennet, E., R. Andorno & B. Elger, 'Does the New EU Regulation on Clinical Trials Adequately Protect Vulnerable Research Participants?,' *Health Policy*, 119 (2015): 925–931.

Gevers, S., 'Withdrawing Life Support from Patients in a Persistent Vegetative State: The Law in the Netherlands', *European Journal of Health Law*, 11 (2005): 347–355.

Gevers, S., 'Abortion Legislation and the Future of the Counseling Model', *European Journal of Health Law*, 13 (2006): 27–40.

Gevers, S., 'Late Abortion in Case of Severe Foetal Abnormality', *European Journal of Health Law*, 20 (2013): 445–449.

Giesen, I. & E. Engelhard, 'Medical Liability in the Netherlands' in B.A. Koch (ed.), *Medical Liability in Europe: A Comparison of Selected Jurisdictions* (Berlin, De Gruyter, 2011): 361–410.

Hendriks, A., 'Kroniek van het gezondheidsrecht', *NJB*, 15 (2019): 1099–1115.

Herringa, J. & J. Dute, 'The Proposed EU-Regulation on Clinical Trials on Medicinal Products', *European Journal of Health Law*, 20 (2013): 347–362.

Janssen, A.J.G.M., 'Informing Patients about Small Risks: A Comparative Approach', *European Journal Health of Law*, 13 (2006): 159–172.

Janssens, P.M.W. et al., 'A New Dutch Law Regulating Provision of Identifying Information of Donors to Offspring: Background, Contents and Impact', *Human Reproduction*, 4 (2006): 852–856.

Laarman, B et al., 'How Do Doctors in the Netherlands Perceive the Impact of Disciplinary Procedures and Disclosure of Disciplinary Measures on Their Professional Practice, Health and Career Opportunities? A Questionnaire among Medical Doctors Who Received a Disciplinary Measure', *BMJ Open*, 9 (2019): e023576, 1–9.

Legemaate, J. et al., 'Palliative Sedation in the Netherlands: Starting-Points and Contents of a National Guideline', *European Journal of Health Law*, 14 (2007): 61–73.

Legemaate, J. & I. Bolt, 'The Dutch Euthanasia Act: Recent Developments', *European Journal of Health Law*, 20 (2013): 451–469.

Legemaate, J., 'Gezondheidsrecht', *Tijdschrift voor Consumentenrecht en handelspraktijken* (2020): 82–90.

Loof, J.P., 'Human Dignity in the Netherlands' in P. Becchi and K. Mathis (eds), *Handbook of Human Dignity in Europe* (Cham, Springer Nature Switzerland, 2019): 643–666.

Markenstein, L.F., 'The Codification in the Netherlands of the Principal Rights of Patients: a Critical Review', *European Journal of Health Law*, 2 (1995): 33–44.

McHale, J.V., 'Reforming the EU Clinical Trials Directive: Streamlining Processes of a Radical "New" Agenda?', *European Journal of Health Law*, 20 (2013): 363–381.

Mevis P. et al., 'Advance Directives Requesting Euthanasia in the Netherlands: Do They Enable Euthanasia for Patients Who Lack Mental Capacity?', *Journal of Medical Law and Ethics,* 4 (2016): 127–140.

Nys, H., 'New European Rules Regarding the Approval of Clinical Trials, the Role of Ethics Committees and the Protection of Subjects', *Archives Immunology Experimental Therapy,* 30 (2012): 405–414.

Ost, S. & A. Mullock, 'Pushing the Boundaries of Lawful Assisted Dying in the Netherlands? Existential Suffering and Lay Assistance', *European Journal of Health Law,* 18 (2011): 163–189.

Pertini, C., 'What Is the Role of Ethics Committees after Regulation (EU) 536/2014?', *Journal of Medical Ethics,* 42 (2016): 186–188.

Ploem, C. & S. Gevers, 'Introduction of a National Electronic Patient Record in the Netherlands: Some Legal Issues', *European Journal of Health Law,* 18 (2011): 191–204.

Ploem, C., 'Handling Unsolicited Findings in Clinical Care: A Legal Perspective', *European Journal of Health Law,* 21 (2014): 497.

Ploem, M.C. et al., *Tweede Evaluatie Wet Afbreking Zwangerschap*, The Hague, ZonMW, 2020.

Quill, T., 'Dutch Practice of Euthanasia and Assisted Suicide: A Glimpse at the Edges of the Practice', *Journal of Medical Ethics,* 44 (2018): 297–298.

Roscam Abbing, H., 'Medical Confidentiality and Patient Safety: Reporting Procedures', *European Journal of Health Law,* 21 (2014): 245–259.

Shaw, D. & D. Townend, 'Division and Discord in the Clinical Trials Regulation', *Journal of Medical Ethics,* 42 (2016): 729–731.

Te Braake, T.A.M., 'Late Termination of Pregnancy Because of Severe Foetal Abnormalities: Legal Acceptability, Notification and Review in the Netherlands', *European Journal of Health Law,* 7 (2000): 387–403.

Te Braake, T.A.M., 'The Dutch 2002 Embryo Act and the Convention on Human Rights and Biomedicine: Some Issues', *European Journal of Health Law,* 11 (2004): 139–151.

ten Cate, K., *Dutch Doctors & Dying. Do Doctors' Personal Views Influence Their Professional Care at the End of Life and Should They?* Amsterdam, PhD Thesis, 2019.

Wade, K., 'Defining the Threshold of Permissible Risk for Non-therapeutic Clinical Trials with Children in Europe', *European Journal of Health Law,* 24 (2017): 414–431.

Westra, A.E., 'Ambiguous Articles in the New EU Regulation May Lead to Exploitation of Vulnerable Research Subjects', *Journal of Medical Ethics,* 42 (2016): 189–191.

Zeegers, N., 'Convergence in European Nations' Legal Rules Concerning the Use of Human Embryos in Research?', *European Journal of Health Law,* 21 (2014): 461.

# Index

*The numbers here refer to paragraph numbers.*

www.ingramcontent.com/pod-product-compliance
Lightning Source LLC
LaVergne TN
LVHW011131300926
849160LV00008B/605